Web-Based Analysis
for Competitive Intelligence

Web-Based Analysis
for Competitive Intelligence

CONOR VIBERT

QUORUM BOOKS
Westport, Connecticut • London

Library of Congress Cataloging-in-Publication Data

Vibert, Conor, 1962–
   Web-based analysis for competitive intelligence / Conor Vibert.
      p.   cm.
   Includes bibliographical references and index.
   ISBN 1–56720–319–1 (alk. paper)
      1. Industrial management—Computer network resources.   2. Internet (Computer
   network)   I. Title.
   HD30.37.V53   2000
   658'.054678—dc21   00–025252

British Library Cataloguing in Publication Data is available.

Library of Congress Catalog Card Number: 00–025252
ISBN: 1–56720–319–1

First published in 2000

Quorum Books, 88 Post Road West, Westport, CT 06881
An imprint of Greenwood Publishing Group, Inc.
www.quorumbooks.com

Printed in the United States of America

The paper used in this book complies with the
Permanent Paper Standard issued by the National
Information Standards Organization (Z39.48–1984).

10 9 8 7 6 5 4 3 2

Contents

Figures

Acknowledgments

In 1997, I started a project aimed at developing examples to show how the free information resources of the Internet might be used to overcome daily work-related hurdles. This book is the outcome of that effort. Here I would like to acknowledge a number of individuals who have supported this initiative.

My wife Sonia and our children Colin, Brendan, and Jennifer are the true inspiration. Her support and understanding, coupled with the children's love, are the real forces behind this endeavor.

The encouragement of my parents, Doreen and Bert, my brother Dermot, and the entire D'Angelo clan also helped to keep the fire burning.

I would also like to thank Celine Gribbon for introducing me to this exciting field of inquiry; Kevin Mills for his unparalleled research skills; Bill McLeod, Stephen Ash, Michael Leiter, and Deborah Hurst for their support and encouragement; and Kendra Carmichael, Shelley Mac-Dougall, Alan McGee, Bob Graves, Phyllis Harvie, Kathleen Martin-James, Jude Nash, Colleen Coollen, Christina McRae, Elaine Benoit, and Ernie Buist for their review efforts. A special thanks is also owed to Sonya Symons, Andre Trudel, and Christina McRae for their chapter contributions.

Mention should also be made of other colleagues at Acadia University including Janice BamBrick, Orlene Bligh-Coldwell, Delores Spencer, Heather Parrish, Joanne Te Bogt, Wanda Demone, Kerry LaFrance, Rosie Hare, Lisa Davidson, and Heather Harvie, whose cheery outlook on life kept me sane for many months.

I would also like to acknowledge the work of a number of Acadia University students in the development of this book. They include Jacqueline Little, Jason Gates, Andrew Baxter, Kelly Dixon, Erin Barrett, Elke Huber, Jeffrey Garber, Patrick Boyle, Christian Keay, Jeffrey Anderson, Joel Dart, Daniel Doucette, Heidi Gallant, Warren Hayes, Jody Nickerson, and Fitri Zainal. Special thanks are owing to Andrew Steeves for organizing the original development of these chapters.

Financially, this endeavor was supported by the Acadia University Teaching Innovation Fund.

Finally, I would like to thank Eric Valentine for giving me a major career break.

Conor Vibert
Wolfville, Nova Scotia

Chapter 1

Introduction

Have you visited an online or bricks-and-mortar retail bookstore recently? If so, you may have noticed the growing industry of publications related to the use of the Internet. Many appear quite similar. However, this book breaks new ground in the area of applied business research. It offers readers a starting point for managing the breadth of information available on the Internet, using online resources, and it suggests how this information can help analysts, researchers, and competitive intelligence (CI) professionals.

A few introductory points are worthy of attention:

- Although this book offers a variety of options to business analysts, the material covered is by no means all encompassing.

- This book is not a beginner's guide. It assumes a basic knowledge of computer and Internet usage. It does not walk readers through existing terminology, explain differences between hardware and software applications, document how firms might create a business presence on the Internet, or discuss many other topics common to "how to" Internet business books.

- This book is not a tool for researchers seeking to delve into the private lives of individuals. References to sources useful for profiling key executives are limited to the content of company press releases and home pages, the news media, and filings with regulatory bodies like the Securities and Exchange Commission.

You will find ideas for effectively using generic search engines, a discussion of the potential impact of literacy shortcomings on future Internet usage, a brief overview of some interesting commercial and noncommercial initiatives that may dramatically alter how we conduct online research in the not-too-distant future, and a theoretical framework for what this book tries to accomplish.

The major contribution of this endeavor is the presentation of a series of innovative analytical approaches useful for researchers in their day-to-day activities. Each unique approach, captured in its own chapter, matches the personal interpretive abilities of CI professionals with an existing or modified theoretical framework and a group of online information sources.

IN CHAPTER 3

As noted in the introduction, we adopt the perspective of the analyst or CI professional seeking to understand the behavior of competitor organizations. Chapter 3 outlines the theoretical basis for this endeavor. In summary form its message is as follows. Analysts and their targets, corporations, are portrayed as participants in an arena hosting a contest of hide and seek. At the end of each contest, the winner holds the knowledge necessary to build an accurate portrait. Target organizations manage and openly disseminate information, hoping to favorably influence the portraits drawn by analysts or ensure that such portraits remain incomplete.

Unfortunately, organizations cannot control all information flows or completely manage analyst interpretations. On the other hand, analysts are challenged in most instances by incomplete information and in many instances by information overload and operational time constraints. Chapter 3 presents a framework for use by analysts seeking to overcome the dual challenges of information uncertainty and noncooperation by target organizations.

IN CHAPTER 4

This book suggests a generic approach to resolving important business concerns. Fortunately, a number of excellent online research approaches are available for finding the information needed. In Chapter 4, Christina McRae, a Nova Scotia–based writer, explores the world of search engines and their potential for aiding CI researchers. If you are looking for specific information, recent advances in search engine technology may simplify your query of what at first appears to be a frustratingly unmanageable amount of publicly available online data. The Web's immense size makes it impossible to locate a particular piece of information by surfing alone. Finding what you need can be a challenge, but using the advanced search options provided by the better search engines will enable you to focus your search and locate Web pages that really match what you are seeking.

IN CHAPTER 5

Which individuals matter in contemporary organizations? Who makes the important decisions that affect a company's direction? How can one identify the true corporate powerholders by using the Internet? This chapter examines the nature of corporate power and explores how to recognize and assess its contenders. A realistic example is that of ABC Corporation.

"The quality of our products makes me sick." Those were Alan Davidson's first words at a meeting on the morning of the first day he was assigned to clean up the quality-control problems rampant at ABC. The current president and CEO of the corporation had held his position as executive VP of Operations for only four short months in the late 1980s when he assumed this role in determining the future of the then moderately successful yet imminently endangered ABC Corporation.[1]

Founded over two decades ago, ABC was the brainchild of Ronald Offen and Stewart Smile, a small, largely family-operated supplier of add-on memory boards. Rising success in its field inspired the company to go public with an IPO on the NASDAQ in the mid 1980s.[2] The computer industry welcomed the newcomer, and sales of its data storage line were strong. Growth of the company was underway when its products began to crash, the cause of which was eventually determined to be a faulty component from an outside supplier. The quality-control problems the company faced placed it at the cusp of extinction. Davidson stepped in, meeting personally with clients and offering to replace faulty components or purchase new systems. He hired engineering specialists who were charged with locating the flaw and for organizing new quality-control measures.[3] His blunt words marked the beginning of an era of awesome success for ABC.

Davidson is credited with having done more than directing the resolution of quality control issues and restoring the status of the company. Upon becoming president in 1990, he redirected the energies of the company to an unexplored aspect of the market, where he saw great potential. Recognizing that companies need to access only 20 percent of their stored data for daily operations, Davidson envisioned ABC Corporation providing a rapid storage system that would allow its clients ready access to their most pertinent information. He made that vision a reality, canceling nine major product lines in order to concentrate ABC's rather limited resources on its fulfillment.[4]

The transformation did not take long, and success came seemingly overnight. Net profits soared from $9 million in 1990 to over $30 million in 1992. Taking over the position of CEO that same year, Davidson sought out yet another unoccupied niche and focused on the development of software for connecting different types of computers to a single storage system. The introduction of Aplex to the market in 1995 established ABC Corporation as a rapidly evolving company, striving to anticipate and adapt to the needs of the business and technological communities. Currently employing 9,700 individuals in twenty-two countries around the globe, ABC is an international contender in the burgeoning gigabyte industry. Design developers for ABC hold over one hundred patents in the United States, with anticipation and innovation providing their leadership in the product development race. With sales topping $5 billion annually, the company's objective is to more than double revenue by 2001.[5]

ABC Corporation has experienced phenomenal success in a niche where keen competition quickly culls the weak. The company and the media alike have identified Alan Davidson as the driving force behind the company's explosive growth. Yet doubt remains. Is Alan Davidson really the savior and godlike figure that he is made out to be? Would or could ABC Corporation survive without him? Who else is influential within the ABC hierarchy? Answers to such queries are the topic of Chapter 5, where we explore how to analyze internal corporate power structures.

IN CHAPTER 6

Does a supplier conduct its affairs in a socially responsible manner? Is a merger target financially stable? Is there evidence to suggest that a client does not respect its physical environment? Are the products and services of a supplier manufactured, developed, and delivered to consumers and clients using the highest available standards? Are there any reasons to accuse a partner of not treating its human stakeholders with dignity and compassion? Is the corporation of interest supportive of local community needs? The answers to these questions can provide valuable insight into more than a company's score on the friendly neighbor scale. Chapter 6 explores the importance of these questions and applies them in an examination of Company A, a company whose mainstay has long been its commitment to society.

"We believe our first responsibility is to the doctors, nurses, and patients, the mothers and fathers and all others who use our products and services."[6] Company A proved to be a staunch supporter of this first item of the company credo when a number of deaths in the Midwest were found to be attributable to product that it manufactured and marketed. The tragedy topped the list for the biggest story on both the crime and the advertising scene in the early 1980s,[7] and its outcome established

Company A as an anomaly amid what is often perceived as an uncaring, profit-driven business world.

The East Coast–based company has a long history in the United States. It was founded in the nineteenth century by three brothers who envisioned the manufacture of ready-to-use surgical dressings to improve the health of the general population.[8] It is unlikely that the trio foresaw that their corporate name would become a household buzzword, encompassing an array of consumer, professional, and pharmaceutical products. The leadership of one brother is touted as having provided much of the impetus and direction for the company's expansion into medical and surgical hardware.

Currently, Company A's operational base consists of almost two hundred companies with locations all over the world. Its ability to gain the attention and loyalty of its enormous target market is further enhanced by the efforts of its thousands of employees and a corporate capability to communicate in almost forty languages.[9] Its reaction to the tragic events of the 1980s demonstrates Company A's consumer-oriented attitude and genuine concern for the well-being of its customers.

The product in question, sold extensively in supermarkets, convenience stores, and pharmacies, had cornered 37 percent of its market[10] and was Company A's single most profitable brand in the early 1980s, comprising 7.4 percent of its revenue and 17 to 18 percent of the corporation's income. In the midst of a multimillion-dollar advertising campaign, a link was discovered between this product and a number of related deaths. The U.S. regulator issued a warning not to purchase the product but did not direct Company A to take a specific action.[11] Uncertainties abounded. It was not known whether the product had been tampered with during the manufacturing process or later; whether the deaths would extend beyond the Midwest; or whether the government would demand a recall of the product. The small group of executives faced with the crisis did know that a recall of the product would significantly impact the bottom line; they knew this loss was not covered by insurance; and they knew that a recall could potentially so damage the product that redemption in the eyes of the public might be impossible.[12] They also knew that their first responsibility was to the public, as their credo mandates, and decided to act accordingly. An immediate recall of the product was issued, and the advertising campaign was cut short.[13]

As anticipated, the company lost tens of millions of dollars and its share value fell drastically, although it managed to regain 96 percent of its market share in the eighteen months following the tragedy.[14] This notable incident has become a textbook example of effective crisis management and a lesson in ethical decision-making. Is Company A still behaving in a socially responsible manner? How might a curious analyst undertake such an assessment? Chapter 6 explores this issue.

IN CHAPTER 7

How can one judge the suitability of another company for collaboration, commitment, or acquisition? Chapter 7 outlines a simple framework for conducting due diligence of a potential alliance partner, supplier, or acquisition candidate. Venturing into the territory of medical equipment and supply, this chapter explores how to utilize these considerations, using B Corporation as a case study.

"Whether you want to pump it up or slim it down, B Corporation's got something for you."[15] So reads an investor's statement and invitation on Hoover's Online for the public and medical sectors to invest their trust and health in products manufactured by B Corporation. With the medical advances of recent decades spurring quality-of-life issues, the invitation has been well received.

Commencing operation over thirty years ago, B Corporation was founded by its current chair and CEO John H. Churchill. Sales and executive offices have been located in the Southwest since the company's inception, with research and manufacturing arms found throughout the United States and in Europe.[16] The outfit was one of hundreds of medical equipment and supplies companies to hit the market during that time, each attempting to capitalize on achievements in the medical field. Many floundered. B Corporation did not, and it survived the media preoccupation with the apparent dangers of silicon breast-implant devices. B Corporation continues to market its product lines, including surgically implantable devices, surgical and diagnostic equipment, and disposable medical and surgical supplies to hospitals, physicians, and patients around the world. Its plastic, cosmetic and reconstructive surgery products include those used for body contouring, breast reconstruction and augmentation devices, erectile dysfunction treatment, and prostate cancer treatment (Axlec 200).[17]

As well as a profitable tapestry of products woven by its research and development department, B Corporation has ventured onto the runway of acquisitions and alliances. Correct-BC and Sunnysky, both bladder cancer products, are marketed by B Corporation through its alliance with DDC Ltd.[18] Concerns regarding product shelf life caused B Corporation to remove Correct-BC from the market recently; Sunnysky, having successfully completed Phase I and Phase II clinical trials, began Phase III within the last year.

In a field as risky as the medical devices industry, are companies such as B Corporation good acquisition candidates? How might an online assessment be made? How would a competitive intelligence professional conduct due diligence in this instance and others like it? These issues are explored in Chapter 7.

IN CHAPTER 8

How can a competitor's corporate communication style be profiled? Is there a normal pattern to its signaling behavior? How does it make use of press releases when implementing its strategies? Such questions are the subject of Chapter 8, which encourages the reader to recognize the importance of attending to corporate communications, illustrating this idea through the example of the Internet Tool Company (ITC).

"ITC is declaring war on rivals Internet Entrepreneur Inc. (IEI) and Communication Portal Corp. (CPC)," read the first line in CNNfn's story *ITC Fights Off Pack*.[19] The cat was already out of the bag. Earlier that week, ITC had initiated a change in its business model, emulating IEI's approach by marketing directly to its customer. It was a strategic maneuver designed to improve its share of the small-business market and yet another signal of ITC's intention to remain an influential player in its fast-changing market.

A Fortune 1000 company, it was and still is the second largest in its industry and the largest global supplier of products in its class. With over one hundred sales-and-service partners worldwide, its portfolio of hardware and software product lines allowed it to provide leading-edge solutions to a range of small and large customers. These product lines included enterprise computing solutions, storage products, and fault-tolerant business-critical solutions. It also claimed status as an industry leader with regard to environmentally friendly programs and business customs.[20]

As the Internet tool wars raged on, ITC discovered that it would have difficulty retaining its status and profitability if it did not imitate the business model of its major competitors. Indeed, a need to regroup had become apparent, as its track record of missing important quarterly earnings projections continued unabated. Analysts suggested a shifting of its corporate focus away from resellers and the use of a direct-selling method to target a more profitable domain. Rival IEI had outdistanced ITC with a 10 percent cost advantage on this front.[21] In the fall of 1998, ITC released word that its new Direct Link line of Internet tools would be available at prices lower than those of resellers when purchased directly from the company. Additionally, ITC announced that a referral fee would be paid for each customer passed on by distributors.[22]

Would IEI be able to read ITC's true intentions? How would an analyst make sense of the deluge of public relations announcements emanating from the ITC Web site? Is a distinctive pattern associated with ITC's communications behavior? How would one know if its public relations posture differs from the norm? Chapter 8 provides the reader with a map for processing the abundant material strewn along the information highway.

IN CHAPTER 9

How can online resources help an outside observer spot an organization in distress, before this knowledge is widely known or disseminated? Are there signals that indicate ahead of time a major competitor transformation in the offing? Signals of impending or ongoing organizational change are the topic of Chapter 9. Garage. When one thinks of this word in the context of famous corporate start-ups, Hewlett Packard is usually a name that comes to mind. It now shares its illustrious beginnings with another well-known entity, BuyFromUs. Less than a decade old and headquartered away from Silicon Valley and the money of Wall Street, BFU has transformed its customer base from personal acquaintances to hundreds of thousands of buyers worldwide.[23] It is among a legion of Web-dependent companies that have experienced astronomical growth in share price, size, and resources without a corresponding increase in profits.[24] The darling of the media, the implementer of a business model envied around the world, and a continual source of innovation, this online storefront now faces a challenge familiar to many other global players—managing corporate growth.

Are there signals that significant change is underway at BuyFromUs? Is the news all good? Questions such as these are addressed in Chapter 9.

IN CHAPTER 10

Who competes with whom? In many industries, the answer to this question is fairly clear. In others, where boundaries are somewhat fuzzy, the responses can be vague and worrisome for analysts. Now consider these different ways of asking the same question. Who does the company think are its competitors? Who does the media think are the firm's competitors? Whom does the investment community consider to be a competitor? Who produces the same products or services? Who is classified under the same SIC code? Who holds similar patents? Responding to such questions is often a trivial exercise. Identifying future competitors, the topic of Chapter 10, is not.

IN CHAPTER 11

The potential of the Internet and the World Wide Web for transforming our daily lives is immense and at times seems limitless. Unfortunately, a number of astute observers are suggesting caution. Dr. Sonya Symons, a research psychologist at Acadia University, is one of those individuals. Her area of expertise is literacy and its connection with technology and the workplace. In this chapter, she suggests that a large portion of the workforce is ill prepared for the literacy demands placed on them today. The rate at which information is made available and the haphazard way in which technology is changing demand more from workers, but much of the populace may not be able to respond adequately. Symons suggests that in order to meet the literacy demands of the twenty-first century, educators will have to emphasize more practical literacy skills, and information technology specialists will have to take human factors into consideration as they develop resources such as the Internet.

IN CHAPTER 12

CI as we know it today may have a limited shelf life. Advances in intelligent software agent applications and research promise to change the way that we look at our competitors and our operating environments. In a fitting conclusion, Dr. Andre Trudel, a computer scientist at Acadia University, offers an overview of this new and exciting world and suggests how close we are to having software that can gather accurate data and make optimal decisions on our behalf.

The Internet and the real-time access it offers to online insights provide both a challenge and an opportunity for those seeking to make sense of an ocean of information. The challenge is to continually identify and make use of meaningful information to resolve important daily business concerns as they arise. The opportunity is the potential of this new medium to simplify that challenge. This book identifies free, publicly available sources of information that might offer a competitive advantage to those curious enough to explore the digital universe. It then integrates these sources with innovative research tools, suggesting a means for analysts to effectively interpret important events in their competitive environments.

Chapter 2

The Challenge

Picture this scenario. It is late in the last spring of the twentieth century. Your four-month leave of absence has been approved by your employer. Within twenty-four hours of leaving the office, you are on a plane bound for New Delhi to start your tour of Asia. For the first time in two and a half years, you are able mentally to leave your work at your desk, work that over the years has kept you preoccupied following developments in the telecommunications equipment industry, now referred to as Internet equipment.

Jump forward to a Sunday evening in early September just prior to the new millennium and your return to work. Completely relaxed but feeling a little out of touch not having read a North American newspaper or glanced at a computer screen in months, you pick up the most recent issue of *Business Week*, the one magazine whose delivery you did not halt during your absence. The cover story is about the ascendance of Cisco Systems as a leading Internet equipment provider.

Instantly, your hunger for a late dinner subsides. As you open the magazine and begin to read, you soon realize what you missed during your journey abroad. In the space of a few weeks, three of the biggest players in the telecommunications industry have moved with dizzying speed to alter the competitive landscape. Cisco Systems has undertaken more than ten acquisitions.[1] Nortel Networks has acquired a number of important players, decided for the most part to get out of the manufacturing business, undergone another reorganization at the senior management level, and announced the launch of an innovative software

driver router that could revolutionize the industry.[2] Lucent Technologies
has done nothing but acquire a series of data networking companies,
another with call-center technology, a messaging technology company,
and a management consulting firm.[3] With this in mind, the notion occurs
to you that tomorrow, your first day back at work, will be somewhat
chaotic.

These changes also sharpen your mind, causing you to think how
sense may be made of such sudden turmoil. Your thoughts soon turn to
your trusted laptop and its accompanying technology. With instant access to numerous commercial databases, information will not be lacking.
Further, you have the luxury of being a recipient of over a dozen regular
subscription services that specialize in technology and the Internet. You
are also privy to analyst reports from the major investment firms of Wall
Street and the City. Along with these external sources, your firm has
developed a sophisticated intranet system that complements its collegial
corporate culture and enables proactive knowledge sharing. Having recently completed a well-developed, hands-on course on the use of search
engines, you are confident that any points of insight not picked up by
the other sources can be found quickly.

Even with all this support at hand, you continue to feel a slight sense
of unease. As with most of your colleagues, you are quite confident of
your ability to predict the near-term future for this industry. You are,
however, feeling less and less comfortable making pronouncements
about the longer-term direction of each major competitor and feel completely ill at ease offering insight as to where the Internet is headed.
Fortunately, your discomfort is shared by many others and, as you also
realize, may be symptomatic of feelings not unique to this era of commerce. Further reflection brings to mind a particularly thought-
provoking economics perspective that you have noticed popping up on
regular occasions in selected business articles.

You recall that for over half a century economists have had at their
disposal a framework for understanding scenarios similar to those currently faced by many industries. However, only within the last decade
or so has such thinking become fashionable. The work referred to is that
of Joseph Schumpeter,[4] an economist who had the misfortune of writing
at a time when Keynesian economics was in ascendance. Hidden on the
shelves of many a library, the ideas of this late Austrian were rediscov-
ered in time to capture the meaning of much of the transformation that
characterized many industries in the late 1980s and early 1990s.[5] In his
writings of 1934, Schumpeter theorized that we live in a truly capitalist
society, one characterized by periods of *creative destruction*. During these
periods, non-innovating industries and corporations fall by the wayside
if they cannot develop the new products, processes, technologies, and
organizational forms demanded by an uncompromising market.

At the heart of Schumpeter's thinking were a number of important points, two of which are particularly relevant for this discussion. One point is that capitalist economies do indeed experience progress over time, even if such progress is messy. A second notion points to the need of organizational or economic entities to innovate continually in order to survive in the industrial marketplace. In view of the changing nature of industries such as railways, airlines, farming, and oil and gas, it is perhaps not too far a stretch to suggest that Schumpeter's thesis is correct.

The telecommunications industry is a good case in point. Currently, corporations such as Nortel Networks, Lucent Technologies, and Cisco Systems are reshaping not only their own industry but others by providing improvements and increasing public access to voice, video, and data networks. As Cisco's CEO, John Chambers, suggests, todays telecom industry is what the builders of the roads, railways, and harbors were during the industrial revolution.[6]

These advances have enabled the development of a body of new technologies, products, processes, and organizational forms that in turn give credence to many of the ideas originally proposed by Schumpeter. Examples of innovations are not hard to find and include online auctions, affordable video e-mail technology, user-friendly Web-based storefronts, virtual university libraries, and virtual corporations with architecturally designed hotelling office spaces useful for contractors or employees travelling for business purposes.

Clearly, the effects of this communications revolution are profound and numerous. Beyond the rise to prominence of e-commerce and e-business operating environments, three of these effects are extremely important for professional analysts seeking to understand or read the behavior of adversaries. One effect is a change for many firms in how strategy is conceived of and implemented. The question "What products or services should we sell?" is one that, in many instances, can no longer be responded to immediately. Among decision makers, increasingly such a question takes a backseat to more urgent queries such as, "Who will my customers be?" and "How will they use the Internet?" To complicate matters, responses to these latter two queries are often intertwined. A response to the former question often depends on the nature of the response to the latter. Place into this equation the chaotic merger and acquisition activity currently characterizing so many industries and one soon appreciates the desire of many senior executives to retire early.

Competitive sense making becomes even more bewildering when one considers the second effect, or challenge, facing analysts. In many cases, customers or potential customers are unsure of how best to make use of Internet technology and the opportunities presented by the World Wide Web. As fiber-optic and microchip technologies improve, applications once only dreamed of quickly become realities. Indeed, previously unheard-of uses often jump out at users. Now, not only is a solid knowledge of one's existing and emerging adversaries and their stakeholders crucial, so too is a general understanding of industry-related technology developments.

The third effect challenging analysts is to understand the impact of two trends apparent in many digitally sensitive industries.[7] The first trend is seen in evidence that numerous corporations are finally "walking the walk" as opposed to "talking the talk" when it comes to focusing on core business activities. When an industry icon as influential as Dun & Bradstreet considers diversifying out of the bond-rating business, one realizes that something important is occurring. A second trend is a restructuring of many existing industry value chains around new business models to incorporate a clearly recognizable brand leader at the head of a group of less well known but very profitable supplier firms.

As you ponder these three effects, it becomes obvious that the progress associated with communications and Internet technologies has had a paradoxical impact on analytical research. At your level, that of the individual analyst or researcher, you observe the advent of the World Wide Web as an information repository and the development of software tools such as Ask Jeeves, Copernic, or Third Voice, useful for navigating or simply using this entity. You also realize that these advances are positive examples of Schumpeter's thesis. Never before has information been so accessible. However, it is also apparent to you that information alone is insufficient for resolving most of the important business concerns facing you or even for tracking the dramatic changes occurring before your eyes. Still lacking are organizing concepts or frameworks.

In particular, you begin to realize that making sense of your company's adversaries and the competitive environment also involves:[8]

- Effectively sharing knowledge with colleagues.
- Structuring your company to most efficiently gather information and make the best use of it.
- Getting the right information to decision makers in your organization.
- Tying intelligence gathering and analysis to the overall strategy of your corporation.

As you contemplate the impact of these recent events on your ability to make informed judgments, you begin to think through some of the ideas that have crossed your professional career path. Where should you look to increase your knowledge of these important processes and improve your own ability to make sense of the telecommunications and

Internet industries? Quickly, one body of insight jumps out as particularly relevant—competitive intelligence (CI).

It has been a couple of years since your introduction to the world of
CI. Out of curiosity, you had attended a half-day information seminar
organized by the Society of Competitive Intelligence Professionals
(SCIP). You discovered an immediate connection between your professional development needs and the resources and interests of SCIP. From
this event and further personal reading, you soon learned that competitive intelligence is the process of monitoring the competitive environment, an environment that includes general business trends and
competitor activities.[9]

You discovered that CI is useful for addressing many issues within
one's competitive environment. These issues include, but are not limited
to, questions such as:[10]

- The identity of emerging competitors
- The behavior of existing adversaries and their impact on your company
- The competitive opportunities represented by the creation of new markets
- Alterations to the existing operating environment and their impact on your
  firm
- The identity of new technologies on the horizon
- New legislation and its potential impact on the existing competitive landscape

Systematic and ethical, this process of monitoring may also be conceived of as the flow of activities involved in a business decision, from
the point where data is collected to the point where a decision is made
and specific desired results achieved. An important goal of any CI process is to develop *actionable intelligence*.[11] A desired scenario is one in
which data is collected and compiled to develop information that is then
analyzed to create knowledge. Knowledge, when communicated, becomes intelligence and, when applied by decision makers, leads to action
and results.[12]

In an organizational setting, CI is not the responsibility of any one
individual. When fully implemented, it is a system in which knowledge
is created and data organized in a meaningful manner. This implies that
understanding business trends and competitive behavior is best done
collaboratively, involving many individuals working together. Within
such a system, as in most organizations, different individuals undertake
different roles. In CI-enabled organizations, people in roles such as analysts, integrators, researchers, and information protectors support others such as decision makers.

As already noted, competitive intelligence is an ethical discipline. As
with those available to academics and colleagues in your industry, information sources useful to CI practitioners are quite extensive. Any rep-

utable list of sources would include trade journals, the shared knowledge of coworkers/colleagues, the opinions of acknowledged industry experts such as trade association representatives, insights from customers or sales representatives of your own company, press releases or the product specifications of competitors and suppliers, government records and regulatory documents, paid research services, newspaper articles, and scientific journals.

With these ideas swirling in your mind, you attempt to refocus your thoughts on your original concern—to make sense in the next few days of the dramatic changes occurring in the telecommunications and Internet industries. Yet, no longer does panic grip your senses. You realize that the team-based, collegial nature of your organization, coupled with a state-of-the-art Web-based intranet, has effectively nurtured an operating culture of knowledge creation and dissemination. A flat hierarchy along with an open-door policy on the part of executives allows informed decisions to be made quickly. A remuneration program targeted at making employees into owners has allowed a climate of loyalty to develop, reducing the need for restrictive external Internet firewalls. The effect has been the retention of a large cadre of competent analysts whose knowledge of, and comfort with, the latest search engines and intelligent software agent technology can best be described as leading edge. Because of these efforts in your organization, you can rest comfortably in the fact that your colleagues are supportive and knowledgable.

You come to realize that, at the very least, you possess the technology, professional training, and supporting infrastructure necessary to make a convincing argument one way or another. Yet once again, despite your confidence, one nagging concern remains—whether you can truly assess the state of the telecommunications industry in a manner that is accurate as well as convincing. You understand that two personal abilities will be both necessary and tested. You will need to integrate, in a meaningful manner, information readily available through the Internet with the concepts and analytical frameworks that form the basis of powerful new areas of inquiry such as competitive intelligence. In this regard, you are confident of your abilities to learn as necessary. You will also have to make use of your intuition, a skill whose acquisition is, in the language of business strategy, both path dependent and causally ambiguous.

Practicing Internet-based competitive intelligence is about mastering the art of integrative and intuitive thinking. The goal of this book is to help readers integrate ideas and information in a manner that is rational and effective. Rational is a term with many definitions.[13] In this context, we refer to technological rationality or an attitude that problems, to be solvable, have to be defined in technical terms and resolved with the aid of scientific knowledge and advanced technology.[14]

Intuitive thinking falls under a different category or set of human qualities. These qualities are acquired over a lifetime, rather than from the pages of a book or the duration of a training course. These qualities also serve to balance the often assured and confident predictions of rational thinking. These qualities refer to an understanding of ethics, a use of common sense, a development and nurturing of creativity, an acceptance of the importance of intuition, and an awareness during decision making of history, experience, and memory.[15] They also instill in your mind a healthy dose of doubt, useful for your upcoming deliberations on the telecommunications industry.

Subsequent chapters, provide examples of how theoretical frameworks and knowledge of specific Web site or information portal content can be integrated to support competent analytical efforts to resolve important business concerns. This book offers tools and ideas that will help CI professionals, analysts, and other users of the World Wide Web improve their ability to reason. It does not replace the human qualities that support decision making. At best, it lays a foundation stone for the lifelong quest for knowledge.

Chapter 3 _____

The Power of Search Engines

Christina McRae

Picture yourself as a twenty-two-year-old, three hours into your dream job. You have recently graduated from a small, relatively unknown laptop college in the Northeast. The college caught the eye of another relatively young junior recruiter from your company. You are the test case for your alma mater. At this moment your feelings are mixed. You are exactly where you want to be in your career. Unfortunately, you are now wondering if your professor's glowing praise of your analytical abilities was a little too optimistic.

The reason for your concern is the task placed on your desk by your boss, a not-quite-as-recent graduate of an East Coast Ivy League institution. You have been asked to present the industry value chain of your company and identify the activities experiencing the most profound degrees of alteration. You are not worried about the alteration issues. New product development efforts are easy to identify using the Transium Business Intelligence Web site. IPOs are easily categorized using the IPO Central home page. Further, alliance announcements and merger and acquisition activity are well covered by online sources such as CNNfn and Yahoo!Business.

What does concern you is your ability to quickly construct a useful industry value chain. You recall a similar challenge put forward a few months ago in class. Instinctively, you pull up the Web site for a search engine titled NorthernLight.com. You then hit the "Power Search" button and click on the "Search the World Wide Web" option. Offered a series of choices, you type "Value Chain" in the "Title" box. In the "Search

For" box, you type in your industry, in this case "Food Processing," and then press "Enter."

Within seconds, you are offered a choice of thirty-three hits. The first hit proves to be an Australian professor's teaching slides on the topic. The second hit originates from the online annual report of a second-tier competitor of your company. The diagram from this digital document bears a strong resemblance to the educator's presentation. A third hit seemingly confirms the validity of the first two ideas. It takes the form of an Industry Canada study available to the public through its Strategis online information portal. Focusing on Canadian aspects of the industry, it provides a solid overview and discusses the potential impact of the Internet on its value chain, although at a fairly high level of abstraction. As the extent of your good fortune slowly sinks in, you realize that your dinner date need not be rescheduled and that other members of your alma mater may soon join you in your workplace.

How far-fetched is this scenario? Probably not far at all. Everything just described is realistic. Although one might debate the accuracy of any value chain found on the Web, the availability of such information is hard to question.

The Internet has fundamentally changed the business world. At an unprecedented rate, new and existing businesses are scrambling to establish a Web presence. Daily, significant volumes of new digital information are being added to the world's largest library. A recent count suggested the existence of hundreds of millions of Web pages, with traffic on the Internet doubling every ninety days.[1] In the second quarter of 1999, venture capital funding in the United States increased 77 percent, to a record $7.6 billion. More than half went to Internet start-ups.[2] The challenge for managers and analysts is how to effectively navigate through this vast pool of material to find necessary information. Analysts can resolve specific business concerns by using free online information resources. Original online sources need to be matched with appropriate analytical frameworks. This chapter outlines a mainstream approach to identifying information sources—the use of search engines.

Few online tools are as appropriate to the practice of competitive intelligence (CI) as a search engine. If we define CI as the business of gathering and assessing information as a means of gaining a competitive edge in today's global marketplace, then it is easy to see where portals such as NorthernLight, Go.com, and Excite fit into the picture. Particularly in the United States, with its easy access to information and databases in the public domain, competitive intelligence is now accepted as a fundamental, technology-driven, management practice. The sheer volume and diversity of data, government, news, business, and company sites from all over the world constitute a wealth of information from which intelligence agents can glean relevant material. Web sites related to your own industry, for example, can provide leads to more specific sources of information; the address and telephone number of an expert writing in your field may be suggested by an article published online. You may come across a reference to an interesting research paper that you can access from a business library. Subscribing to an industry mailing list can keep you abreast of industry-related news while keeping tabs on your competitors. Company Web sites, eager to establish their businesses online, are notorious for providing more information than they should. A competitor's site may offer "a gold mine for corporate sleuths, an electronic road map to [their] organization and product range."[3] For example, U.S. Robotics used to list the technical specifications for every product it sold. The Web site of Mail Boxes Etc., a global mailing service based in California, described a typical franchise operation, including its square footage, operating hours, and number of employees. Other corporate Web sites may include extensive insight into specific marketing strategies, advertising campaigns, and manufacturing information.

Despite the easy access to information, there are a few drawbacks to using the Web for research. Contrary to popular belief, you cannot find everything on the Web. The reliability of data can not always be assured, and the exponential growth rate of the Web is making it more difficult to locate specific data. In addition, technical problems such as downed networks, poor connections, busy sites, and long downloading times still persist.

Software developers have responded to the growing use of the Internet for business with new intelligence gathering and analytical tools that can help managers stay in the game. A number of these are discussed in the final chapter of this book. For the moment, however, you may be aware of some of the new high-tech software products that can quickly sift through vast amounts of market research or financial data to find just about anything online. Cognos Inc., based in Ottawa, Ontario, sells software tools that can gather information from competitors, combine it with internal information, analyze the data, and then run it through models. This software could, for example, predict the effects of spending more money on advertising, so that the manager has additional criteria on which to base his or her business decisions. Verity Inc., based in Sunnyvale, California, sells a system based on "knowledge mapping." Searching is refined by combining machine-derived intelligence with human intelligence to create rules of evidence and families of topics and then mapping these domains of knowledge. Their corporate starter kit includes an information server to maintain the index, a spider server to search the Internet and intranet, and an agent server that automatically alerts specific agents of relevant information. This cutting-edge intelligence-gathering technology comes at a price—most corporate-wide systems run into hundreds of thousands of dollars.[4]

Luckily, a host of free Web sites and services are designed to make competitive intelligence gathering easier. These are discussed extensively in the following chapters. However, here is a sampling of sites that offer pertinent business information. For general data on the technological industry, the Corp Tech Web site maintains a business database for primary information on over 50,000 high-tech manufacturers and developers. A list of 300,000 company profiles organized by country, as well as links to non-American market research reports, accounting policies, laws, and court decisions can be found using the Corporate Information portal. Recruitment and job-posting sites, such as *Career Path* and Monster.com, are also popular with intelligence gatherers. The IBM Intellectual Property Network Server lists over two million U.S. government patents dating back to January 5, 1971, and provides images for the last twenty-four years. Demographic and economic data are available through the home page of the United States Census Bureau. If these are not helpful enough, a number of Web sites now suggest detailed processes for researching corporations or industries along with links to relevant sites for each step in the process. Examples of such processes may be found on the Virtual Pet and Corporate Watch home pages.

Search engines are indispensable for sorting through the millions of pages of information on the Web. Learning how to use the available search engines most effectively is one of the easiest ways to gather specific information quickly. An example of a fairly sophisticated search engine that points to the future is Ask Jeeves. It has the ability to find online information using natural language.[5] Its claim to fame is an ability to match specific questions with specific answers by independently constructing a Boolean search of its proprietary database of seven million (and growing) answers. Not all search engines work in the same manner as Ask Jeeves.

In order to understand how search engines work, it is useful to review the differences between Internet providers and Internet browsers. *Internet service providers* (ISPs) such as IBM, Voyager, and Sprint provide a direct connection to the Internet. Online services such as America Online (AOL), CompuServe, and Genie also offer a search engine to access information on the Internet, but they specialize in providing more of an online community with services like chat rooms and shopping areas. *Internet browsers* are software systems that are installed on your own personal computer. This browser software enables you to read Hypertext Markup Language (HTML) documents. At the moment HTML is the standard programming language used to create Web pages. The browser options allow you to manoeuver between Web pages, set home pages, reload badly transmitted information, copy, save, or store pages, text, and images offline, print pages, find specific words on a page, and so on.

Internet search services such as Hotbot, Excite, and GO.com use automated software agents, known as spiders, robots, or crawlers, to travel through Web sites and catalogue their contents word by word. This information is recorded in the search service's proprietary databases. Search engines, the programs used to search through these databases, use specified terms, phrases, or topics to find matches. It is important to remember that no single search engine can search the entire Web. Even the largest search engines are working from indexes that contain less than half the pages posted on the World Wide Web. Altavista, for example, indexes only slightly more than 160 million pages out of an estimated Web total of 400 million pages. Therefore, it is essential to use combinations of different search services to achieve the best results.

All of the better search engines have advanced search options that help you to define more precisely what information you want to find. For example, when using Altavista, click on "advanced search"; on Hotbot, use "more search options"; and on NorthernLight, click on the "power search button." Specific search queries return fewer results, and most of these results will be good matches. Most search engines focus searches with Boolean logic. Boolean searching allows word and phrase combinations using "and," "or," and "not." Placing the word "and" between two words or phrases results in returns containing both the words or phrases. Using the word "or" between the terms or phrases ensures that all the matches returned contain at least one of the two terms or phrases. A search for "United Kingdom or U.K." would find pages mentioning the country by either name. "Not" is used to exclude words from a search. A search for "mutual funds and not bonds" would eliminate all the pages containing the word "bonds."

Another way to refine your search query is to use phrase searching, specifying that the selected words must appear in a certain order. For example, in Altavista, Hotbot, or Netscape, the phrase "distribution equipment demographics" in quotation marks would direct the search engine to return only pages containing that exact phrase.

Field searching[6] can be used to restrict your search to certain parts of the document, such as within the site's title, the image description, or the URL. In Altavista and GO.com the keyword (title, image, link, etc.) should be in lowercase and followed by a colon and the word or phrase you are looking for. For example: title: "emergency aid" would find documents having "emergency aid" in the title; url:bank would find pages with the word "bank" in their World Wide Web address; host:www.firstenergy.com would find pages on a specific computer; domain:edu would find pages with .edu as the domain; and link:www.ford.com would find pages with that specific link. On some search engines, field searches can be combined with a Boolean or phrase search. This advanced search option is known as nesting. For example, title: "navigational products" and Internet would locate documents with "navigational products" in the title and the word Internet anywhere on the page. In Altavista, title: ("navigational products" and Internet) would return pages with both terms in the title. Hotbot allows nested searches through its pull-down menus, while Northern Light's Power Search Page also provides options for nested searches.

Two additional advanced search options are truncation and proximity operators. *Truncation operators* allow searches for words with similar patterns, so that at the end of the search for the word "manager" a truncation operator would also find "managers," "managerial," and the like. In Altavista an asterix is used for the truncation operator; other search engines sometimes use a percent sign or a question mark to replace characters. In Hotbot there is an option to allow for word stemming, or grammatical variations of your search term. The search for the word "thought" would also find "think" and "thinking." Proximity or nearness operators allow searches in which terms are specified to be near to other terms. For example, "stock market" near "shareholders," or "corporate takeovers" near IBM. Altavista can find words within a dozen words of each other, and Lycos-Pro within double that.

Speaking of good Web sites, which are better than others? This is a good question with no easy answer. Search Engine Watch does, however, try to answer it. If its efforts are any indication, "it depends" appears to be among the most appropriate of responses. This Web site offers a Search Engine Reviews Chart that documents the results of performance surveys conducted by magazines such as *PC Magazine*, *Cnet*, *Internet World*, and *Family PC*.[7] If gold, silver, and bronze medals are still indicative of excellence in a field of endeavor, then its review suggests few search engines that are not exceptional or award winning. To forego controversy, let's assume that performance is question driven and in many instances resides in the eye of the beholder.

In addition to using specific, well-defined queries on individual search engines, there are metasearch sites that can search several other search engines. Three of the most popular of these are Dogpile, Metasearch, and Savvysearch. The major drawback of these large search sites is that some do not account for the unique ways in which the individual search engines work.

Some metasearch engines do stand out, however. Copernic 2000 is such an example. It allows users to target searches using nearly sixty search engines grouped into six categories. As it searches, this efficient tool filters out and eliminates digital documents that are found on more than one search engine.[8] It also provides detailed search histories and allows users to download documents as needed.

Hundreds of other search engines offer specialized services and have often done some initial work on collecting and reviewing. News search engines, for example, can be a useful means of gathering intelligence information. You can specify how far back in the news you want to look, and you usually can set up a folder that follows developments related to particular topics or companies. Examples are numerous, some of the more common are Newsbot, which carries news of the digital world, as well as News Index and Total News, two sources that carry news of interest to the general public. The digital dialogue from thousands of Internet news and chat groups are also indexed and searchable. Keywords can be used to look for discussions on a wide range of interests, companies, products, and people. Among the more specialized discussion forums are The Motley Fool and Silicon Investor. For online sources that allow topic-specific discussion forums to be identified, consider using Deja.com and Reference.com.

Of course, a variety of help is available online. One should always read the tips or help section at the search engine site to become familiar with its features and benefits. Additional information on different kinds of search engines, how they work, Web tutorials, reviews of search engines, and so on can be found on the Web sites of Search Engine Watch, Notess.com, and Search Engineers.

If you find a relevant piece of online information, you may want to make a note about it to a group of colleagues. An interesting tool for accomplishing that is Third Voice.com. Billed as a "browser companion service," it allows users to post their ideas through online notes on any Web page.[9] Simply sign yourself and your colleagues up as a group, post notes where you please, and then direct your group members to the note markers. Invisible to others, you can hold your own private discussions on the Web sites of some of the largest and most powerful companies in the world.

As is evident here, the Internet offers tremendous opportunities for finding business information that is relevant and useful. Formulating your search carefully, being specific, using several different search engines, and taking advantage of the advanced search options will help to make the task manageable. It is a good idea to take notes as you work. Bookmarks are indispensable for establishing sources that you want to review on an ongoing basis or for marking something you would like to come back to. Using keystrokes (control "C" to copy, control "V" to paste, control "F" to find information within a text) to copy text into your word-processing program (Word, WordPerfect, PowerPoint, etc.) enables you to store and reformat information off line.

It is a good idea to review the basic rules of gathering competitive information on the Web.[10] First, abide by any legal restrictions. For example, if you are doing research for your own company, you may need clearance to e-mail suppliers or potential clients. Remember to follow the usual rules of communication when using e-mail, such as not exchanging price information with competitors or offering bribes. There are Internet service providers that allow you to look at a competitor's site while protecting your identity (such as Anonymizer), but if you are sending e-mail, posting to newsgroups, or subscribing to mailing lists you must identify yourself by name and/or company. If you are collecting information for a report, your purpose should be made clear to those you are communicating with. Of course, it is vital that you post credible information yourself and not try to hack your way into private intranets. Operating in good faith and accessing only public information are the key elements of competitive intelligence.

There is no question that the latest high-tech software systems and the advanced options of online search engines can be used to effectively track down relevant, competitive information from the Web. These tools can accomplish in minutes work that would take months to do manually. As André Trudel notes in the concluding chapter of this book, search engines as we know them probably have a limited shelf life. Indeed, advances in software agent technology promise to dramatically improve the ability of online researchers to find relevant and accurate information quickly. Ask Jeeves and Copernic are but two examples of the tools that agent research will continue to make available to the general online public.

Complementing the development of agent technology is a growing awareness among Internet knowledge creators of the need for an ontology to organize the information of the World Wide Web. Concern over digital information overload and disorganization is shared globally by users of the Internet. Unfortunately, efforts to classify or meaningfully organize such information have been inconsistent and fragmented. Increasingly, the community of researchers is recognizing this shortcoming and attempting to develop a specification or knowledge base of concepts and relationships that govern the classification of Web-enabled information and knowledge. Should an ontology be successfully created, it will enable knowledge to be shared and reused in a far simpler manner than exists today. It will also provide a consistent and coherent vocabulary. In a digital world where the use of intelligent software agents such as Copernic and Ask Jeeves becomes the norm, a common vocabulary, or standard,[11] would allow these digital spiders to query each other and make assertions when undertaking specific tasks.[12] Such an ontology would also be capable of evolving, allowing researchers to build on previous knowledge and incorporate changes as needed. For the CI professional, in the long run, this should enhance the accuracy and speed of search efforts as well as the level of sophistication of responses.

In the not-too-distant future, software agents and knowledge ontologies will play an increasingly important role in the world of competitive intelligence. However, for the time being, the responsibility still lies with the human mind to make sense of it all, to follow intuition, and to find ways to make the reams of information effect positive change. The next chapter moves us in this direction by outlining the theory underpinning this book.

Chapter 4 ─────────────────────

A Theory

Do the ideas of the following quotation sound familiar?

Capitalism involves a process of change that revolutionises the economic structure from within, destroying the old and creating a new one. This is the process of creative destruction. . . . Outside of the theoretical world, the most important form of competition is not from existing firms selling similar products but from the new product, technology, source of supply or other innovation, that will replace the existing industry standard product with a commanding cost or quality advantage. This competition does not pressure the profit margins of firms like the perfect competition of Adam Smith, but strikes at their foundation and very reason for existence.[1]

Few would suggest that these ideas have no relevance to today's world of commerce. As many of us experience the breathtaking excitement associated with technological progress and the changes in our daily lives, so too do we realize that we are at the dawn of a new era, one increasingly being characterized by long-term or perpetual uncertainty.

One important aspect of this new time has been the scope of alterations to the competitive landscape. Although the phrase "develop products and services and then sell them" still captures the bulk of what firms do, the context within which these tasks are accomplished is not so simple to describe. A number of characteristics[2] describe this new environment, one faced by all forms of organizations, be they private, public, or not for profit.

To begin, risk and uncertainty of all forms are increasing, while in many industries the ability to forecast beyond a few weeks' time is diminishing rapidly. In some of these cases, the boundaries that differentiate one competitive setting from another are no longer easy to define. For instance, in what industry does Microsoft compete? Can you draw a map of the telecommunications industry? Answers to such questions do exist. Whether or not they are accurate is anyone's guess. Consider the quandry facing many executives. How does one manage a new collaborative relationship with a long-time competitor, who only weeks before was considered the number-one threat to the long-term survivability of the organization?

Further, add to this a new collaborative relationship, a contractual agreement that dictates a partnership in certain but not all product lines. Unfortunately many executives have no choice but to accept such risky propositions and then strive to make them work for both parties. Finally, order and disorder appear to be an accepted part of the competitive landscape. Despite the apparent chaos associated with changing boundaries and an increasing risk, successful firms are managing and doing so with increasing profitability.

These and other aspects of the competitive environment are placing a number of unavoidable demands on serious corporate players. Dramatic improvements in communication technologies, increases in computer usage in the workplace and in homes, user-friendly enhancements in work-related software, and a growing acceptance of the future role of e-commerce in the marketplace have made available to businesses tools that dramatically decrease the transaction costs associated with day-to-day operations.[3] These time- and cost-saving improvements are now, in many instances, considered a necessity for gaining and retaining clients, customers, distributors, and suppliers.

In response to these demands and opportunities, we are now witnessing the creation of new organizational forms, a never-before-seen accountability in the corporate suite, and the rise of knowledge and its application as the main competitive lever available to corporations seeking a sustained advantage over their competitors.[4]

Especially important in this new competitive landscape are the current advances in electronic communication systems, which in turn are facilitating new ways of organizing.[5] These new communication-friendly organizational forms have been variously referred to as the adhocracy,[6] technocracy,[7] internal market,[8] virtual organization,[9] knowledge linked[10] and network organization.[11]

How might this new form of electronically based organization be described? One suggestion is that it is small or located in a subunit of a large organization, with an operating mandate typically in the area of automated production or of the service or information variety. If not, its technology is computerized, with a division of labor that is informal and flexible. Further, its management structure is functionally decentralized, eclectic, and participative.[12] Along with these efficiency-enhancing structures, advances in electronic communications have also given rise to increasingly transparent operations.

In turn, this transparency suggests an alternative metaphor for describing leading organizations of the new millennium—*interpreters* of the competitive landscape. Such a metaphor may not be too far-fetched, as interpretation is argued by some to be a basic requirement of individuals, influenced by such things as the nature of the answer sought, the characteristics of the environment, the previous experience of the questioner, and the method used to acquire it.[13] "A key maxim of CI is that 90 percent of all information that a company needs to make critical decisions and to understand its market and competitors is already public or can systematically be developed from public data."[14]

Organizations may be thought of as interpretation systems. In turn, analysts and executives in their employ respond to opportunities and threats by scanning the competitive environment, collecting relevant data, and interpreting it. From these interpretations, actions are taken and insights fed back to help respond to the next important issue.[15] Describing a corporation in this manner highlights the vital role played by CI professionals in the new economy.

The implications of operating transparency do not end here. Never before have the abilities of the top management teams of our major corporate institutions been subject to such close scrutiny from all quarters. Gone are the days of long-term privilege based on suspect profitability and poor share-price earnings. Transparency in reporting practices, powerful regulators, and a rise of activist pension and mutual fund managers have helped to generally increase the accountability of corporate boards of directors and in turn to focus attention on bottom-line results. Examples of this attention include a renewed interest by writers and scholars on the topic of leaders and the role of the CEO. One recent study went so far as to suggest a reason for the recent rash of CEO firings—a need for CEOs to execute the fundamental strategies of their organizations. One quote from this article is quite revealing: "So how do CEOs blow it? More than any other way, by failure to put the right people in the right jobs."[16]

Not only the pressures to deliver solid financial results are increasing; so too are the demands placed on executives from an operational point of view. Simply consider the corporate success factors suggested by one group of leading organizational thinkers. To them, success is offered to those who can guide boundaryless organizations[17] to prosperity. Success factors include speed in everything that companies do, flexibility in people and operations, integration of specialists and nonspecialists, and a constant search for innovation in all corporate functions.

Add to this formula a competitive landscape that is often unforgiving to companies that make mistakes or managers who are too hesitant to make or implement critical decisions, and one begins to realize the relevance of practices such as employee empowerment or effective hiring practices.

Simply put, the operating environments of most organizations are too complex to be managed from atop a hierarchy. Corporations depend on employees at all levels to decipher and navigate environments rife with uncertainty. The implication of this is knowledge as a basis for competition, and knowledge accumulation and deployment as the most effective route to competitive advantage.[18] Indeed, future economic and strategic advantage may rest with organizations that can most effectively attract, develop, and retain the best and the brightest human talent in the marketplace. In this book, our attention focuses on one specific form of knowledge worker—the competitive intelligence analyst.

Our underlying argument is quite simple. Managers and analysts face uncertainty when seeking to make sense of complex competitive environments. In order to make sense of this complexity, these same individuals have at their disposal two forms of aid: analytical tools and information sources. Analytical tools are, in many instances, nothing more than existing or modified theoretical frameworks. Successful analysts develop accurate interpretations of the environment by matching these tools and sources. Alone, each of these three components is at best incomplete. Together, in the mind of an experienced CI professional, interpretation, analytical frameworks, and information sources spell knowledge. It is knowledge that organizations seek to protect and analysts seek to uncover. Matching appropriate theoretical frameworks with ideal information sources is the subject of most of the remaining chapters. The issue of ideal or relevant information sources is the topic of the remainder of this chapter.

CRITICAL SOURCES OF INFORMATION

Within a few years, every important news story, news picture, wire service report, and major press release in English . . . will be commercially searchable and retrievable using a personal computer with a modem, subject only to the cost that a company is willing to incur and the time it is willing to spend. Vast amounts of other information will also be available simply by *going to the net*.[19]

A few years ago, print media outlets were abuzz. The popular media reported that the sum total of material printed on paper throughout the world was multiplying at an astronomical rate. At the time, informed commentary questioned the usefulness of amassing such large volumes of text. It had become evident in previous decades that no one person could possibly process or comprehend all available knowledge in subjects such as biology, chemistry, or literature. With growing fields of inquiry, it became increasingly obvious that access to, not knowledge of, specific information was the key to individual prosperity and growth.

The Internet has made apparent the truth of this last point as never before. When a search portal returns 759,103 "matches" to an inquiry, one begins to understand the magnitude of available information. One also begins to understand how crucial reliable research methods are for identifying the useful information strands. In their efforts to build an accurate portrait of a company, analysts need to identify relevant information sources. This book is about providing a framework for analysts who "go to the Net" to resolve their business concerns, with attention on free online sources of information, not those available on a commercial basis.

For our purposes, the information available on the Internet can be classified into ten categories of information portals: legal, regulatory, news and journalism, educational, specialty business, general, corporate, special interest, public relations, and personal interactive.

Legal information portals are Web sites that direct users toward information falling within the domain of the judiciary. Particularly useful current examples of these online sources belong to the Federal Judiciary, the Stanford Securities Class Action clearinghouse, and the University of Virginia School of Law. Portals such as FindLaw Internet Legal Resources and LawCrawler Legal Web Search offer resources that enable researchers to query courts operating at both the federal and the state levels. These pages link analysts to Supreme, federal, and circuit court case transcripts, as well as to other important administrative decisions and opinions.

Despite the popularity of government bashing in corporate executive suites, cafes, and bars, competent business analysts have long recognized the importance of government regulators in leveling the domestic economy playing field. *Regulatory information portals* are government-sponsored Web sites that offer researchers insight into and information on the functions of government and market regulators. The home pages of the U.S. Securities and Exchange Commission, the U.S. Patent and Trademark Office, the Federal Trade Commission, and the Food and Drug Administration fit into this category, as do those of the National Technology Transfer Center and FedWorld.

A business analyst's first online stop should be the Securities and Exchange Commission (SEC) Web site. The SEC is an independent, non-partisan, quasijudicial regulatory agency whose role is to ensure that securities markets operate fairly and that investors have access to current financial data and material information regarding publicly traded securities.[20] Since 1996 it has adopted EDGAR, an electronic filing system that offers the public free online access to regulatory documents. Arguably, the most important sources of corporate information for any analyst are two SEC filings: Form 10K and Form S1.

Form 10K is a firm's annual financial report. Part one of a 10K Form[21] can be revealing. Not uncommonly, it contains an in-depth industry and market overview of a corporation, a portrait of its competitive environment, and a detailed business description that includes major risks or future litigable concerns. Form S1 is a corporation's prospectus, or initial business plan. It offers information on firms that have recently gone public. This information is important to watch, of course, as occasionally a new entrant alters an industry overnight. The S1 form provides an overview of the company, its history, and the major risks it faces. The organization's business model is often available in the overview section of the management's Discussion and Analysis section. The espoused strategy of the top management team is included in the business section of the report. The risk factors section will normally discuss the competitive environment, the potential impact of competitors and technological change on the organization, and the role of regulators.

Other important forms available on the SEC Web site are:

- Form 10Q: a quarterly financial report that provides an up-to-date view of a company's financial position at various points throughout the year
- Form 8K: documents the occurrence of any material organizational changes that affect the corporate bottom line
- Forms 3 and 5: specify the executives who own enough of a firm's stock to be classified as insider traders
- Form 4: documents recent insider trading activity
- Forms SC 13D and 10C: document major share purchases
- Form DEF 14: a proxy statement that informs designated classes of shareholders about matters that will be brought to a vote at the next shareholders' meeting

Once a particular corporate filing has been identified, analysts can make use of the Internet browser's built-in word search function to help find specific information quickly. Reading the entire report in detail may save time in the future and help to clarify the content of other reports, press releases, or financial statements.

Although situated on the SEC Web site, the EDGAR documents and their definitions may also be accessed through most company home pages, other online information sources such as FreeEdgar and Edgar

Online, and most business information portals including Hoover's On-line, JustQuotes.com, and Market Guide.

In many instances, industry overviews are not easily available. This requires business analysts to be creative in piecing together the information they need from the regulatory filings of competitors. The Power Search capabilities of the IPO Central Web site allow users to identify Initial Public Offerings (IPO) by industry. If a relevant IPO can be found, an exploration of that company's S1 and 10K forms may provide sufficient details to paint a meaningful portrait of the market. A second approach is to use the FreeEdgar Web site to search for filings by SIC code, enabling analysts to access comparative industry descriptions quickly.

Regulatory information portals also offer other means of building an industry portrait. Government agencies such as the Food and Drug Administration, the Department of Agriculture, and the Department of Transportation occasionally invite comments from interested parties when they seek to alter or improve regulatory policy. For instance, from time to time the Food and Drug Administration requests input from the pharmaceutical industry on the role of technology in testing procedures. As pharmaceutical firms or their agents lobby for alterations that best meet their needs, they often provide detailed explanations of industry or corporate behavior. Many regulatory bodies make these written suggestions available to the public through their Web sites. These portals may be accessed through the home pages of FedWorld or the National Technology Transfer Center.

In some instances creativity is not necessary. For selected industries, the U.S. Census Bureau maintains a series of free industrial reports on its Web site. Topics available up to 1997 for online researchers included steel mill products and truck trailers, as well as fertilizers, metalworking materials, and glassware.

News and journalism information portals are commercial, not-for-profit Web sites that provide current information, journalistic analysis, and links to information sources. Included under this banner are online local newspapers, national newspapers such as the *Wall Street Journal* and the *New York Times*, media outlets such as MSNBC or CNNfn, and electronic magazines like Red Herring and Forbes.com.

As with their print versions, online newspapers, magazines, and news media often contain articles profiling particular firms or industries. Many dedicate a considerable amount of digital space on an issue to discussing a certain sector, industry, or market related to it. When searching the current or archived online issues of these organizations, researchers should look for special reports, end-of-year reviews, and regular industry discussions.

Underlying the value of online media articles is the value of those specialty portals such as NewsDirectory.com, the National Newspaper

Association, the Newspaper Association of America, CEO Express, and Transium Business Intelligence that effectively guide researchers to pertinent electronic publications. Transium Business Intelligence is particularly effective at identifying relevant publications. A feature that differentiates it from most of its competitors is its sorting capability. A search by a company name on its home page directs users to a series of article abstracts categorized by function, geography, industry, journals, and products and services. Sorting these abstracts by journals provides not only a listing of online publications but also the number of articles of each publication that mention the company. It is most effective to look at the magazines or journals with highest article counts for industry or market summaries and for details of company behavior.

Educational information portals are those not-for-profit Web sites associated with universities, libraries, and other educational institutions focused on serving the general public. Examples include the library systems of the University of Virginia, Widener University and the University of Michigan. These portals also refer to online scholarly publications.

Specialty business information portals form a growing legion of Web sites dedicated to providing highly detailed, real-time business data to paying customers. Luckily, most of these sites also offer a significant amount of free information. These portals can be divided into two subcategories. The first includes portals that offer analysts the information necessary to effectively profile a firm, its industry, and its competitors. The second includes portals that offer information centering around one particular issue. The home pages of the Thomas Publishing Company, Monster.com, and Report Gallery.com fall into the latter group.

Hoover's Online, Zack's Investment Research, JustQuotes.com, and Quicken.com belong to the first category. Hoover's Online is one of the best known and most user-friendly profilers. It provides easy-to-read company capsules and industry reports with links to profiles of major competitors, SEC filings, insider trading activity, employment opportunities, and frequently read online magazines, including information on the most recent articles.

JustQuotes.com and the Web site of the Wall Street Research Network (WSRN.com) approach the topic of corporate and industry profiles from a different angle. After identifying a company, each offers a myriad of web links to other pertinent online information sources. For instance, WSRN.com guides users to profiles on MarketGuide, Silicon Investor, Yahoo!, and Zack's Investment Research, Inc. Web sites. JustQuotes.com uses the services of Yahoo!, Quicken.com, InvestQuest, and Edgar Online. Both WSRN.com and JustQuotes.com offer users company-specific news, profiles, financial statements and ratios, earnings data, discussion forums, and analyst recommendations.

Researchers can obtain shareholder annual reports through any number of links, including most company home pages, specialty business information portals, general information portals like Yahoo!, and through online annual report services like Reports Gallery. Generally, a good picture of industry conditions can be found in an annual report's letter from the chairman of the board. However, like corporate home pages, annual reports are written by communication professionals who largely write what their employers and constituents want to read.

Users wishing to conduct their own industry analysis should investigate Virtual Pet.com's home page. It offers a detailed, thirteen-step analysis process that includes links to important information sources.

General information portals include subject guides and search engines. Yahoo! is an example of a subject guide that hierarchically organizes indexes of subject categories, allowing searchers to browse through lists of web sites. NorthernLight, Excite!, and Infoseek are examples of search engines. These permit users to enter keywords that search against a particular online database.

Offshoots of general information portals, such as Yahoo!Business, are included in the category of sophisticated business information sources. Yahoo!Business is an excellent example of how large, older general subject directories or search engines are now striving to compete for the same corporate dollars as portals such as Hoover's Online or WSRN.com. Its typical profile provides readers with a brief description of a company's operations, links to the company home page, raw SEC filings, company public relations offerings, insider trading highlights, stock price summaries, detailed research reports, descriptions of employment opportunities, selected financial statements, subsidiary links, product and service descriptions, and dedicated chat groups. Yahoo!Business also offers free annual reports when available.

Another angle of attack is fairly simple. Try searching Excite! or Infoseek using key words such as "petroleum industry" or "petroleum" and "industry analysis." Frequently, this style of query uncovers useful academic reports and scholarly articles.

Two categories of Web sites fit under the umbrella of *corporate information portals*. One set provides links to or consists of company home pages. Accessed through online services such as Companies Online and Company Link, many of these home pages provide excellent business summaries. Descriptions of basic business postures, marketed products and services, mission statements, office and facility locations, top management team profiles, employment opportunities, news releases, executive speeches, and corporate values are available in varying levels of detail. Readers should be aware that these home pages are usually developed to show the company at its best, hence the optimistic tone of the Web site and the general absence of details that might be considered unflattering or controversial.

The second category of Web site belongs to industry associations or advocacy organizations acting on behalf of industry participants. For obtaining a picture of an industry or market, few sources are as effective as this one. Quite common are "year in review" or "market overview" speeches made by executives to association conferences or a selection of articles or press releases, many of which may describe the competitive environment in detail.

The home page of the American Society of Association Executives offers a link termed "Gateway to Associations." Among a number of subsequent links, one guides readers to the "Directory of Associations Online." From this web page, users may search for associations by key word, alphabetical order, or category.

Special interest information portals are Web sites sponsored by organizations attempting to influence public opinion. Examples of such sites include those of the Better Business Bureau, Corporate Watch, Macrocosm USA, Inc., the Institute for Global Communications, Multinational Monitor Online, Consumer World, and Consumer Reports Online.

The information these sites contain is often at odds with what is stated on corporate home pages. Special interest portals dig up dirt on companies and use what they find to inform the public and, at times, to promote the organizations' ideologies. The opinions, research reports, essays, and dialogues found through the use of these portals are not normally carried by Web sites such as Hoover's Online, CNN Financial, or the Wall Street Journal Online. Readers who want to undertake their own research effort should investigate the Corporate Watch home page. It offers readers excerpts from a detailed guide to how to find dirt on transnational corporations.

Public relations information portals are commercial Web sites dedicated to the dissemination of corporate or organizational press releases to the news media and general public. These portals give analysts insight into the views of industry insiders. Executive speeches outlining the state of the company or the state of the industry are particularly useful. This information is most easily obtained through company home pages or through portals such as PR Newswire and Business Wire. As with many other online instruments, information in these portals is found by querying the name of a company or executive using the search window.

Personal interactive portals include chat groups, message boards, and discussion forums that offer users the opportunity to share their opinions and insights with other users. Portals such as Deja.com, the Raging Bull, and the Motley Fool can be useful in obtaining a company or industry profile. Simply join in a discussion and pose a question such as, "Can any one pass on the address of a Web site with a good analysis of the West Coast forestry industry?" or, "Could someone recommend an online journal or magazine that profiles the domestic petroleum industry?"

What should be apparent from this discussion is the difference between a portal and an information source. A company's 10K annual report and its home, the EDGAR database, are information sources. The
Web site of the Securities and Exchange Commission, where it is found,
is a portal. What makes the World Wide Web confusing is that the SEC
Web site itself may be accessed through any number of different portals.
One might use a specialty business information portal such as Hoover's
Online. In this instance, a direct link would probably be found by scanning the target company's capsule. One might also access a specific 10K
annual report through a corporate information portal such as the company home page. Increasingly, many corporations are providing direct
hyperlinks to these documents. Further, one may also find a path to the
document by creatively using the advanced search options of a general
information portal such as Northern Light.

It should be clear that depending on information portals without being
aware of specific information sources can often lead to ineffective results
and an inefficient use of research time. Indeed, the ease of online information access can be a liability if the identity of the most useful or relevant information source is unknown. The following simple example
illustrates this idea.

A rookie analyst is tasked with identifying any important legal challenges facing
a potentially important future supplier. As a result of discussion around the
office coffee machine, he has learned that one important source of such information is the corporate annual report. Unfortunately, he is unaware that in most
instances two versions exist. One is normally offered with a glossy finish and
may usually be found in the reception area of most corporate offices. A second
and more reliable version is the one filed with the Securities and Exchange Commission under the heading, "10K Annual Report." Although he may find information regarding important litigation in both versions, the latter offering will
probably contain much more detail.

Finding information on the Web is only the first step in Internet research. Assessing the information is the second. The exponential increase
in Internet usage has given rise to a need for effective evaluation processes. How good is the information found on a Web site or through the
use of a particular portal? How might one assess its believability? Fortunately, analytical frameworks are becoming more and more common.
Excellent evaluation techniques are offered online by the Wolfgram Me-
morial Library of Widener University as well as by the References Services Division of the Olin* Kroch* Uris Libraries of Cornell University
Library.

The framework used in this book is much less complex than the foregoing. It ranks the levels of information integrity by category and is

Figure 4.1
The Concept of Portal Types

Portal Type	Online Examples	Higher Level of Information Correctness
Legal	Findlaw Internet Legal Resources Law Crawler Legal Web Search	
Regulatory	Securities and Exchange Commission Food and Drug Administration	⇑
News & Journalism	CNNfn The Wall Street Journal Fortune.com	
Educational	University of Virginia School of Law	
Specialty Business	Transium Business Intelligence Hoover's Online justquotes.com	⇑
General	NorthernLight.com Yahoo!	
Corporate	ASAE Gateway to Associations Companies Online	⇓
Special Interest	Better Business Bureau Corporate Watch	
Public Relations	PR Newswire Business Wire.com	⇓
Personal Interactive	Deja.com Motley Fool	
		Lower Level of Information Correctness

illustrated in Figure 4.1. The categories marked by consistently correct information are the legal and regulatory information portals. They are followed, in descending order, by news and journalism information portals, educational information portals, specialty business information portals, general information portals, special interest and corporate information portals, public relations information portals, and, finally, personal interactive portals.

Unfortunately, even these rankings are estimates, at best. The reason is the increasingly vast reach of many portals. More and more, the motto of most successful Web entities appears to be, "the more the better." While such a strategy may increase the potential for online traffic, it does pose a problem for analysts seeking reliable information.

A case in point is the growth of online versions of traditional print newspapers. News and journalistic portals such as NewsDirectory provide access to most online offerings, ranging from that of the *New York Times* to weekly small community publications. For this reason, information sources obtained using this type of portal are ranked in the middle of the pack. This ranking is, at best, an average. Within the population of Web sites that might be categorized under this heading, some may be described as extremely correct in their information offerings. Others may belong at the opposite end of the scale.

A case in point is the online version of the *New York Times*. This organization is normally very dependable in terms of what it publishes under its name. Indeed, the occurrence of inaccurate information is, in many cases, a scandal in and of itself, and occasionally a career breaker. Unfortunately, the majority of news publications do not possess the same reputation or have access to the same resources as the *New York Times*. As a result they are unable to consistently meet the same high standards of information integrity as this sterling publication.

ANALYTICAL TOOLS: FIRMS COMPETE THROUGH HIDE-AND-SEEK

A categorization scheme for online Web sites and a framework for assessing information are but pieces of the puzzle facing analysts in their quest to make sense of the uncertainty facing them. Other pieces of equal importance are the analytical tools used by online researchers. As described in the following chapters, these include frameworks for assessing signals of organizational change, socially responsible corporate behavior, and internal power structures. Yet to effectively make use of these frameworks, analysts might find it helpful to think of themselves and their quarry, the corporations or organizations, as competitors in a sporting arena.

In this arena, analysts and researchers of all stripes attempt to build accurate portraits of target organizations. Hide-and-seek is the game played between analysts and corporations, with information as the object of interest. At the end of each contest, the winner holds the knowledge necessary to build an accurate portrait. Target organizations manage and openly disseminate some of the information, hoping to favorably influence the look of portraits or to ensure that such portraits remain incomplete. Unfortunately, corporate information officers cannot control all information flows about their organization, nor can they completely manage analyst interpretations. On the other hand, analysts are challenged in most instances by incomplete information and in many instances by information overload and operational time constraints. They strive to overcome these challenges by identifying and matching relevant sources of information with appropriate analytical frameworks and personal interpretation. Realistic portraits arise in the presence of competent CI professionals. These portraits or solutions to important business concerns are also what we term *knowledge*.

The Analysts' Quest: Seek

Executives ignore human resource talent at their peril. Uncertain operating environments increasingly necessitate the inclusion of insight from all levels of the hierarchy. Yet analytical insight is not without its own failings. In order to make sense of corporate dissemination efforts, we would like to suggest the following step-by-step process for use by online researchers.

1. Identify the business concern of interest. In other words, clarify the nature of the task facing the analyst.
2. Clearly define a research question. Put simply, reword the concern in a manner that makes it testable.
3. Search for existing theoretical support. Find an existing theory or develop a new one that responds to the research question.
4. Match theoretical support with expected online information sources. Reduce first-order theoretical construct to a series of second-order theoretical constructs. Match second-order theoretical constructs with portal types. Examples are suggested in later chapters.
5. Identify the expected dissemination strategy of the target organization. In the context of each concern, will the firm want the public to know about the issue (y/n), and will it be considered good or bad news?
6. Collect relevant online data. Use insights regarding the expected dissemination strategy of the target organization to identify and explore specific online information sources for relevant data.
7. Interpret the data. Examine the data in light of the theoretical framework.
8. Form a conclusion. Respond to the research question.

Such a process offers a formal approach for addressing complex matters of online query. It also provides a means to understand the challenges facing many analysts in their quest to reach a satisfactory solution to a business concern. Business concerns vary by degree of complexity and clarity of solution. To grasp this idea, think of a two-by-two matrix, as illustrated in Figure 4.2. In one quadrant lie business concerns with resolutions that are complex. In these situations, success is not easily defined and relevant information sources are not immediately known. In another quadrant may be found business concerns that are relatively simple to resolve. In these instances of low complexity, analysts recognise the relevant information sources before beginning their quest and

Figure 4.2
Categorizing Business Concerns and Analytical Shortcomings

	Known Source	Unknown Source
Well Defined Solution	• Simple Concern • Competence Shortcoming	• Moderately Complex Concern • Methodological Shortcoming
Poorly Defined Solution	• Moderately Complex Concern • Interpretive Shortcoming	• Highly Complex Concern • Learning Shortcoming

are also able to clearly define a successful solution ahead of time. In the remaining two quadrants, one would find problems of moderate complexity. These combine well-defined solutions with unknown sources of information or poorly defined solutions with known sources of information.

This categorization scheme also suggests reasons that research efforts may fall short of the mark. Four shortcomings may be particularly relevant. *Competence* challenges refer to situations where supposedly well-trained analysts are unable to successfully prosecute searches for problems with well-defined solutions and known sources of information. In these instances, corporate efforts to rectify a failed search may be well served by questioning the involvement of the particular analyst in the overall process. An inability to identify the officers of an established and publicly traded U.S. corporation would be a characteristic of an analyst whose competence should be questioned.

Interpretive challenges refer to instances where analysts are unable to successfully resolve a concern, given a known information source but a poorly defined solution. An appropriate strategy for managing the future is to increase the formal training of the analyst in areas such as financial analysis and accounting. More specifically, we refer to existing theoretical approaches such as the steps involved in a social responsibility audit or the constructs involved in an assessment of internal corporate power.

Methodological challenges describe instances where an analyst is unable to capture information from unknown sources to resolve a problem with a well-defined solution. An example of this shortcoming would be understanding how to conduct a social responsibility audit but not knowing where to look for product recall notices involving a particular firm. Resolution of future concerns would involve coaching the analyst in the art of information sourcing.

Finally, challenges of the *learning* variety refer to tasks that demand professional training. Failure to resolve highly complex concerns occurring in this quadrant result not from personal incompetence on the part of the analyst but from the nontrivial nature of the task. A poorly defined solution coupled with unknown information sources demands learning on the part of the organization to ensure future success in resolving similar concerns. An example of this type of concern would be an assignment to discover the future computing needs of private companies that do not wish to participate in the online study

Despite the promise of the wired world, increasing levels of formal education and training, and instant access to almost limitless information, analyst predictions and explanations are often dead wrong. Competence, methodology, interpretation, and learning effectively categorize many of the shortcomings that hamper effective resolution of key operational issues. In many respects, however, they do not address the underlying reasons for analytical failure. An all-encompassing list is beyond the scope of this endeavor. However, many research efforts fail for the following reasons.

First, definitions of knowledge are inconsistent across organizations. Operating entities have different orientations to knowledge, and even the best of analysts may be unaware of the differences. Knowledge may take the form of an application, a creation, an assemblage, or the reuse of an existing process. An audit process used by a particular accounting giant differs considerably from a research activity in a pharmaceutical firm whose new-product development efforts build on an existing template.

Second, analysts are subject to competitive blind spots resulting from a mistaken or incomplete view of an industry and competition, the poor design of the competitive analysis system, inaccurate perceptions, or ineffective organizational processes. The most serious blind spots are misjudging industry boundaries, poor identification of the competition, overemphasis on where, not how, rivals will compete, overemphasis on competitors' visible competence, faulty assumptions about the competition, and paralysis by analysis.[22]

Third, researchers have a tendency to complicate justifications for issues and activities that can be explained in simple terms. In short, the complexity of models and measures exceeds the complexity of the phenomena under study.[23]

Fourth, when confronted with feedback that chosen courses of action are not working out, analysts often escalate their commitments to previously chosen research strategies or hypotheses.[24]

Fifth, researchers have a tendency to find what they look for. They should be looking for disconfirmation of their notions. Instead, they often become trapped by their own selective perceptions and selective attention to information.[25]

Sixth, analysts unintentionally omit information on a regular basis. The use of at least three different information-bounding strategies is fairly common. Consultation is often limited to a handful of habitual and key strategic information sources. The types of environmental signals monitored, such as the monitoring of key trends or specific critical events, are rarely as broad as possible. Likewise, attention to emerging issues is frequently and unnecessarily bounded by initial definitions and group consensus.[26]

Finally, at a philosophical level, analysts may focus too much of their attention on rational as opposed to human qualities.

Reason detached from the balancing qualities of humanism is irrational. The promise of a sensible society lies in the potential reality of a wider balance. And in that equilibrium, reason has an essential place.[27] But a balance of what? What is this equilibrium that the humanist seek? A reasonable list of human qualities might include ethics, common sense, imagination or creativity, memory, history or experience, intuition and reason.[28]

Despite these shortcomings, it is not outrageous to suggest a desire on the part of most corporate decision makers to simplify the typical business concern faced by their analysts on a day-to-day basis. Subsequent chapters suggest examples of analytical frameworks that match a Web site categorization scheme, online information sources, and relevant theoretical frameworks. Each chapter's intent is to help managers and CI professionals move the resolution of many important business concerns away from the high and moderate complexity categories to that of a concern with a simple resolution.

The Corporate Answer: Hide

Analysts, their failings, and the tools at their disposal account for but one team in the game of hide-and-seek. On the other side of the coin lie corporations and their communications professionals.

In operating environments such as those of the pharmaceutical, computer peripheral, and software industries, the possession and application of knowledge often serve to differentiate winners from losers. An understatement in industries such as these is that the protection of intellectual property and information is serious business.

An important assumption is that firms that do a better job of protecting their unique knowledge from being stolen, observed, or imitated will have an advantage over those that don't. We here define knowledge, from the point of view of the CI professional, as a mix of interpretation, accurate information sources, and analytical frameworks. In some instances, analytical frameworks can be dropped from the formula when certain information is available. In particular, we refer to some forms of codified or tangible information such as written documents and blueprints, as well as tacit or intangible information such as routines.

These forms of information are normally part of an organization's formal intellectual property protection program. Practices seeking to protect tangible forms of information can include patents, trademarks, copyright, and trade secrets. Unfortunately, these forms of protection are often weak and costly to write and enforce. When referring to intangible forms of information, common protective mechanisms include employment contracts, structural organizational features, and work design characteristics such as team-based projects.[29] Although increasingly holistic in their coverage, these protective efforts are unintentionally incomplete. Fortunately, this shortcoming is being recognized and addressed by many major entities.

One solution adopted by the most sophisticated of organizations is a cloaking program that identifies and hides information worthy of protection. "Worthiness," in many instances, encompasses information that is difficult for a competitor to develop without tacit cooperation, time-sensitive data, data crucial to completing a profile of one's firm, and information crucial to completing a comprehensive analysis of the industry.[30]

A third approach to information protection is the topic of this book. We assume that in their efforts to mold a positive public image and manage the information available to analysts, corporations and their communication professionals make use of fairly sophisticated information dissemination tactics. These strategies match different information types with different dissemination tactics. Information types are judged from the point of the view of the corporation under study and are categorized as either good news or bad news. Dissemination tactics take one of two forms, as illustrated in Figure 4.3. Companies either actively disseminate information or disseminate information solely to meet legal or regulatory requirements. The challenge facing analysts is to beat corporate information managers at their own game.

In instances where companies want the public to know about good news, we suggest that they use a *promote* strategy. A safe tactic is the use of corporate and public relations portals by corporate communications professionals to spread the news. On the other hand, good news is often most valuable when it is not openly disseminated. On these occasions, we expect sophisticated management teams to *bury* such information. In such a case, documents found in regulatory portals seem to be particularly valuable to curious researchers. On some occasions, corporations will be quick off the mark to publicize bad news about their

Figure 4.3
Corporate Information Dissemination Strategies

	Good News	Bad News
Actively Disseminate (Want you to know)	Promote	Justify
Disseminate to Meet Legal or Regulatory Obligations (Don't want you to know)	Bury	Protect

operations. In these instances, efforts will be intense to *justify* any such shortcomings. We would expect public relations and news and journalistic information portals to be especially revealing for online analysts. Finally, a fairly common occurrence is a situation of bad news that few concerned internal stakeholders want publicized. A *protect* strategy best describes a corporate response to this challenge. When this is the case, CI professionals will be hard pressed to uncover relevant information. Legal, personal interactive, special interest, and regulatory information portals should be the best sources for discovering information that most organizations might not want you to know.

In this era of perpetual uncertainty, few organizations can afford to ignore the insights of well-trained CI practitioners. In the new millennium, serious corporate players recognize that the basis of sustained competitive advantage lies in the nurturing, protection, and application of knowledge. As in a game of hide-and-seek, firms operating in the new competitive arena will strive to protect their knowledge through numerous means, including well-thought-out information dissemination strategies. On the other side of the coin, CI analysts seek to uncover this knowledge by identifying and matching relevant sources of information with appropriate analytical frameworks and personal interpretation abilities. At the end of each game of hide-and-seek, the winning side holds the information necessary to resolve an important concern regarding the organization of interest. We now move on to the application of these ideas.

Chapter 5 _____

Identifying Power Holders

Power is a funny topic. Sociologists, philosophers, and historians have played dominant roles in teasing out what we know about power. The mention of names such as Giddens, Lukes, and Foucault almost always brings forth immediate and lively responses from academics educated beyond the confines of the strictly empirical sciences. The ideas of these thinkers and the ensuing battles between academic revisionists and traditionalists over power point to the importance of increasing our understanding of its use and effects.

Why then does corporate North America shy away from the term? In fact, the use of the word "power" often intimidates a Western audience. Many do not want to be openly referred to as powerful. It is sometimes difficult, then, to determine who the powerful are in companies. If, however, we look at company "leaders," we will undoubtedly find those holding power, as the corporate world often uses "leadership" as a euphemism for "power." It is these individuals who are of keen interest to business analysts.

For obvious reasons, it is beneficial for an analyst to determine if her or his competitor, for example, is reliant on the capabilities of a particular individual or group of individuals. If so, a competitor's ability to compete might be seriously harmed by the loss of a certain manager or vice president. This type of information is invaluable in determining a variety of things, including who should top your list of acquisition targets. The Internet provides a wealth of ways to identify the executives your competitor does not want to lose. Reading online industry journals, newsletters, and magazines can be helpful. Before we turn to these sources, it is important to consider how an individual obtains power in a large organization.[1]

The old fashioned way for most individuals to obtain power is to be promoted up the hierarchy. In the world of corporations, a vice president is usually more influential than a junior manager. A second tactic for gaining power is to bring much needed resources or new business opportunities to an organization. Research on professional service firms suggests that partners who bring in new clients are those who last the longest and are frequently found on executive governance committees. A third opportunity open to those in search of power is to make one's employer or colleagues dependent upon oneself for the accomplishment of important tasks. For example, given the role of regulators, employees of electrical utilities might find it useful to be among the select few who understand the functioning of the company's nuclear power plant simulator. A fourth effective means for gaining power is to be visible. Choose assignments that are high profile. Do things that people notice. Finally, powerful individuals are those who are seen as capable time and time again of reducing important sources of organizational uncertainty.

PEOPLE IN AUTHORITY

There are two clear indicators of those employees who possess formal authority within a company:

1. the company's organizational chart
2. those employees who participate in the ownership pool

When analysts examine an organizational chart, they should pay attention not only to obvious levels of hierarchy but also to who is doing what in the organization. In plain language, this means looking at job titles. More often than not, individuals with line authority will have more say than individuals with staff authority. In addition, employees with titles comprising more than one area of responsibility are often less influential than those with only one area of responsibility, as the grouping of two areas under one usually indicates a lack of clout in each of the individual areas.[2]

Useful on-line information sources for unearthing people in authority include the company's 10K annual report filing with the SEC, online versions of its annual report, and its Web site. To find companies with an Internet presence and for quick links to that site, try the Infospace business search engine or the Companies Online Web page.

A second, obvious signal of authority is ownership. It is not uncommon for members of a top management team to possess relatively large numbers of company shares. One way to find out who has a large interest is to identify those who are considered inside traders by the SEC. Examine forms 3, 4, or 5 of the EDGAR database for this information.

VISIBILITY

Unfortunately, titles rarely tell the whole story. In many instances, visibility is a better indicator of influence. Given the increasing importance of public relations professionals and an awareness of the potential impact of negative or positive information on a company's share price, it is not surprising that most corporations are very careful about whom they choose to mention in their communications. One place to begin a "power" assessment is the news release section of a company Web site. If the company does not make these available, it may be worthwhile to scan the offerings of PR Newswire and Business Wire.

A second means for assessing visibility is to enter the company name or the names of key executives in a general search engine. Three of the easiest and most useful search engines are AltaVista, Northern Light, and Excite. When using AltaVista, put quotation marks on either side of the search request for a more precise search. For example, if searching Maurice Worth, COO of Delta Airlines, Inc., enter the search as "Maurice Worth."

To find out who is quoted on a regular basis in the media independent of company news releases, try any number of general news search sources. An interesting and very detailed site is the DLJ Direct home page. This site is essentially a financial services page, although its search capabilities return a detailed list of news information dating back just over one year. In the same category, Newsalert and CNNfn services Web sites provide similar resources.

Although time consuming, it is often worthwhile to check newspapers in and near the towns where a company has its headquarters and divisions. Fortunately, many of the major daily newspapers offer a search capability by keyword on their Web sites. For information within the United States, two useful and easy-to-use Web sites are those of the Newspaper Association of America and PPPP.Net.

RESOURCE ACQUISITION

An acknowledged and proven ability to acquire resources for a firm usually marks an individual with significant influence.[3] Companies live and die by their balance sheets. Unfortunately, few firms publicly link revenue generation figures to specific individuals. However, numerous means exist by which to identify those who have succeeded or are succeeding in this regard. One way is to determine which units within a company have been growing. A second is to identify whose department or unit has recently acquired a larger proportion of the budget of a particular division or operating entity. Major capital expenditures, equipment purchases, or a sudden increase in job postings often point in this direction. A third effective means to distinguish the overachievers from the mere achievers is to learn which of the company's products and services have been extremely successful or are being marketed heavily.

In all three instances, the ability of the Transium Business Intelligence Web site to meaningfully sort articles by topic can reduce research time immensely. Company home pages, accessible through Companies Online and SEC filings such as a 10K company annual report and DEF 14A proxy statement, should provide the names of key individuals if the previously noted articles do not. The 10Q quarterly reports, 10K company annual reports, and shareholder annual reports obtainable through the Report Gallery Web site should also highlight areas of a firm that are growing. A search by company name using general information portals such as NorthernLight generally provides a list of stories that document positive or negative change. Finally, the most useful sources are often a firm's press releases found on its home page. Most companies trumpet their own successes. These documents can also be queried using public relations portals such as PR Newswire or Business Wire.

The area that brings in resources may also be signaled by a larger than average share of company job-specific hiring. Why is one area of the company growing and not others? Decisions to boost personnel dramatically are not made lightly. In most cases, one or more executives need to support such a decision and one or more need to do the suggesting. Those who are given the right to hire are more often than not those who have been effective at doing the suggesting.

A variety of options exist for online sources of job postings. Many of the same media sources noted earlier are applicable in this instance. The most obvious source is, of course, the company Web site. Other useful and user-friendly sources are online job listings. One excellent Web site is Monster.com. It allows users to search by industry, company name, profession, and geographic region and offers in-depth job descriptions. The Yahoo job listing board is another effective site. It will search for specific companies and the job openings that they list.

Researchers might also want to consider the information found in local newspapers using NewsEdge and the Newspaper Association of America. In many instances, online local newspapers will offer a search tool and/or archives. Most will also provide access to recent job postings or classified ads.

Another way to tackle the "who's hiring?" question is to identify industry-specific publications and then search their career sections by company name or area. The Industry Zone of Hoover's Online and the Transium Business Intelligence Web site allow researchers to do just that. A search by company or industry provides a listing of recent articles. The Transium Web site also allows researchers to sort article abstracts by different criteria such as product or service and merger and acquisition activity.

UNCERTAINTY ABSORPTION

Who in the company has a track record for being innovative, for getting the company out of tight spots, or for being creative and keeping the company ahead of the competition? One approach for identifying those who absorb uncertainty is to make use of the search capabilities of an online media source such as the Newsalert service or the financial news services of CNN. Searching these sites using the name of the company and/or the executive of interest is often successful. A second approach is to make use of the Transium Business Intelligence search tool. By providing a count of articles written about a firm in specific magazines, journals, or newspapers, the site allows researchers to identify the media sources read by industry insiders. In turn, these sources will likely be the location of most insights regarding uncertainty absorbers and are good targets for highly focused searches. A third source is, again, a firm's news releases. In this case, look for "heroic" stories or records of individual achievement.

DEPENDENCE

Power can also be understood by examining previous cooperative experiences or identifying those employees with rare or unique skill sets. Are any members of the executive team dependent on other members? Have any senior managers followed other colleagues into the upper echelons? Did one executive give a second executive his or her big career break? If you know who the "leader" is, you might be able to determine which team members are also handpicked. This information can be very useful for those seeking to understand who is most trusted and who might jump ship with an appealing offer.

Dependence can also mean possessing a skill that is unique within a firm, such as a leading brokerage house's only mining analyst or an employee with work experience in a competitor organization. Another relevant example is an employee with experience managing complex organizational change. Outside of the investment banking or legal industries, few executives have extensive experience with mergers and acquisitions. Given that many firms prefer to buy revenues rather than create them, identifying such individuals can offer a competitor an advantage when battling head-to-head for a particular acquisition target.

Piecing together the necessary information to build a personal portrait can be a challenge, but it is possible. Corporate home pages offer career highlights of key personnel either openly or through press releases. SEC filings also contain relevant information. In particular, S1 prospectus and DEF14A proxy statement filings normally include extensive executive background material. Most firms are also dependent upon great minds in their midst. The U.S. Patent and Trademark Office offers a searchable Web site that allows the easy identification of these individuals. Finally, make use of the Deja.com Web site, by joining an online discussion regarding the firm or industry of interest. Pose a question and see what response you receive.

THE ANALYSTS' CHALLENGE: THE EXPECTED DISSEMINATION STRATEGY

As noted earlier, with the exception of the officers of the corporation, most firms do not openly identify powerful employees to the general public. One very good reason for this is that they fear losing these stars to competitors. Thus, in most instances, a curious analyst should expect little proactive promotion of employees by the company to stakeholders beyond a regulator-mandated disclosure of the identities and backgrounds of senior executives and write-ups of only the most senior of management team members.

When seeking to build a "power" portrait to identify these key employees, it might be useful to think of issues of authority and visibility as good news that ABC Corporation will actively promote to the business press and general public. In line with this, we expect ABC's 10K and DEF 14A SEC filings, its company home page, and press releases to play a large role for analysts seeking to determine the identity of these individuals. Correspondingly, corporate, public relations, specialty business, and regulatory portals should be quite popular.

On the other hand, knowledge about employees who reduce uncertainty, own significant numbers of shares, and acquire resources is probably considered sensitive. Indeed, we expect that ABC will not proactively disseminate such information and instead will seek to bury it away from the business press and general public. In their quest for details of this nature, analysts will most likely spend much of their time reading independent business press coverage of ABC as well as interpreting its SEC and patent office filings. Thus, specialty business and regulatory portals should be popular tools.

We expect that ABC will also seek to protect, or at least not openly

Figure 5.1
Expected Information Dissemination Strategies—Identifying Power Holders

	Good News	Bad News
Want You to Know	• Promote • Individuals in positions of authority • Individuals who do visible things	Justify
Don't Want You to Know	• Bury • Individuals who own significant numbers of shares or stock options • Individuals who acquire resources for the company • Individuals who reduce uncertainty	Protect • Dependence relationships

identify, dependence relationships within its organization. Not surprisingly, most organizations do not want to be dependent upon the skills and abilities of a limited number of individuals. As a result, the curious will likely spend much of their efforts reading independent business press coverage of ABC and as well as interpreting its SEC and Patent Office filings. Figure 5.1 displays these expected strategies.

A Hypothetical Example

Now consider the fictional case of BDA Corporation, a computer peripheral manufacturer that designs and develops components for personal computers. Employed by the new business opportunities group of one of these latter organizations, you as a CI analyst are to identify potential upstream acquisition candidates. One firm in particular is extremely attractive, given that it supplies five of the major PC manufacturers, including your firm. A successful end to this pursuit will not only allow your firm to move closer to its goal of becoming a participant in all sectors of the industry value chain but will also disrupt the supply chains of key competitors. While the firm's products are well known, the same cannot be said about its human resource talent. Your immediate challenge is to identify the real brains behind the company.

As with most of your assignments, a starting point is SEC EDGAR data. An examination of the firm's most recent 10K annual report filing and its DEF 14A proxy statement suggests a list of six executive officers who occupy positions of authority. Luckily, within the last month, it has also filed its most recent Form 3, which lists those individuals employed by the organization who own enough shares or stock options to be considered insider traders. Nine names appear on that list, seven of which correspond to the list of executive officers. Of these, only four own a material number of shares. In order to round out this portrait of authority, you scan the company's home page and identify a section called "people." It discusses the identities and backgrounds of the employees and gives information on one other individual: Ms. Pearson, the director of research.

With this list of individuals in hand, you query the archived press releases found on the company home page. Only two of these individuals are mentioned there. The company president, Chantal Latour, receives the vast majority of the attention, while the vice president of marketing, Bob Smith, is also mentioned favorably in a number of online dispatches. Under the home page section titled "Executive Speeches," two are evident, given by Latour to the company's industry association.

Next, you examine dependence patterns among the executive team and its employees. A first indicator is evident from the profiles found in the company DEF 14A filing. From this information, it becomes apparent that both Latour and Smith worked at the same previous employer. In that instance Latour was also at a higher level in the corporate hierarchy than Smith. Latour joined BDA company six months prior to Smith, strongly indicating a close professional bond. The other five executive officers are all long-term members of BDA.

Given that BDA is in a technology-intensive industry, you assume that patents may play a role in identifying key individuals. The Hoover's Online company capsule of BDA strengthens your assumptions when it lists the U.S. Patent and Trademark Office as an important regulator of BDA. You find that BDA owns nine patents, each registered over the last three years. A closer examination of the patents available through the Web site of the USPTO indicates that the director of research at BDA is listed as the inventor on all the patents.

Figure 5.2
An Assessment of the Internal Power Structure of BDA Corporation

	Chantal Latour	**Bob Smith**	**Charlotte Pearson**
Hierarchy	CEO	Vice President Marketing	Director of Research
Ownership	3% of Outstanding Common Shares Options to purchase 500,000 shares	1% of Outstanding Common Shares Options to purchase 100,000 shares	Less than 1% of Outstanding Common Shares Options to purchase 100,000 shares
Visibility	The company is Chantal. Two Business Week articles on her and three in the local newspaper. Twenty press releases mention her name. Two industry association speeches are available on the company home pages along with a lengthy profile.	Four press releases mention Smith. One speech to the National Marketing Association is available on the company home page as well as a brief profile.	With one exception, no mention in press releases or in the popular press. No profile is offered on the company home page.
Dependence	Latour worked with Smith at a previous employer. She hired him six months after her arrival at this company	Smith is dependent upon Latour.	Pearson is the inventor listed on the firm's eight patents filed with the USPTO.
Uncertainty Reduction	Latour is credited by the business press with turning this firm around through creative cost-cutting that shed no workers.	No evidence.	No evidence.
Resource Acquisition	Latour arranged short-term debt financing two years ago, buying the company valuable time as it cut costs.	Sales have risen 300% since the arrival of Smith. The number of new major clients has doubled.	No evidence.
Relative Level of Power	Highest	Equal to that of Pearson	Equal to that of Smith but less visible and deliberately so.

You still have to discover the individuals who acquire resources for BDA and those who reduce uncertainty. A scan of the Internet using the Northern Light search engine suggests Latour, again, as the key figure-head in reducing uncertainty. A search with "BDA Corporation" in the title and "Chantal Latour" in the text offers three *Business Week* online articles in which Latour is described as the savior of BDA, responsible for a successful turnaround effort two years ago that saved the organization from bankruptcy.

Finally, on the topic of resource acquisition, two names are noteworthy and these are once again Latour and Smith. Your examination of the company's income statement indicates that sales have risen more than 300 percent since Smith's arrival at BDA. Further, the same *Business Week Online* articles noted above mention Smith's major client base, which is twice that of his predecessor. The profile of Latour offered on the company home page suggests that one of her important contributions to the organization was successfully obtaining the short-term debt financing that kept the firm afloat during a difficult period.

Given these facts, who is powerful in BDA Corporation? As Figure 5.2 illustrates, Latour is certainly calling the shots, with Smith as a visible second. Evidence also suggests that Pearson is an influential stakeholder whom the corporation wishes to protect from predatory competitors. Thus, she fits in the second tier.

This concludes our discussion of how the Internet might be used to identify those who hold power in an organization. To further illustrate these ideas, we present the case of ABC Corporation in the chapter appendix.

APPENDIX: POWER AT ABC CORPORATION

OVERVIEW

ABC is an S&P 500[a] company that designs, manufactures, markets, and supports hardware and software systems that are used to store computer information. Clients include airlines, banks, governments, universities, retail chains, and telecommunication firms, to name just a few. Unlike its competitors, who are for the most part diversified in the technology sector, ABC concentrates on computer storage devices, making it unique in its industry and a recognized leader in the field. ABC was originally founded as a supplier of add-on memory boards in the late 1970s. Following successful growth in the memory storage market, the company went public in the 1980s and efforts focused on improving the quality of the company's product line. As worldwide demand for data storage increased in the 1990s, so did the firm's success; ABC has grown to employ 9,700 employees working in twenty-two countries.[b] The firm has numerous manufacturing and customer support facilities throughout the world and boosts annual sales of over $5 billion, with projected plans to exceed $10 billion in revenue by 2001.

An Issues Statement

ABC's success has not gone unnoticed. Increasingly, analysts are touting it as an attractive takeover candidate. The identities of the key figures underlying its success are thus of great interest. If the firm becomes an acquisition target, whom should suitors be talking to? The current CEO, Alan Davidson, is featured prominently in corporate press releases and other business press articles and is believed to be the driving force behind the firm's success.

THE RESEARCH QUESTION

How might theoretical ideas concerning power help inquisitive analysts? By identifying existing power holders, analysts will also be targeting key decision makers. Thus, an acquisition team seeking to acquire ABC would want to know which individuals have influence in the corporation and who holds the most power.

An Assessment and Identification of the Important Variables

In order to identify internal ABC power holders, CI professionals might want to find out:

- Which ABC employees are in positions of authority?
- Who within ABC owns significant numbers of shares or has been granted large numbers of stock options?

- Which employees are seen to be openly affecting change, or which members are promoted to the general public and business press by ABC?
- Who has a track record of successfully acquiring resources for ABC?
- Who reduces uncertainty for ABC?
- Who has made ABC or some of its employees dependent upon themselves for its continued success?

Prediction According to the Model

How will ABC manage this information? To answer this question fully, it is helpful to break the concept of power into parts and offer a separate prediction for each. In this instance, with the exception of individuals who do visible things or are in positions of authority, members of ABC would probably not use the terms "good news" or "bad news" to describe information. Thus, for the sake of classification, all information is placed under the category of "good news." What is of most interest in this scenario is whether or not ABC wants the general public to be informed of the information.

We expect that ABC will actively *promote* to the business press and general public those employees who have authority and who do visible things. We expect ABC's 10K and DEF 14A SEC filings, its company home page and press releases, and the business press to be important sources of information for analysts seeking to determine the identity of these individuals. Correspondingly, corporate, public relations, specialty business, and regulatory portals would also be useful.

We expect that ABC will seek to *bury* from the business press and general public information about employees who reduce uncertainty, own significant numbers of shares, and acquire resources. In order to uncover such information, analysts would most likely spend much of their time reading independent business press coverage of ABC and interpreting its SEC and patent office filings. Thus, specialty business and regulatory portals would also be good sources of information.

We also expect that ABC will seek to *protect*, or at least not openly identify, dependence relationships within its organization. Once again, analysts would most likely concentrate their efforts on reading independent business press coverage of ABC, as well as interpreting its SEC and patent office filings.

ANALYSIS

Who is powerful in ABC? To whom should potential suitors pay attention? Who should not be put on hold when they call? Let's consider the following sample analysis.

Hierarchy

How stable is the top management team of ABC? Who is in charge, at least in terms of the organizational chart? From a historical perspective, it becomes apparent that a major transformation has been ongoing for a number of years. Two separate portraits can be developed from a series of ABC's 10K annual report form filings. One assessment highlights a large team of fourteen members, but in four years this team had been reduced to seven members. Where did everyone go? Some had moved on to other careers, others to lower positions within the firm, and still others had retired. Is this a case of power being concentrated into the hands of a few? The answer is, "probably." Although ABC started out as a family business, family members have had a declining influence in the firm. The bulk of the company's power seems to have shifted to the new CEO, Alan Davidson.

Visibility

Alan Davidson is the most prominently featured employee at ABC. Hyperlinks found on the company Web site direct readers to business and industry press articles featuring the firm, its products, or its people. In these articles, Davidson serves as spokesperson for the firm. His name and image also appear a number of times on the company's Web site, in the company's annual report, and in most, if not all, press releases. Other employees and executive officers are not as strongly featured.

Uncertainty Reduction

Upon joining the company, Davidson focused his attention on improving the quality of the product line that was endangering the company. Because of faulty components from an outside supplier and the failure of ABC's engineers to find those faults, all shipped ABC equipment was causing system crashes when installed in client computer networks. ABC replaced the faulty parts or replaced the product with similar models, and Davidson developed and implemented a system to improve product quality. Nine major product lines, comprising 80 percent of ABC's revenues, were cancelled, and attention was given to securing customers and undercutting competitors' prices. Within six months, ABC was controlling the market, all without damaging company profits. Davidson's hard work eventually paid off, and he was appointed CEO. Since assuming this position, Davidson has had continued success, and ABC profits have increased from $30 million to over a projected $1 billion in just a few years.[c]

Resource Acquisition

As CEO of the firm, Davidson has used his power to direct his firm's activities. The current executive vice president of markets and channels, George MacDonald, also has some control over ABC's resources. For example, well over half of the employment positions fall under his jurisdiction. This is impressive, especially considering that MacDonald is fairly new to the firm. There is some evidence of a dependence pattern within the top management team; there seems to be a strong bond between MacDonald and Davidson and a possible dependence of MacDonald (the newcomer) on Davidson. Other than these two leaders, there do not appear to be any other shining stars within the organization who have control over important resources.

Dependence

Under the guidance of Davidson, ABC has become one of the top producers of mainframe computer disk memory hardware and software.[d] A number of online articles cite Davidson as the catalyst for the firm's success. However, he did not do it alone; system and software engineers implemented his vision. The production team created the quality products that the sales department promoted, and the technical customer service staff maintained the quality product flow to the end users. But to be fair, all of these factors were directed from the top by Davidson. Who else might be critical to ABC? Consider the numerous holders of the firm's patents, listed on the USPTO Web site. At one point the top four filers held twenty-six of the company's 100 patents for that year.[e] Yet, these individuals are not included on the corporate home page. As with many corporations, ABC does not actively promote to the public the members beyond the most senior of managers who have played a crucial role in its success.

Who is powerful at ABC? On the surface it appears that Alan Davidson definitely calls the shots, with George MacDonald a distant but rising second in the batting order. There is still some family influence in the corporation, but it seems to be secondary. As with many contemporary organizations, little mention is made of individuals who are not executive officers. Yet, the existence of one hundred patents and at least four highly active inventors suggests a subgroup of individuals who are extremely valued by ABC and worthy of protection from predatory competitors. These ideas are summarized in Figure 5.3.

PREDICTIVE ACCURACY OF THE THEORY

How well did our model work? The answer is, "fairly well." As expected, those individuals who were actively promoted to the public were all executive officers of ABC. Individuals in positions of authority, as well as those who do visible things, were discussed, but for the most part attention focused on the very top of the pyramid. Put simply, Davidson is ABC, at least in terms of publicity. As expected, ABC actively buried or protected from the media information about others who might acquire resources for it, reduce uncertainty, or be influential enough to suggest a state of dependence.

How believable is the information used to make this assessment? Even taking into account the subjective nature of interpretation, the information is still fairly believable. Much of the assessment, including the identities of the patent inventors and the backgrounds of the executive officers, was based on information from corporate regulatory filings, such as ABC's SEC 10K annual report filing and its registered patents available from the online database of the U.S. Patent and Trademark Office. The corporate press releases and home pages were also used, but often they served to reinforce points made in independent business press articles, such as those found in *Business Week* online and CNNfn.

Figure 5.3
Case Illustration: An Assessment of the Internal Power Structure of ABC

	Davidson	MacDonald	Family Member
Hierarchy	Top	Second	Third
Visibility	Highest	Lower	Lower
Dependence	Highest	Unknown	Moderate
Uncertainty Reduction	High	Unknown	Moderate
Resource Acquisition	High	High	Moderate
Relative Level of Power	Highest	High	High

Chapter 6

Performing a Social Responsibility Audit

Among the many important transformations altering the global marketplace of the last millennium, few have been so profound in their impact as the newly acquired ease of information access. Never before have the actions and intentions of our leading individuals, institutions, and corporations been so transparent to the public at large. A consequence of this transparency is a growing requirement for socially responsible corporate behavior.

Socially questionable or irresponsible behavior is bad news. In the Internet age, bad news travels fast and frightens away investors, analysts, and other important stakeholders. How might one define socially responsible behavior? The answer is not straightforward. One means to assess such behavior is to imagine a Christmas tree, with each light representing an indicator. Positive performance on an indicator allows the light to turn green. Poor performance leads to a red light. A socially responsible company is one whose Christmas tree lights are primarily green. A deviant firm is colored in red.

Finding fault with a major operating entity is not normally a difficult task. Assessing whether it acts in a manner that is not socially responsible is a completely separate issue. Given that this concept encompasses so many different concerns, an analyst may choose to seek answers to a series of general questions:[1]

- Is the firm financially stable?
- Is there any evidence to suggest that the organization does not respect its physical environment?

• Are the organization's products and services manufactured, developed, and delivered to consumers and clients using the highest available standards?

• Are there any reasons to accuse the firm of not treating its human stakeholders with dignity and compassion?

• Is the corporation supportive of local community needs?

Despite the obvious importance of responses to these questions, attending to broader social interests has long been viewed by many corporations as an unnecessary expense. Traditionally firms have found it easier to lay off a female employee than to endure the cost and disruption of repeated maternity leaves. It is often cheaper to dump chemicals down a drain or into the ocean than to pay for their proper disposal. In the same manner, in many instances, it is cheaper to use Third World children as laborers than pay First World, unionized adults First World wages. Whether a company is simply unaware of the impropriety of its actions or is intentionally negligent, socially irresponsible corporate behavior is unacceptable. Recent high-profile examples involving the use of child labor indicate that there is a price to pay for deviant behavior.

How might these issues impact a manager on a daily basis? The following scenarios offer a few clues.

You are an executive of a textile company. One of your customers has changed locations and is asking that its orders be shipped to a new destination. You recognize the country in question and wonder what prompted your customer to move. The country's status as a Third World nation leads you to fear that your customer might be making use of a low-cost labor market where safety standards are questionable. Perhaps even child labor is being used to transform materials into finished goods. Even if you have no moral qualms about this behavior, others might. You wonder if your company can afford to get caught in a potential controversy. Some online research about your customer may yield useful insights regarding its standard practices and whether it is about to become headline news.

Your company is one of the biggest names in sportswear. After years of building a reputation for quality, you have found that the most efficient way to meet the growing demand for your products is to contract out the manufacturing processes and devote your company's time and energy to design and marketing. You soon realize that dozens of small manufacturing companies are willing to assemble your products. As sales depend on name recognition, you can not afford to become embroiled in any type of scandal. After narrowing the list down to a few of the most capable, it becomes evident that the makeup of these firms and the manner in which they conduct business is still a mystery. A background check on the final candidates may be the only way to ensure the long-term survival of your firm.

As the CEO of a midsized commercial bank you have been heavily involved in merger negotiations with another industry player from a nearby state. It has recently become apparent that there are no women on the other firm's top management team. It also appears that their employees are, for the most part, uncomfortable dealing with your female executives. Does this company have a discrimination problem? What is their personnel makeup? Should you be worried about a significant conflict of corporate cultures?

Clearly, assessing a company's social responsibility does matter. The challenge for analysts is to do so in a thorough yet time-efficient and inexpensive manner. Addressing five specific concerns should capture much of the information necessary for making an accurate portrayal.

ECONOMICS

Determining how socially responsible a firm is is usually much easier when you consider its financial health.[2] At first glance, the basic profitability of a company may seem irrelevant to your research. However, downturns in financial performance can drive many firms to the point of organizational crisis, a state with which most top management teams have little experience.[3] In these instances, survival often means that important decisions are made on the run, without taking the time to explore potential consequences. These situations may also entail radical restructuring and drastic actions, including layoffs and plant closures.

In times of crisis, individuals occasionally cross the line, placing entire organizations in jeopardy. Where profitability is questionable, evidence suggests higher rates of illicit behavior as well as the use of suspect reporting practices that intentionally or unintentionally paint a false portrait of financial health.[4] Information found in the archives or online articles of numerous financial news organizations like Hoover's, Zack's, CNNfn, or InvestQuest can jump-start any analytical effort. Simply search by company name. Poor performance and improper accounting practices are issues that few interested observers ignore. Neither do news services or professional analysts.

Other windows for assessing poor performance are those that contain online annual reports or company filings to the Securities and Exchange Commission's EDGAR archives. Read through its 10K and 10Q reports by using the quick forms search. This may not only give you an idea of the company's general financial condition, but it will also probably mention ongoing investigations by government agencies or special interest groups.

THE ENVIRONMENT

How is a firm handling its environmental responsibility? Is the firm the subject of close examination by any particular organization? What is the extent of regulatory control or monitoring? Is it in the news for reasons that might not be considered favorable to its corporate image? To answer these questions, researchers might want to consider the opinions of special interest groups, legal archives, the publicly available information troves of the concerned regulatory authorities, and mainstream online news sources.

Special Interest Groups

Special interest groups are an excellent source for information on controversial practices such as illegal dumping or other environmental infractions. It is not uncommon for organizations like Greenpeace, who are sensitive to these issues, to report and act upon alleged corporate wrongdoings before anyone else, making them an excellent source of environmental data. Greenpeace is among the best known of activist organizations. At least two other Web sites are also useful in determining a company's level of environmental responsibility.

The Macrocosm USA Web site, an all-purpose information source for concerned citizens, offers links to a vast library of socially active online organizations. It also allows researchers to search for and categorize these organizations using an extensive list of keywords. It can, for example, categorize online resources, interest groups, and self-described socially responsible organizations according to market features such as products or services.

A second important resource is the Corporate Watch Web site. It contains a detailed series of critical, analytical processes for researchers seeking to examine transnational corporations and industries. Each of these processes in turn also documents important sources of information. Analysts may also find its well-organized "Hot Links" useful. They neatly direct users to environmental watchdog groups that often clearly identify environmentally suspect corporations.

Legal Archives

Environmental lawsuits are often high profile and, occasionally, precedent setting. Examining key legal briefs, stories in the legal press, and archived court transcripts for evidence of environmentally unfriendly activity often turns up information on questionable environmental treatment. Consider using the advanced search option of a legal portal such as LawCrawler and search using terms such as "environment" and the company name. One might also move directly to the environmental law section of these portals and read about the issues that appear to be common to the industry in question. In many instances all major firms will be dealing with the same concerns.

Regulatory Authorities

If the firm you are examining is truly environmentally irresponsible, it has probably attracted the attention of a number of government regulators. In many industries, it is not uncommon for a firm's behavior to be impacted by more than five regulators, with a significant number of these operating at different levels of government. A word search of a firm's 10K annual report will normally suggest its major regulators. A second approach is to follow the links from the company profile section of the Hoover's Online Company Capsules or Industry Zone profiles. In most instances, the key regulators will be identified by means of a hyperlink. Once in the relevant regulator Web site, a search using the company name will often lead to a series of related press releases and regulatory documents that may include information about warnings, fines, and other disciplinary actions. Regulatory bodies also normally allow online observers access to company specific decisions and, occasionally, also to cases under review. The University of Virginia Law School portal, for example, allows users to search for actions in progress or decisions previously rendered against a particular organization.

If you are in a hurry to discover the identities of regulators that might deal with or at least mention firms with poor environmental track records, check the home pages of the following organizations: the Securities and Exchange Commission, the Environmental Protection Agency, and the state governments.

If you are unsure of the regulator in question, the National Technology Transfer Center Web site allows a researcher to follow an educated guess.[5] It offers links to all government information sources through the World Wide Web Virtual Library. Another site that offers links to all U.S. government agencies and Web servers is the Federal Web Locator.

Online News Sources

Public media sources also have a role to play. More than ever, journalists consider environmentally unfriendly behavior to be worthy of front-page coverage. One example, the News Page home page, provides fairly detailed information on companies, including press releases and news articles. Just click on the "Companies" button and fill in the search form. Other organizations of note include a more specialized media source, the Environmental Journalism Home Page, which offers links to numerous other environmental organizations.

A different angle to pursue when using online news media is to use general news and information portals such as the Newspaper Association of America or NewsEdge to track down the local papers that are near company facilities. However, be diligent when making use of local online newspaper content, as many receive much of their ad revenue from the same employers that you may be seeking to critique.

PERSONNEL AND DISCRIMINATION

Among the topics encompassed by the umbrella term "social responsibility," few are as important as the way a firm treats its employees. Is the organization family friendly? Are its wages competitive? Are employees promoted based on merit? Does the company provide access and employment opportunities for the physically challenged? Are men and women treated equally?

Companies ignoring these concerns are increasingly being noticed and rebuked by the popular press, special interest groups, or employees themselves. Unfortunately, positive corporate behavior is often not given the media attention it deserves. However, the consequences of being invisible are superior to the potential harmful loss of valued customers and talented workers that negative publicity might bring.

One way for you, the analyst, to simplify your efforts in researching this important area is to ask two questions. First, what does the company do well? As noted, most firms will highlight any positive efforts on their part to improve standards in the workplace. In particular, an analyst might want to consider whether a firm actively strives to upgrade its workers' skills or offers a comprehensive training program. Information of this nature is often found on company home pages accessible through the Companies Online Web site and in online annual reports. For a more specific search, try using keywords such as "education" and "training" in sites like PR Newswire or Business Wire.

The second question is, what does the company not do well? For obvious reasons, negative points are normally a little trickier to identify. To begin your research, consider whether there are direct indicators of problematic work environments. To do this, you might examine the company's 10K annual report filing with the SEC, because corporations are required to disclose their involvement in litigation that might lead to material damage. You may then want to search the online court case databases available through legal portals like LawCrawler. Is there an abundance of online state and federal level court cases involving employees with the firm in question as defendants? If time permits, compare the number of cases pending or recently completed with the firm's major competitors, keeping in mind the relative differences arising from companies' sizes. Are there great disparities? If so, then trouble is probably brewing internally. Finally, a series of regulatory actions against the firm is not good news. The following regulators are empowered to deal with workplace issues, and all list regulatory actions on these Web sites:

Occupational Safety and Health Administration Violations

Employment Standards Administration Wage and Hour Division Violations

National Labor Relations Board Unfair Labor Practices

Equal Employment Opportunity Commission Equal Pay Act and Age Discrimination in Employment Act Violations

Immigration and Naturalization Service Work Site Enforcement Records

Federal Trade Commission Complaints, Consent Agreements and External Court Cases

Health and Human Services Cumulative Sanctions

Environmental Protection Agency National Emission Standards for Hazardous Air Pollutants and Asbestos

Federal General Services Administration Excluded Parties List

Again, decisions, actions, and directives of these regulators may be accessed through the portals of the National Technology Transfer Center and the University of Virginia Law Library. The latter source offers direct access to an online list of links to the federal administration's actions and decisions.

Indirect indicators are often equally powerful in researching fair labor practices. Look for suspicious employment trends that might indicate a high turnover rate. Portals such as Yahoo! and the Monster.com employment Web site are two online sources that allow you to monitor company hiring. Of interest to analysts might be an abnormally high number of job openings for a particular position, operating division, or geographical region. Although this may be indicative of nothing more than a growing organization, if unjustified it can signal a sinking ship. A strong indicator might be a recurring series of openings for the same position.

If the company has an active union, the union home page may contain a description of workplace concerns. If the company has been the subject of a boycott, detailed explanations may be found on the union site, or by using a general information portal like Yahoo! The "Hot Links" section of the Corporate Watch home page will also point analysts to a well-organized listing of unions and activist sites. The Labor Net Headlines

Archives is also a good source for this type of information, as are the WomensNet section of the Institute for Global Communications Web site and the Corporate Watch home page.

You should also be sure to surf the company home page in your research. Find out where information related to human resource management is offered and look for patterns. Who is being promoted? Do the successful candidates typically have similar backgrounds? How many females are in the top management team, and are they in positions of real influence? Do minority employees tend to get promoted, but to be given tougher assignments? Do a lot of minority employees quit after a certain amount of time with the firm? There probably won't be too much saying that the company outwardly discriminates, but read between the lines.

Where else might indirect indicators of poor work environments be found? Try any number of chat groups or discussion forums such as those available through Deja.com, the Motley Fool, or Biz.Yahoo! Business Web sites. Look for discussions where employees or stakeholders are actively criticizing their employers. Are employees openly complaining about the workplace or improper behavior? Is it typical "I wish I made more money" chat, or does there appear to be widespread disenchantment? How many individuals are active in the discussion? How many appear to be outsiders and how many are insiders? Does there appear to be any evidence to support allegations? One can search by subject or by the company name. If particular authors or contributors are of interest, analysts may also have the option of exploring past insights. Have these individuals been actively critical of the organization in the past? If so, why are they still with the employer?

PRODUCTS

Product or service quality and the accuracy of information surrounding it is an extremely contentious issue for many consumers and consumer groups. Just how pure is that store-bought baby food? How safe is that child's toy? Is 24-hour qualified service support really available on that 1–800 line? Despite the rise of the TQM movement and the ISO standards, few firms have yet to develop the perfect product or provide flawless service.

Analysts seeking to explore such issues have a number of sources at their fingertips. In many industries, regulators and the law courts serve as effective deterrents to extensive illicit behavior. In other cases, the attention of special interest groups and the potential harmful publicity that they can bring serves to moderate behavior. Finally, nothing sells like bad news. The general news media love a good story and controversy always makes for an interesting read. Few firms want to be featured front and center on any news source for activities deemed inappropriate by others. The Web sites of CEO Express and Transium Business Intelligence and articles linked to the company profiles found on Hoover's Online are fairly effective at pointing out stories written on the companies of interest.

A number of organizations provide searchable databases allowing the identification of offending companies and an opportunity to explore the offences in detail, be they alleged or proven. The Web site of the *Better Business Bureau* offers readers company-specific alerts and news briefs. The Federal Trade Commission allows real-time analysis of its Formal Actions Opinions and Activities. The U.S. Consumer Product Safety Commission documents companies disciplined for placing problematic products on the market. The *Arent Fox Advertising Law Internet Site* directs readers to advertising-related violations. Finally, another angle for researchers to examine is the Consumer Opinion links in Yahoo!'s business and economy section. These links direct researchers to online watchdog groups that are targeting specific companies for boycotts or public critiques.

COMMUNITY INVOLVEMENT

Is your firm an active community participant? Does it support local community events? How do its charitable donations rank compared to its competitors'? Is it active in promoting activities of benefit to the greater populace? Few firms do not trumpet their goodwill toward the local community, and most do so using their press releases, various sections of their company Web site, and local online newspapers available through portals such as the Newspaper Association of America. With luck, the company will also offer an online version of its internal newsletter, another vehicle by which it communicates its good deeds to the world. Finally, firms will often mention high-profile community events in their online annual reports. Access to these will often be found on the company or the Annual Reports Online home pages. Online analysts should, of course, be particularly concerned if there is an absence of such proactive publicity.

THE ANALYSTS' CHALLENGE: THE EXPECTED DISSEMINATION STRATEGY

What should be evident is that positive, socially responsible behavior is good news that most firms will want to publicize through tools such as their press releases, corporate speeches, and annual reports. Thus analysts seeking to obtain a positive spin on a firm's behavior should spend some time examining the content of the corporate Web site, the output of online public relations organizations such as PR Newswire and Business Wire, online annual reports, and industry association home pages such as those found through the services of the ASAENET portal.

On the other hand, with the exception of financial instability, most firms will wish to protect examples of socially irresponsible actions or behavior from the media. Although in many instances, the corporation in question cannot block public disclosure of a problematic incident or dilemma, most will certainly not go out of their way to publicize it, preferring instead to adopt a protective stance while quietly rectifying the concern. As a result, unless exposed to the general public through popular press portals such as Reuters.com or CNNfn, most analysts will have to dig deep to find dirt. Digging deep in this instance means examining online court case transcripts and actions found on regulatory Web sites that implicate the firm in question. Although clearly in the public domain, these are not sources of information to which most firms will draw the public's attention. Reading the online magazines that lawyers read may also shed a different light on a publicity-shy organization. An analyst can also expect to find a personal interactive portal such as Deja.com extremely useful when building a case on a firm, although the information it contains is usually somewhat subjective.

Financial instability is an exception as far as negative news goes. When such news is made public, few firms will not actively attempt to justify poor financial performance by putting a positive spin on events. Thus, when assessing the extent to which a firm's activities are socially responsible, analysts should expect firms to promote their good news and protect themselves from bad news. Figure 6.1 below highlights these points.

A Hypothetical Example

For analysts seeking to assess just how socially responsible a corporate player really is, few tools are more useful than the Internet. Before offering the activities of Corporation A as an example, it might be valuable to present a fictional case. Consider the instance of a CI professional seeking to build a portrait of XYZ Corporation, a major Midwest auto parts supplier.

A starting point is, of course the corporation's most recent SEC 10K form filings found on the Securities and Exchange Commission Web site. A brief glance at its income statements and balance sheets indicate a positive upward profit and revenue trend with no abnormal levels of debt or inventory. Benchmarking its key financial figures relative to its major competitors and the industry as a whole using tools found on Market Guide indicates a firm that is average on most counts, with the exception of a slightly poorer return on shareholders' equity. Overall, these figures lead one to conclude that XYZ is financially stable.

Figure 6.1
**Expected Information Dissemination Strategy—Performing a Social
Responsibility Audit**

	Good News	Bad News
Want You to Know	Promote • Good financial stability • Good environmental track record • Good record in terms of personnel and discrimination • Good track record in terms of product and service quality	Justify • Poor financial stability
Don't Want You to Know		Protect • Poor environmental track record • Poor community involvement • Poor record in regard to personnel and discrimination • Poor track record regarding product and service quality

Despite the appearance of solid financial performance, this company's environmental track record is shaky. An online local newspaper near one of its plants has been repeatedly attacking XYZ for not being diligent in monitoring the flow of pollutants into a nearby river. Evidence to support these charges is found on the Environmental Protection Agency Web site, where XYZ has been cited twice on pollution charges.

On the issue of product and service standards, XYZ Corporation does not appear to be a role-model company. In each of its last three SEC 10K filings, it mentions the existence of numerous product recalls as well as its efforts to resist the associated regulatory pressures. A search of the Consumer Safety and Protection Commission Web sites indicates that at least three products have been pulled off the market in each of last four years. In one of these instances, it also highlights a paper trail of efforts by the CSPC to have XYZ voluntarily pull its products. When the topic of XYZ appears on a number of discussion forums and chat groups, commentary is scathing, with participants more often than not accusing

Figure 6.2
Social Responsibility Audit of XYZ Corporation

Issues Important for Assessing the Level of Socially Responsible Behavior of a Firm	Assessment of Socially Responsible Behavior	Summary of Evidence to Support the Assessment	URLs of Pertinent Sources Used in This Case
Financial Stability	High	No mention of regulatory action in SEC 10K or 8K filings. Revenues growing at an average of 15% per year over the last five years. Share price is in line with industry average.	www.sec.gov www.marketguide.com
Respect for Physical Environment	Low	Regulator warning letter regarding waste disposal at plant. Negative spin on corporate conduct in the local press.	www.epa.gov www.newsdirectory.com
Product & Service Standards	Low	Regular occurrences of product recalls. No mention of the firm's products as award-winners with consumer product raters. Evidence of unfavorable gossip in chat groups.	www.cpsc.gov www.consumerworld.com www.deja.com
Treatment of Human Stakeholders	Excellent	No record of legal or regulatory action against the firm in search of U.S court documents or SEC 10K or 10Q filings. No evidence of high employee turnover.	www.lawcrawler.com www.legalnewsnetwork.com www.sec.gov www.monster.com
Community Involvement	Suspect	No mention of charitable donations or participation in community activities in local newspapers, home pages, press releases, or annual reports.	www.annualreports.com www.newsdirectory.com www.businesswire.com www.companiesonline.com
Overall	Questionable		

the firm of simply not caring about its customers. A final point of evidence is the absence of XYZ's products on the most recommended or best-buy lists of online consumer testing groups. Clearly, XYZ is not leading the pack in terms of product quality. It is interesting to note, however, that this has yet to affect its share price or profit margins.

Despite its seeming lack of respect for the environment and questionable attention to quality, there is no evidence to suspect that XYZ Corporation does not treat its employees fairly. A search using LawCrawler of all U.S. circuit courts as well as the courts of states where the company has facilities offers no track record of litigation. A search of commentary by the legal press also suggests that XYZ is a good employer. In this instance an indirect indicator of a poor work environment would be a significant number of online job postings relative to its competitors. A search of the Monster.com Web site indicates that XYZ corporation is high but not at a level that would indicate a problem. Further, an examination of its online press releases and its SEC DEF14A indicates no significant changes in its top management team in the last two years.

Unfortunately, the same cannot be said about the company's involvement in its local and stakeholder communities. No mention is made of charitable donations or support for worthwhile activities on its home page, in its press releases, or in its online annual reports. Furthermore, when the archives of the local online newspaper are searched using the term "XYZ Corporation" as well as the names of its executive officers, no information is provided beyond stories of new product launches, personnel promotions, and yearly financial performance indicators. Thus, although one cannot conclude that XYZ does not involve itself in the local community, analysts have strong reason to be suspicious.

With these points in mind, does XYZ Corporation act in a socially responsible manner? Unfortunately, the evidence summarized in Figure 6.2 suggests it does not. Despite strong financial performance, without significant changes to its operating culture investors should be wary of this organization.

This concludes our discussion of socially responsible corporate behavior. The example of Corporation A is presented in the following appendix.

APPENDIX: SOCIALLY RESPONSIBLE BEHAVIOR
AT COMPANY A

OVERVIEW

Company A was originally founded as a supplier of surgical dressings used to prevent the spread of postoperative disease. It grew throughout the war years to become a multinational, diversified health care product maker specializing in consumer, pharmaceutical, and professional products. Company A shares a portion of its revenues with the world community by donating products and money to worthy causes. The continued growth and profitability of this firm would suggest it to be a popular and wise investment.

An Issues Statement

The name Company A is associated for many with a socially minded organization; its history of philanthropic action is well documented, and it has a reputation of treating employees and customers fairly. However, Company A may be guilty of occasional negligence, as it has not been entirely free from litigation and some products have had defects. In addition, Company A has been openly criticized and has come under the scrutiny of industry regulators. Analysts are interested in determining if the company is deserving of its reputation as a socially responsible organization.

THE RESEARCH QUESTION

Are the behaviors of Company A consistent with those of a socially responsible organization?

Assessment and Identification of the Important Variables

Are the behaviors of Company A consistent with those of a socially responsible organization? Given the large size of this organization, it is best to break this question down to five more-specific questions:

Is Company A financially stable?

Is there any evidence to suggest that Company A does not respect its physical environment?

Are the products and services of Company A manufactured, developed, and delivered to consumers and clients using the highest available standards?

Does Company A treat its human stakeholders with dignity and compassion?

Is Company A supportive of local community needs?

Prediction According to the Model

How does Company A manage the dissemination of information? If the news, activity, or information can be considered "good news," then we can assume that Company A will actively try to promote them to the general public and business press. Thus, predictions can be made for each area of social responsiveness: financial stability, respect for the environment, respect for human stakeholders, quality of products and services, and community involvement. In these instances we can expect Company A's home page, press releases, online annual reports, executive speeches, and 10K SEC filings to play a large role in its dissemination efforts. Thus, corporate, public relations, specialty business, and regulatory portals should be quite popular for CI professionals.

On the other hand, with the exception of financial instability, when news, activity, or information falls under the category of "bad news," chances are that Company A would try to *protect* the business press and the general public from this knowledge. There would be no effort to disseminate this information widely. Analysts would find most of this information in online transcripts of court cases, regulatory actions and decisions, chat-group commentary, and the Web sites of critical, special interest groups.

If there is some question of financial instability, then we would expect the firm to *justify* its performance through the use of company press releases, executive speeches, and its own online annual report.

In summary, a combination of corporate, public relations, and regulatory portals would be the most useful to analysts when assessing this organization.

ANALYSIS

Company A's social image and reputation have been enhanced through a long association with a well-known charitable foundation that works to improve the delivery and availability of quality health care. Also, Company A seems able to survive and prosper in a changing, competitive landscape. It is financially stable; its share price is strong and continues a five-year growth trend. Indeed, in 1998, Company A shareholders received 12.1 percent[a] dividend payout, the result of years of continually increasing annual revenues. In addition to senior debt ratings of AAA with S&P,[b] Company A earnings are expected to be greater than the anticipated rate for the broader market.

Does Company A respect its physical environment? Once again, the evidence suggests that it does. Company A has established an environmental program to reduce levels of energy consumption, eliminate accidental releases of toxic, chemical, hazardous, and nonhazardous waste, and efficiently package its products. As an EPA Climate Wise Company Partner,[c] it has been credited with substantially reducing energy usage and yearly paper and package material consumption by 2,600 tons, for a total saving of $3 million. In terms of air quality, Company A is credited with a 29.2 percent indexed energy reduction since 1991, and it has reduced its CO_2 emissions by 1,950 tons.[d] Although the evidence is largely positive, a search of EPA defendant reports using the Right to Know Network Web site lists two instances in the last five years where a Company A

Figure 6.3
Case Illustration: Social Responsibility Audit of Company A

Issues Important for Assessing the Level of Socially Responsible Behavior of the Firm	Assessment of Socially Responsible Behavior	Summary of Evidence to Support the Assessment	URLs of Pertinent Sources Used in This Case
Financial Stability	Strong	Continued growth through sales and acquiring good fit firms.	www.sec.gov www.disclosure-investor.com
Respect for Physical Environment	Moderate to Strong	Praise regarding performance but evidence of past problems.	www.jnj.com www.corpwatch.org www.mcspotlight.org www.epa.gov www.rtk.net
Product & Service Standards	High	Past behaviors in best interest of consumers.	www.jnj.com www.cpsc.gov www.fda.gov databex.transium.com
Treatment of Human Stakeholders	High	Awards for such from national organizations.	www.jnj.com www.osha.gov
Community Involvement	Strong global	Company home page, Grantee home pages.	www.jnj.com
Overall	Excellent		

facility was fined for pollution.[e] Although not perfect in its operations, this company does actively encourage and support environmental efforts in-house and through its philanthropic programs.

Company A offers a wide range of products through its current base of consumer, pharmaceutical, and professional lines. It demands from its workers and suppliers high standards of quality assurance that meet or exceed regulatory compliance levels.[f] In addition, its consumer question (support) service provides prompt replies to inquiries and product difficulties. Written documentation available online through Food and Drug Administration (FDA)[g] and the Consumer Product Safety Commission (CPSC)[h] Web sites indicates a history of quickly responding to product concerns and voluntarily recalling products when necessary. Indeed, a search of these two Web sites suggests a proactive management style when dealing with potentially defective products. Company A usually pulls its products prior to being ordered to by these regulators but, in all fairness, there have been few problems.

How well does Company A treat its human stakeholders? If we take into account online court cases at the both the federal and the state levels, filings with the Securities and Exchange Commission, article abstracts obtained through the Transium Business Intelligence search tool, and documents from the Corporate Watch homepage, evidence suggests that it would be difficult to build a negative case against this company. It has been credited by a number of diverse organizations, online journals, and magazines as being an outstanding employer of working mothers, people with disabilities, women executives, and minorities, including minority students. Its home page lists a number of honors including being named as one of the best places to work for black students by *Black Collegian* and being among the top twenty-five employers for executive women and top fifty for minorities by *Working Woman* magazine and *Fortune* magazine respectively.[i] It has also been recognized on numerous occasions by national organizations for being mindful of the needs of employees, consumers, society, and other human stakeholders. In addition, a search of online documents offered through the Occupational Safety and Health Administration[j] homepage revealed no warning letters or administrative actions targeting Company A.

How active is this company in the community? Some might suggest that it serves as a role model to other high-profile organizations. Complementing its reputation as a producer of quality child-care products, its philanthropic program focuses on improving the health and welfare of mothers and children around the world.[k] This commitment to social responsibility is reflected in the company's credo, which serves not only as a mission statement but also as a code for corporate behavior. How generous is Company A financially? In 1997, it contributed $146.3 million in cash and products to programs and activities that it deemed worthy of support.[l] Funded areas of social concern include hundreds of nonprofit, worldwide organizations in the disciplines of health, education, employment, the environment, and culture.

Is Company A socially responsible? The evidence suggests that it is (see Figure 6.3), and this statement is supported by numerous accolades, including its placement on the Council of Economic Priorities "Honor Role" for distinguished achievements in the area of corporate social responsibility.[m]

PREDICTIVE ACCURACY OF THE THEORY

How well did our model work to substantiate Company A's claim of being a good corporate citizen? The answer is very well. An online examination of relevant information from various information portals was able to show that Company A does operate in a socially responsible manner.

Information from Company A's own site was easily verified by other sites, and its open information policy made it easier to gather the necessary facts. Regulatory bodies, news, watchdog, and specialty business sites offered very little additional information to that available on the company's own site.

How credible is the information used to make this assessment? Favorable information generated through the company's Web site and the popular online press was easily confirmed by regulatory bodies and special interest sites. Indeed, the most damning information obtained through the regulatory bodies was, for the most part, fairly innocuous. Although, Company A may or may not overplay its contribution to society, it certainly does not go out of its way to endanger it.[n]

Chapter 7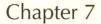

Performing Due Diligence

We are taught at an early age to be cautious and to protect our own safety. Although all motorists are obliged by law to stop for pedestrians at crosswalks, we still teach our children to be cautious and wait until approaching vehicles come to a full stop. As adults we follow the same rules. By doing so we hope not to become accident victims.

Due diligence applies in much the same way to business transactions. Despite all the possible reassurances that a potential alliance partner, acquisition candidate, or promising supplier might offer, it is in the best interest of all parties to take the time to verify written guarantees or assertions. Whether defined as sizing up the risks of a deal or increasing the level of believability of a business proposal, the aim of a due diligence exercise is to reduce the uncertainty surrounding a transaction by accurately assessing its risks. When might a due diligence exercise be of use? Consider the following example.

Recently, an interested party approached your company offering prices and quality products that are superior to those of your current supplier. Unfortunately, you have no record of prior transactions with this firm, and its reputation is unknown. Do you jump at this chance and risk ruining a long-standing business relationship? The answer is not always obvious.

In your capacity as vice president for market development of a mid-sized consulting engineering firm, you are quite familiar with the conduct of transactions and firms in many of the developing nations of the world. A phone call from a frequent partner on domestic projects invites your company into a consortium recently awarded a contract to build and manage a gas pipeline in the Russian Far East. Although your knowledge of the American partner is extensive, the same cannot be said for the Russian partners and their U.S. subsidiaries. The invitation to collaborate expires in six days. What should you do?

Finally, like many others, your industry is consolidating. In order to compete successfully with a newly merged adversary, your firm is seriously considering acquiring one of two major competitors. Unfortunately, your bid team is faced with a dilemma. The corporate culture of one target is a good fit despite a similarity between your products and geographic markets. On the other hand, although a history of hostility characterizes your relationship with the second target, its existing geographic base and product line complement yours. Which should your bid team recommend?

How might one reduce the risks associated with efforts to merge, collaborate, contract, or acquire other companies?[1] Here are some ways:

Assess the other group's financial ability to live up to future commitments.

Assess the strength of its top management team.

Assess the soundness of its previous critical strategic decisions and existing management systems.

Assess its core organizational values.

Assess its reputation within its industry.

Assess its legal situation.

Assess the existing level of customer satisfaction with its products and services.

With this in mind, let us begin our discussion of where an analyst might look to obtain the financial information necessary to practice effective due diligence.

FINANCIAL ABILITY

Does a potential business partner have the financial ability to carry out its commitments? Is it on sound financial footing? Is it stretched to the limit and consistently worried about the adequacy of cash flow? Surprisingly, it is not uncommon for the answers to these basic questions to be overlooked during the excitement and momentum of a sale.

Given the necessary information, a high-level assessment is not beyond the reach of most business school graduates. Performance history during past periods of economic downturn, ratio analysis involving issues of profitability, leverage, and liquidity, financial projections based on current performance, and examinations of three-to-five-year income and cash flow statement data are all subject matter normally found in most basic accounting textbooks. Of interest to most researchers are questionable practices such as unfunded company pension plans or confusing changes to accounting methods that drastically alter corporate inventory values. A change of a firm's auditor or a major write-off of an important asset might also be cause for concern.[2] A full discussion of financial risks is beyond the scope of this chapter, however, with instant online data access, information necessary to undertake such an analysis may be as close as your fingertips.

A starting point is to examine the firm's most recent annual report (10K), quarterly report (10Q), and material change report (8K) filings found in the EDGAR Database of the Security and Exchange Commission Web site. These somewhat somber reports pull no punches regarding information disclosure. The "reference" area of the FreeEDGAR site offers analysts an easy-to-read explanation of the typical content of a 10K report. For a more optimistic view of firm performance, analysts may also be interested in perusing the top management team's version of the annual report written by communication specialists for shareholders and the general public. CNNfn offers links to online annual reports in electronic format, as do the Wall Street Research Network and the Annual Reports Library Web sites.

What are the potential pitfalls and information blind spots of an annual report? In the online Guide to Understanding Financials section of its home page, IBM provides a tutorial for assessing what may or may not be missing. This tutorial is obtainable through IBM's home page, as well as through business sources such as Hoover's Online and Business Wire.

As noted above, 10K annual reports are often different in style from annual reports created for shareholders.[3] One should carefully consider the differences between the contents of these documents. Does one mention the threat of litigation while the same issue is ignored in the other? Is the loss of a key employee not noted in the shareholder-targeted annual report? Why? Regardless of the version of the report you are considering, be sure to read the notes accompanying the financial statements or the auditor's comments. Changes to accounting practices and a discussion of restrictive loan covenants are examples of useful information that might be hidden in the small print.

Just as access to annual reports is increasing, so too is information related to share price performance. Indeed, there is no shortage of avenues for retrieving data and insight on recent share price movements, comparative financial figures and firm-specific indicators, assessment tools, and historical data. JustQuotes.com is an excellent source for links to a large array of performance indicators. The Web sites of Quicken.com, Market Guide, and Quicksource are especially effective for comparative assessments, be they by company, industry, or financial ratios.

Have you noticed that Wall Street analysts are suggesting that a particular firm's shares be held, sold, or bought? Is the firm outperforming the most recent analysts' predictions? Links to brokerage industry assessments and reports of a particular firm's situation may be found using the JustQuotes or Zack's Web sites. Despite the obvious subjective nature of such predictions and subsequent performance pronouncements, researchers might want to make note of predictions and justifications that differ from their own. One need simply ponder the name "Bre-X" to realize that analysts are occasionally wrong.

What does the market think about the company's ability to repay its debt? Check the company's credit rating. Pay special attention to any recent downward changes in their ratings. The two major players, Standard and Poor's Ratings and Moody's Investors Service, offer rating summaries on their Web sites. Once again, ratings found through these sources should not be a surprise to knowledgeable analysts.

TOP-LEVEL GROUPS: CEOs, EXECUTIVES, BOARDS OF DIRECTORS

Financial indicators offer the most accurate portrait of past and present performance. However, they may not be very effective in gauging the future. Trouble or riches on the horizon may be spotted by other means. Consider the following: Who are the members of the top management team, and do they have a track record of doing what they say they can do? In the event of a merger or a decision to offer a vital contract to a new supplier, one wants to be aware of the true talent in the organization and to be reassured that those individuals will be around to implement the agreed upon deliverables. Surprisingly, many managers fail to carefully examine this important issue. Luckily, there are a number of good online sources, including the online media and company Web sites, available for those undertaking such an assessment.

Once again, a good starting point is the content of the documents the company has filed with the SEC. In many instances, a firm's 10K filing will detail the ages, remuneration, and titles of the individuals in question. Form 8K is the filing used to disseminate information regarding material changes to a corporation. If there has been an important turnover in the top management team, it should be noted there. If the company has only recently gone public, then an in-depth profile of the key figures should be available in its 1S filing. Finally, those individuals who are considered to be privy to insider information or who hold significant company shares are identified in filings of Forms 3 and 5. The latter information is important to know as these individuals typically have a lot to lose if the firm goes belly-up. To this end, you should note the departure of any inside traders from the corporate family. The most useful form available may be the proxy statement. As executive compensation regularly attracts the attention of shareholders, top management teams will frequently make use of form DEF 14 A to justify generous pay packages and, in doing so, offer a fairly detailed description of an officer's background. The information on these forms may be accessed in several ways. The most direct is the EDGAR database found on the Securities and Exchange Commission Web site.

Next, one might want to peruse the company Web site and any associated press releases. Researchers can use company press releases to amass a significant historical record of notable employees. A research-friendly disclosure policy may mean, among other things, the existence of a searchable archival database of press releases. Press releases often mention new or existing high-profile employees and their particular areas of expertise. Who are their colleagues? Where do they come from? Are details of their professional backgrounds or education listed? Also note when they joined the company. Take a look at family names and record any connections that might point to empire building. Unfortunately, press releases are unlikely to list those who have left the organization for reasons other than retirement.

If the firm posts its company newsletter online, look there for insight into its employee turnover rate. Are a large number of new employees being introduced into a particular department? If more than one newsletter is available online, look for areas of the organization with a high rate of new employee announcements compared with the rest of the company or with the company's competitors.

Information regarding individuals obtained from SEC filings will normally be limited to a corporation's officers or directors. Press releases may also be largely limited to these two types of stakeholders. However, important contributors are regularly found outside of the executive suite. How does an analyst track these contributors down? If the firm holds patents or trademarks, an online examination of its filings with the U.S. Patent and Trademark Office will reveal who developed the processes or technologies that underpin the company's fortunes. If you are concerned that crucial researchers may have left the organization, a keyword search by inventor name may reveal these individuals conducting groundbreaking research for another organization.

Analysts may also be interested in those individuals who staff an organization's far-flung operations. In this instance, the searchable archives of an online local newspaper can prove invaluable. Who is responsible for the success of a local auto plant or regional airline hub? Who is the project manager of the new hospital facility soon to be opening in the community? In many instances, the exploits of these individuals, which are not covered in the national press or even in the press releases issued from head office, are of interest to readers living near the company's facilities and therefore appear in the community newspaper. The Web sites of the Newspaper Association of America and NewsDirectory.com offer links to local newspapers throughout the world.

CORE ORGANIZATIONAL VALUES

Due diligence practitioners should also assess the potential cultural fit a suitor or target firm. What are the values that guide the behavior of corporate officers and employees?[4] If one assumes that executives can build and maintain values that are accepted and shared by their entire organization, then corporate home pages can be useful places to visit. Often, however, the answer isn't that simple. In an era when multiple job offers for talented individuals are not rare and when entrepreneurial ventures are an increasingly attractive alternative, the manner by which firms define themselves matters.

With information freely and instantly available, curious and well-prepared job seekers no longer limit their research to the annual report holdings of their local libraries. Most also pore over the human resources section of a potential employer's home page for evidence of fringe benefits such as casual Fridays, flextime, office hoteling, or stock option plans. These pages often provide a portrait of a firm's culture. Some sites detail the values the company seeks to instill in its stakeholders. Most post their mission statement. Others offer brief profiles of individual role models. It is worthwhile to take note of the specific traits documented in these profiles, as well as to read company leaders' public speeches, if they are available. These are all examples of how corporate communication teams strive to communicate espoused values and beliefs that support a long-term strategy.

If you are unconvinced of the relevance of a corporate Web site for assessing corporate values, then consider this: What message is communicated by a home page that is disorganized, contains spelling mistakes, is difficult to follow, lists outdated links and fax numbers, or has not been updated for months? In the same vein, how appealing to potential new hires is a firm whose online job advertisements are confusing and riddled with grammatical errors? Careless errors of this nature send a powerful, negative message. Corporate home pages can be accessed through a Company Locator link on the home page of NetPartners Internet Solutions, Inc., the search engine of the Companies Online Web site, and the Web site of NewsEdge.

Where else do corporations communicate their image? Press releases. Most generic search engines, like GO.com Yahoo!, Excite, and NorthernLight, will guide readers to company announcements, which in many cases are links from the Business Wire or PR Newswire online services. Examine the "typical" release. Does the firm publicize bad news such as failed project bids? Does it react swiftly to Food and Drug Administration alerts regarding its products? Does it admit fault from time to time? Does it normally follow through on its announcements? Few firms wish bad news upon themselves. However, admitting failures often creates an image of honesty and integrity in the eyes of stakeholders. Trust is also a deciding factor when companies consider an alliance partner or merger candidate. On a more positive note, project and alliance successes will often be highlighted in company newsletters, which can be found on company home pages.

Regardless of grammatical Web site errors or politically correct responses to bad news, evidence suggests a powerful role for subcultures in most organizations. Despite the warmth of public relations announcements and the hopeful justifications offered by corporate leaders for large-scale change efforts, controlled chaos is, in many instances, an accurate description of contemporary work environments.[5] Researchers may also want to take note of responses to questions such as: How warm is the corporate culture? Is morale a concern, or are there indicators that point to an organization in turmoil? These are often indicative of viewpoints not in line with those of the top management team.

The Internet offers a window for exploring this somewhat less optimistic side of corporate values and cultures. Ongoing economic decline, high-profile project failures, or a recent record of layoffs usually point to a workplace riddled with tension and strife. These occurrences are normally well documented by the popular business press. If this is the case, the particulars will probably be found using online business information sources such as Transium Business Intelligence and NewsEdge, as well as generic search engines like NorthernLight.

Other signals are less obvious but well worth exploring. Is it difficult to rationalize recent heavy hiring activity? Online job-advertising Web sites such as Monster.com or direct links to a firm's job postings such as those found on Yahoo! offer a means of monitoring this behavior. Hiring of this nature may signal a time of prosperity; it may also point to an unwanted loss of talent.

Finally, gossip should never be ignored. The Internet's contribution to gossip is a powerful one, opening the ears and minds of discussants around the world. Chat groups are an increasingly common feature of most major generic search engines. Yahoo!, Motley Fool, and Silicon Investor all offer ongoing discussions regarding an assortment of companies and industries. Excite's Money & Investing message boards allow researchers to browse discussions of company stock performance sorted by alphabetical order. Deja.com's online chat capabilities are among the most sophisticated. In many instances, the chat subject possibilities are limited only by one's imagination. How do junior associates feel about the work environments of the major national law practices? How much do the major law firms pay their new recruits? What is it really like working for that soon-to-be-publicly-owned biotechnology firm? Is one insurance firm having problems with its agents in a particular geographic region? Approximately how high is the turnover rate of software engineers in a major competitor? Answers to or at least insight or rumors regarding these issues often turn up on computer screens. Unfortunately, readers should also be wary of these information sources. They are not unknown to stock promoters.

SOUNDNESS OF PREVIOUS CRITICAL STRATEGIC DECISIONS

A fourth important area of inquiry for those seeking to assess the fit of a potential partner is managerial capability. How can one assess the ability of a top management team to effectively perform in a future fraught with uncertainty? How able is a partner's executive team to manage competently? The past often sends signals regarding the future. Two indicators are particularly useful for assessing the soundness of previous critical strategic decisions: the absolute and relative performance of a firm's share price over time and the stability of the top management team.

How has the firm's stock performed over the last two or three years? How has it performed relative to the market, its industry, and its competitors? These represent broadbased indicators of effective and ineffective decision making. Simply put, below-average performance in any of these three areas should sound a warning to investors. Comparative charts and financial figures are available through a number of Web sites, including Market Guide and the Wall Street Research Network. In both cases, locate the research button on the home page and search by company name. In the case of Market Guide, comparative figures are found using the "financial" hyperlink. The Big Charts Web site offers good visual diagrams, and for absolute figures, use the "industry comparison" hyperlink in Research Net.

Closely examine these same charts for sharp drops or increases in price. Make a note of the approximate date of these occurrences. Then, make use of a research tool like the searchable archives of CNNfn or NorthernLight to hunt for explanations of the changes. In particular, look for independent analysis of company activity on or around these dates. Are outside observers attributing the changes to market or economic factors outside of the corporation's control or are they attributing these events to poor management or ineffective decision making?

The stability of a top management team is useful for assessing the effectiveness of previous decision making.[6] For instance, have new entrants to and departures from the executive suite been a bit too common over the last few years? Are there any particular positions that just do not appear to fit any one person all that well? Is it difficult to keep track of who is who in the company? These occasions signal a frequent lack of consensus among managers regarding the style and content of decision making. The most accurate sources for information of this nature are the 10K Annual Report and Def 14A Proxy Statement filings found in the EDGAR database on the SEC Web site. Look at each of these filings for the last three or four years and note the names of the officers in each case. Any changes should be obvious.

INFORMATION SYSTEMS CURRENCY

Hidden risks may still lurk beneath the surface of companies with sound financial performance, capable talent, motivated employees, and a track record of success. Is a potential supplier's technical infrastructure up to snuff? How compatible is your firm's MIS system with that of an acquisition target? Thanks to cyber trails left by systems operators and the like, there are several places to find the answers to these questions.

Trained in school to work collaboratively, many technology professionals naturally gravitate toward online chat groups where they openly query each other in the hopes of quickly resolving concerns. Whether asking for technical support or assisting others, their online interaction offers insight not only into the existing corporate culture but also into the weaknesses or strengths that pervade its management technologies.

InterNIC Directory Service, developed in 1993 as a collaborative project between AT&T, General Atomics, and Network Solutions, Inc., to provide a directory to the Internet, extracts registration information that includes the names, addresses (e-mail and street), and telephone numbers of a domain's administrative, technical, and billing contacts (simply enter a company's domain name in the search box). In many cases the information also includes the system running the site (computer hardware and software). It will also provide information if an ISP operates the site as a host master (i.e., if the company site is maintained on CompuServe and not its own equipment).

With knowledge of the firm's hardware and software, chat groups and computer industry publications become a source of potential competitive advantage. For instance, Deja.com or other chat sites may contain groups discussing the pros and cons of computer hardware or software configuration used by the company you are examining. Although the firm of interest may not be named, problems consistent with the equipment it operates may arise in discussions offering you insight into sensitive issues. A similar logic applies to computer industry publications. Are there any articles addressing the shortcomings of a particular system type? Members of your firm's MIS department may prove to be an invaluable means of uncovering the identities of industry publications.

Researchers may also want to make note of the issues discussed in other related chat groups and articles. If a representative of a company of interest is active in a particular discussion and is asking for help on a software matter, then one might be interested in understanding why he or she is not contacting the technical support services of the software seller? Perhaps a software license agreement is not in place. Assuming that an agreement is in place, why is the representative not contacting its supplier's technical support services? Further, one might want to question if chat group feedback is the dominant form of training for software operators in this firm. If so, how rigorously does the firm enforce intellectual property safeguards and how much value does it place on its management information systems?

LEGAL STATUS

Litigation or the potential for litigation in any industry is bad news. Few companies win when involved in dogfights. Practitioners of due diligence should be interested in litigation for at least four reasons. First, there should be no surprises. Legal spats are supposed to be well documented in 10K or 8K filings and in online annual reports. Second, court transcripts often expose details of operating behavior not normally openly discussed elsewhere. Careful examination of these transcripts can provide useful insight into areas of risk not previously addressed by the suitor or target firm's top management team. Third, this same information can work against a company by offering a competitor an unnecessary and often confidential portrait of its internal operating systems. Finally, a litigious history may point to a future of acrimonious relations, be it with a partner or its satellite of allies, customers, and suppliers.

A number of online sources are helpful when seeking to discover who is being sued by whom and why. One of the most effective tools is LawCrawler. It offers real-time access to transcripts of all U.S. circuit, federal, and Supreme Court decisions as well as those of other jurisdictions. A second information source is the University of Virginia School of Law Library Web site. It links analysts to the online transcripts of the U.S. federal regulatory bodies under the heading "U.S. Federal Administrative Decisions." Each is searchable by name or topic.

Court transcripts and legal proceedings represent the past and present. Other online resources are available to help predict the future. In an era where the role of government in the marketplace is increasingly being questioned, special interest groups have arisen as a major force for monitoring and moderating the behavior of for-profit organizations. For example, research conducted by Greenpeace recently resulted in the voluntary recall of a large number of soft plastic children's toys from the marketplace. Affected child toy manufacturers acted in their own best interests by foregoing the threat of future legal action. A number of activist online organizations allow researchers to search their archives and databases for company-specific articles or news releases. These organizations include Macrocosm USA, Corporate Watch, the Society of Environmental Journalists, and the Multinational Monitor. By definition, these organizations are critical of our major institutions. One may not agree with a particular group's slant on an issue. It is, however, important to know what that slant is as these views may be precursors to future litigation or problems.

Also of interest to those seeking to reduce the uncertainty surrounding a potential deal should be a growing number of boycott listings. Why are these firms being punished? Are firms of interest associated with any of those targeted for action? Baobab's Corporate Power Information Center and Yahoo! direct researchers to such lists. Yahoo! lists each company under scrutiny and provides links in its consumer opinion subdirectory to related news articles or critiques.

INDUSTRY REPUTATION AND SATISFACTION OF EXISTING CUSTOMERS

What do industry stakeholders think of a particular firm? Are its products of the highest quality, and does it maintain a stellar image? Two fairly direct approaches to identify industry views are to monitor what chat group participants are discussing and to browse the same magazines and journals that industry participants read. How might one assess the level of customer satisfaction with a company's products or services? Chat groups, share price performance, brokerage firm recommendations, online product reviews, industry publications, and testimonials all have a role to play in uncovering views that may not be in line with those of a potential partner.

As the tone of independent product assessments are often shared by industry participants and commentators, online customer or product review sites are worthy of examination when assessing industry reputation or customer satisfaction. Of interest should be responses to the following questions: Has the organization recently been forced to recall a number of products? Are its products mentioned only rarely in positive product reviews found on product review services such as Consumer Reports Online and Product Review Net? If not, why aren't its products mentioned and why are its products being recalled? Neither occurrence may be characterized as good news, and they often point to quality concerns as well as a stressful work environment. As many online organizations are hesitant to offer negative reviews of a particular product, a lack of attention or silence may be a cause for alarm, although it may simply be a sign of a poor marketing effort.

One might also examine the testimonials found on a company's home page. What is important to note are testimonials that should be present but are not, as well as the sophistication or importance of the firms that have chosen to offer to support its products. A testimonial from Coca-Cola is probably a stronger endorsement of quality than one from the corner Mom and Pop coffee shop.

Online industry publications normally address issues of interest to industry participants. Hoover's On-line directs researchers to electronic magazines and journals as it profiles particular firms or industries. The Transium Business Intelligence Web site queries users to specify a company and then offers links to online articles sorted by magazine or journal. By listing the number of articles associated with each journal or magazine, this tool allows an observer to identify which publications are probably read on a regular basis by industry insiders. The higher the number of "hits," the greater the probability that the publication has a wide following in the industry. In instances where geography may play a role in the origin of a publication, as in the case of a regional leisure magazine or a city restaurant review, the home page of News Edge may be of use. If a user simply wishes to browse through a large number of industry journals, CEO Express is also a good place to look.

A final angle is also useful. Has there been a recent change in share price performance? Is the stock unusually in or out of favor with analysts? Why is a buy, hold, or sell recommendation being suggested? In many instances, online purchase recommendations are accompanied by an explanation. These are accessible through the home page of Just-Quotes.

The chat group approach is straightforward. Discussion forums such as those found on the Raging Bull and Deja.com Web sites allow researchers to target dialogue on specific products, services, industries, or firms. Simply pick one of relevance and monitor what is being said. A word of caution before accepting insight from these sources as truth. Professionals employed in the areas of investor relations, corporate communications, and public relations within the brokerage industry are increasingly realizing the value of online discussion forums for portraying a positive image of an industry, company, product, or service. The implied image of a corporation or organizations may be one that is well developed but different from that held by employees, customers, or suppliers. Chat group participants are routinely blunt in regards to product or service quality. If doubters do exist, they will often be found sharing their thoughts with online colleagues.

Legal scholars, organizational economists, corporate strategists, and operating managers have long recognized the shortcomings of legal contracts for managing business relationships.[7] Despite the best of intentions, few competent lawyers will openly claim an ability to construct a foolproof legal agreement for managing complex relationships involving multiple future contingencies. This shortcoming captures the essence of due diligence. Despite the most thorough effort, uncertainty can at best be reduced but never removed from large business deals. By providing access to timely, relevant information, the risks associated with the managerial capabilities, corporate values, information technologies, reputations, and business practices of a potential partner may be clarified and brought to the fore prior to locking one's firm into a long-term, potentially disastrous relationship. We now move on to the important topic of identifying signs of corporate change ahead of their occurrence.

THE ANALYSTS' CHALLENGE: THE EXPECTED DISSEMINATION STRATEGY

Practicing due diligence is not easy at the best of times. In a world where opportunities appear boundless, analysts face two challenges not prevalent even fifteen years ago. First, the amount of information available to the curious may often appear overwhelming. Second, the increased use of digital operating environments has opened the door to data and information manipulation in ways that are not always in the best interest of an acquirer, supplier, customer, or business partner. Of the two concerns, the second is perhaps the most serious. Despite an onslaught of information, should they choose, most players can fall back on a number of professional practices and methods developed to focus efforts and reduce risks. However, attempting to get a true picture of an organization when it is actively constructing an image for public consumption is a difficult task. For this reason, knowledge of useful online information sources can be vital.

Given that most firms will not choose, in most instances, to actively disseminate bad news about themselves, once again, serious researchers should have a picture in their mind of a probable information management strategy in use by a target organization. Consider Figure 7.1. In an age of alliance relationships and close ties beyond normal corporate boundaries, a reasonable assumption is that indicators of positive customer satisfaction will be promoted to the business press and the general public through online testimonials, press releases, and links to external supporting stories. Promotion would also be a useful term to describe expected dissemination behavior that shares with the online readership competence-enhancing data on key executives, media or association coverage that places its industry reputation in a good light, corporate success stories that support a past of effective critical decision making, and statements regarding corporate values that may be deemed attractive by in-

Figure 7.1
Expected Information Dissemination Strategy—Performing Due Diligence

	Good News	Bad News
Want You To Know	Promote • Strength of its top management team • Previous critical strategic decisions • Core organizational values • Industry reputation • Financial capability to live up to commitments • Customer satisfaction	Justify • Financial capability to live up to commitments • Customer satisfaction
Don't Want You to Know	Bury • Legal situation	Protect • Strength of its top management team • Previous critical strategic decisions • Core organizational values • Industry reputation • Legal situation • Customer satisfaction

demand, skilled job candidates. We would expect that its home page, press releases, and public relations portals would be largely instrumental in disseminating these ideas to the public at large.

We would also expect positive news on the financial front to be promoted, increasing the confidence of existing or future investors. However, bad news on the financial front will probably not just be hidden or protected, it will be justified in order to mold future performance expectations. Unlike many other operational concerns, poor financial performance is difficult to hide, especially given quarterly and annual SEC filing requirements. In both instances, explanations should be available in corporate press releases, found on a company's home page and public relations portals, as well as in chat groups and discussion forums where investors and investor relations professionals are known to actively participate in the image maintenance of many corporations.

Litigation and involvement with the courts is an issue unto itself. In instances where an organization is not a defendant, a bury strategy may prove prevalent, keeping detailed information away from the business press and general public. In order to uncover the necessary information, analysts will likely spend much of their efforts reading independent business press coverage of the organization at hand, as well as searching legal and regulatory portals for specific reference to the targeted firm. One can expect an organization accused of wrongdoing or activities not in the best interest of the general public to actively protect such information. Protected information might include unhappy clients or suppliers, corporate or divisional reputations that are not industry friendly, outdated or inefficient operating systems, top management teams that do not evoke confidence in stakeholders, or core values that are not in line with those portrayed in corporate press releases, executive speeches, and home pages. Where might analysts expect to find such sensitive information? A safe bet is a group that encompasses special interest portals, personal interactive portals (chat groups), online broker recommendations, independently written online business news articles, and, in many instances, online local newspapers. In some cases, the actions and warning letters of industry regulators may also be of use. Dissatisfied customers may represent an exception to this rule, however. Look for a strategy of justification accompanied by concrete moves to fix the problems. These would be found in the usual places such as company home pages and corporate press releases.

A Hypothetical Example

For analysts seeking to practice due diligence, few tools are more useful than the Internet. Before offering the activities of B Corporation as an example, it might be valuable to present a fictional case. Consider the instance of a CI professional seeking to build a portrait of XYZ Corporation, a major Midwest auto parts supplier. A logical starting point for assessing the attractiveness of this organization is its most recent 10K annual report filing with the SEC. A first-pass examination of its financial statements suggests a healthy state of being, with an after-tax gross margin of 12 percent and no obvious problematic financial ratios or expenses. From its company capsule found on Hoover's Online, our analyst identifies the company's major competitors. With this information in hand, the analyst turns to the Market Guide Web site to compare various performance indicators with those of the competitors and the industry in which they compete. From this analysis, it becomes apparent that, although financially stable, when overall revenues are taken into account, XYZ Corporation's profit lags significantly behind its three major competitors' in both absolute and relative terms. Returning to the 10K form filing of XYZ, it appears that revenue growth over the last three years is almost flat, with profit growth originating with expense improvements. Thus, our analyst may surmise that, although currently quite sound, XYZ may be in trouble in the not-too-distant future.

In an effort to understand the core organizational values of XYZ Corporation, the analyst visits its online job postings. Listed through Yahoo!, these postings lead our researcher back to the company Web site posting, where XYZ describes itself as a "dynamic and exciting organization where employees can grow personally and professionally." Interestingly, ten of these opportunities are for immediate postings in the company's marketing department. Unfortunately, little further information is available, except for a message asking interested parties to contact the human resources department of XYZ via e-mail.

Continuing the quest to understand the company values, the analyst peruses the 10K annual report form filing. He undertakes a word search for terms such as "values," "beliefs," and "culture" and finds only a description of corporate culture. For the most part, that suggests that XYZ is a leading-edge manufacturer of car parts and an employer of choice, but little else. A scan of the press release section of the company home page fails to clarify the issue of corporate values in our researcher's mind, as financial statement overviews appear to occupy most of the outreach activities of the organization. The analyst searches online for speeches by XYZ executives to industry associations or elsewhere. The XYZ Web site contains no executive speeches. However, the ASAE Gateway to Association home page suggests four different associations that might have XYZ as a member. In two of them, a speech by the XYZ CEO is available. In both cases, its topic is XYZ's solid relationship with one of the major car manufacturers. In neither case is any mention made of values. Finally, the analyst finds a discussion forum dedicated to XYZ using the Deja.com Chat portal. In it, a number of former employees openly lambast the company for its shoddy treatment of smaller customers. The basis of their complaint is the growing degree of inertia at the firm as a result of its new strategic alliance with one of the former Big Three auto manufacturers. The discussion suggests that the firm was built by providing quality parts to a series of small-end users but that in its new status as a major, but dedicated, parts supplier, it appears willing to forget its roots by becoming increasingly impersonal and bureaucratized.

An examination of XYZ's most recent 10K and DEF14a proxy statements points to a stable top management team of eight individuals whose makeup has remained virtually unchanged in more than four years. Six of the eight are engineers from major North and Midwest engineering schools. None are females. All of the members have significant experience in the auto industry, and indeed five of the eight were formerly employees of the new strategic alliance partner. The two individuals tasked with marketing are also former employees of this same partner. Having discovered what appeared to be a fairly competent top management team, the researcher turns his attention to the issue of the soundness of previous critical decisions. Scanning through two years of press releases on the corporate home pages reveals the importance of the strategic alliance to XYZ. Seeking to better understand the relationship, the researcher scans through the previous three years of the SEC 8K Statement of Material Change, looking for more detail, but finds none that mentions the arrangement. He then searches through the XYZ Corporation's 10K filing that followed the announcement. It states that a memorandum of understanding (MOU) had been signed encouraging XYZ to increase its supply of auto parts. Becoming suspicious, the analyst decides to look at the press releases on the home page of a major car manufacturer partner. On it he finds that the announcement is worded in a similar fashion but specifically indicates that the MOU is not a formal purchasing agreement. Putting two and two together, our researcher comes to the realization that XYZ is still quite susceptible to the cyclical sales fluctuations of the auto industry and that "betting the farm" is perhaps a good way to describe its move away from its traditional customer base.

With this in mind, curiosity overtakes our analyst. He decides to examine the major partner in a little more depth and discovers that the online business media community was not in awe of its performance. Use of the Transium Business Intelligence Web site leads him to eighteen different abstracts of articles, none of which paints a rosy forecast for the partner's future. A theme common to most of the abstracts is the company's expected poor performance relative to competitors should no major changes occur in its current operations. In particular, writers suggested an excess number of suppliers and alliance partners at a time when competitors were moving towards fewer but more versatile and longer-term relationships. To add strength to this conclusion, recent productivity figures carried by CNNfn suggest that, when ranked in terms of profit per automobile, this major producer does not fit within the top ten worldwide.

Continuing the process of due diligence, our analyst makes use of LawCrawler to query the online federal court and state court judgments in search of cases involving XYZ. None is found, even in the courts of Michigan, where XYZ has its major facilities. In terms of customer sat-

Figure 7.2
Performing Due Diligence—XYZ Corporation

Issues Relevant When Practicing Due Diligence	Assessment: Is There Cause for Concern?	Summary of Evidence to Support the Assessment	URLs Pertinent to Sources Used in This Case
Financial Ability	Yes	Sound but lags competitors in terms of revenue growth as per SEC 10K Annual Report, and information obtained through Hoover's and Market Guide company profiles.	www.sec.gov www.hoovers.com www.marketguide.com
Strength of Top Management Team	Perhaps	Homogeneous. Experienced in auto industry but closely aligned with major customer as per information available on SEC 10K Annual Report and DEF 14A proxy statement.	www.sec.gov
Key Decision Track Record	Yes	Key risky decision to focus revenue generation efforts on one major customer.	www.sec.gov databex.transium.com www.cnnfn.com databex.transium.com
Core Organization Values	No	Very little information to be found through search of XYZ Corporation home page online job boards, industry association homes pages and online media.	www.xyz.com www.deja.com www.monster.com www.asaenet.org
Industry Reputation	No	Solid. No bad news.	www.asaenet.org
Litigious Track Record	No	Good record.	www.lawcrawler.com www.sec.gov
Level of Customer Satisfaction	No	Fine, as a scan of regulatory body actions, recalls, warning letters, and business press articles suggest.	databex.transium.com www.dot.gov www.cpsc.gov www.bbb.org
Overall	Questionable		

isfaction, a quick search of Better Business Bureau complaints, Consumer Protection and Safety Commission recalls, and Department of Transportation actions and warning letters, left no reason to suspect that XYZ products were defective.

With these points in mind, is XYZ Corporation a sound acquisition target? The evidence summarized in Figure 7.2 suggests "perhaps." However, despite strong financial performance, the company appears to be developing an overdependence on one large customer that might become troublesome in light of growing pressure for it to streamline its operations.

This concludes our discussion of the practice of due diligence. We present the example of Corporation B in the following appendix.

APPENDIX: DUE DILIGENCE OF CORPORATION B

OVERVIEW OF CORPORATION B

Corporation B is a progressive firm at the cutting edge of modern surgical technology. Its products and techniques have been employed in surgical suites around the world for the past thirty years.[a] Corporation B produces numerous medical products, including surgical implant devices and diagnostic equipment. They are best known for their plastic/cosmetic and reconstructive surgery products, such as "body contouring" (liposuction), breast reconstruction and augmentation devices (saline implants), and products for the treatment of bladder and prostate cancers. Included in this latter category are offerings designed to assist men afflicted with erectile dysfunction (ED) and disposable urinary incontinence products designed with the dignity of the user in mind. Corporation B is positioned in a sector that has a decreasing number of players because of the increasing and constant threat of litigation. Corporation B has remained as a provider of medical products designed to improve the quality of life of clients around the world.

An Issues Statement

With the inherent regulatory and liability hazards associated with the medical supply sector, Corporation B must be vigilant in its efforts to protect its long-term prosperity. Whether dealing with nuisance court cases filed to catch the wave of litigation madness or with those brought forth from legitimate pain and suffering caused by product failures or human error, companies in this sector must be cautious. The challenge for analysts seeking to make an investment or assess an acquisition, partner, or alliance target is to obtain enough good data to make an informed judgment.

THE RESEARCH QUESTION

For suitors of Corporation B, what concerns might the free online resources of the Internet allow them to respond to? Put another way, what issues should an investor be aware of before purchasing Corporation B?

An Assessment and Identification of the Important Variables

Prior to building a relationship with Corporation B, most decision makers want to perform due diligence. In undertaking such an assessment, responses to the following questions would be helpful.

- How financially able is Corporation B to live up to future commitments?
- How strong is Corporation B's top management team?

- How sound are Corporation B's previous critical strategic decisions and existing management systems?
- What are Corporation B's core organizational values?
- What is Corporation B's reputation within its industry?
- Does Corporation B have a track record of litigious involvement?
- How satisfied are customers with Corporation B's products and services?

Prediction According to the Model of Chapter Two

In a scenario where Corporation B is being pursued in a friendly manner, diligent analysts would need to dig beneath the surface to uncover the truth.

How does Corporation B manage its image? To begin with, it may actively seek to *promote* to the business press and the general public examples of positive customer satisfaction through online testimonials, press releases, and links to external supporting stories. It may offer to the general online readership corporate success stories that demonstrate effective critical decision making, statements that support corporate values that it wants shared, background data on key executives who show extreme competence, and any media or association coverage that enhances its industry's reputation. We would expect that its home page, press releases, and public relations portals would play a large part in disseminating these ideas to the public.

In terms of its financial position, analysts would expect Corporation B to *promote* positive news, but to *justify* bad news, given the ongoing need for many medical products sector firms to attract funding. In both instances, the firm will probably make heavy use of press releases, available through its home page and public relations portals, as well as chat groups and discussion forums where investors are known to actively discuss the firm and its fortunes.

Involvement in litigation is never good news. In instances where Corporation B is not a defendant, we would expect it to *bury* detailed information away from the business press and general public. In order to uncover such information, analysts would most likely have to read independent business press coverage of Corporation B and search legal and regulatory portals for further details. One would predict heavy use of the SEC and USPTO homepages as well as the Food and Drug Administration Web site. In instances where Corporation B is a defendant, one would expect it to actively *protect* the press and general public from such information, leaving analysts to explore the same Web sites just noted.

Dissatisfied customers, examples of core values not consistent with those portrayed by Corporation B, reputations not in line with industry expectations, nonoptimal operating systems, and weak top management teams are all extremely sensitive matters. In all instances, with the exception of dissatisfied customers, we would expect Corporation B to *protect* the press and public from this information. Thus, analysts would find special interest portals, personal interactive portals (chat groups), online broker recommendations, and independently written online business news articles especially revealing. In some cases, the actions and warning letters of industry regulators may also be of use. Dissatisfied customers present a different case. In many instances, a firm like Corporation B might choose to *justify* this concern by announcing that concrete actions have been taken to fix the problem.

ANALYSIS

How Financially Able is Corporation B to Live Up to Future Commitments?

Over the past few years, Corporation B has demonstrated its ability to adjust to the challenges of its core business. Based on the available data, the firm has experienced double-digit sales increases while reducing the firm's operational cost.[b] Although primarily a manufacturer of surgical/medical products, it is diversified within that sector and not dependent on a single product line. It maintains a solid reputation among industry combatants of providing premium products and after-sale support that effectively complements a strong domestic and foreign marketing program. Corporation B has a proven record for continued product developments and improvements. The USPTO issued ten U.S. Patents to Corporation B over a recent eighteen-month period.[c] Implant competitors have faced media and medical sector scrutiny, and Corporation B faces continual litigation. It was involved in substantial product liability litigation in the early 1990s, but was able to settle these claims via a combined payment program between Corporation B and its insurers.[d] Other litigation-related issues appear to be the norm for this sector, but industry analysts look favorably upon Corporation B and its chances for future prosperity and growth.[e]

How Strong is Corporation B's Top Management Team?

Corporation B's top management team reflects the strength of the firm. It's members hold straightforward titles, and there is no confusion as to individual roles. Of the seven current members of the executive team, only one individual has joined the company in the last decade.[f] This stability and coherence has guided Corporation B during the turbulent times that have threatened its survival. For example, a recent announcement of a new CEO appointment did not have a major impact on share price.[g]

How Sound are Corporation B's Previous Critical Strategic Decisions and Existing Management Systems?

The soundness of Corporation B's previous critical strategic decisions can be best demonstrated by the firm's reaction to its greatest crisis—namely, claims that silicone gel and saline-filled breast implants are linked to illnesses in the women who received them. With media attention in the 1990s focused on its sector of the health industry, Corporation B came under a great deal of scrutiny. In retrospect, its decision to quickly settle the breast implant case, as opposed to dragging it out in court, appears to have been a sound one, given the fate of some of its competitors. Corporation B remained in the mammary implant business when other firms bowed out, fearful of potential litigation. It corrected identified problems and did so in a manner that provided reasonable disclosure to the public.[h] It also branched off into other product lines at a time when competitors were retracting. Its international expansion and R&D programs demonstrate a desire to broaden its industry share. If its track record can be summarized in one brief statement, then perhaps "Corporation B's reaction to previous critical strategic decisions has resulted in its continued growth" is the most accurate.

What are Corporation B's Core Organizational Values?

Through analysis of the available information, it appears that Corporation B's core organizational values are customer centered. The firm provides a wide range of medical products that improve the quality of life of the end user. Corporation B provides a toll-free phone service to give clients and potential clients greater access to information on products and service access. For example, there is a service designed to assist women looking for information on breast reconstructive options. Women can access the specialized Web site or call Corporation B and speak with a registered nurse to address concerns for treatment options.[i] Similar information services exist for other product categories including ED, liposuction, and cancer treatment products. Corporation B has a record of dealing with product concerns quickly and continues to manufacture products with a risk profile that many other firms consider too high to work with.

What is Corporation B's Reputation Within Its Industry?

Corporation B has a good reputation within the industry as a company that develops and markets products that improve quality of life and maintain the dignity of the user. The sheer number of devices implanted annually is a testimony to the industry's support of Corporation B products. It appears that unlike OTC products, such as pain relievers, doctors discuss treatment options "in clinic" and not to the general public. Corporation B's consumer line connects patients with doctors, but surgeons tend to consult with patients on the options best suited to their individual needs. Surgeons repetitively access Corporation B's diverse product line, but the FDA has expressed concerns with some of its products. However, in those cases it appears Corporation B has worked with the FDA to rectify the concerns.

Does Corporation B Have a Track Record of Litigious Involvement?

As is the case with most firms in this sector, Corporation B has been actively involved in litigation. Claims related to product liability are regular and ongoing in the medical device industry. Corporation B's legal counsel appears quite savvy when faced with legal claims, attempting to resolve high-risk challenges as quickly as possible. However, evidence suggests that it does not back down in most cases. Indeed, it regularly uses wording such as, "Management believes

Figure 7.3
Case Illustration: Performing Due Diligence—Corporation B

Issues Relevant When Practising Due Diligence	Assessment: Is There Cause for Concern?	Summary of Evidence to Support the Assessment	Sources Used in This Case to Assess Social Responsibility	URLs Pertinent to Sources Used in This Case
Financial Ability	No – Sound	Data obtained from the SEC 10K Annual Report.	SEC	www.sec.gov
Strength of Top Management Team	No – Strong	Business news stories.	Transium Business Intelligence	databex.transium.com
Key Decision Track Record	No – Strong	Business news stories.	Transium Business Intelligence	databex.transium.com
Core Organizational Values	No – Strong	Company Web site statements.	Corporation B Home page	www.bcorp.com
Industry Reputation	No - Leader	Business news stories.	CNNfn	www.cnnfn.com
Litigious Track Record	No – Ethical	Data obtained from the SEC 10K Annual Report. Business news stories. Scan of the U.S. FDA Web site.	SEC Home page Transium Business Intellgence	www.sec.gov databex.transium.com www.fda.gov
Level of Customer Satisfaction	No – High	Positive chat group commentary.	Deja.com	www.deja.com
Overall	Positive			

that this matter is without merit," in its SEC 10K annual report filings in response
to product concerns.

How Satisfied are Customers with Corporation B's Products and Services?

Customer satisfaction levels are hard to judge in this industry. Corporation B
provides telephone customer support services staffed by medical professionals
to assist consumers and potential consumers. Direct customer satisfaction reports
are not comparable to other industries. The opinions of the medical doctors who
use the equipment and implant devices are a better gauge of the company's
degree of customer satisfaction. Medical personnel continue to use the products,
and the FDA reviews all complaints for merit. Individuals who have experienced
apparent medical complications from implants have founded support groups.
These groups continue to address concerns with health-related issues and act as

watchdogs for the industry. Evidence suggests that Corporation B is forthcoming and provides requested information to current and potential consumers. Corporation B has proven to be cooperative with the FDA over concerns with manufacturing processes.[j] Judging from the commentary on chat groups, Corporation B's behavior appears to leave a positive impression with customers and consumer groups. A recent billboard-based market campaign and a run of print ads in national magazines were criticized for targeting women with negative body images and insecurities,[k] but the firm's overall image remains positive. Also, it must be remembered that Corporation B offers a large catalog of diverse medical and surgical products.

PREDICTIVE ACCURACY OF THE THEORY

The model proved to work well. Although information regarding a number of topics was sparse, its quality was high. Statements could be confirmed through publicly available sources of information. The information dissemination tactics, for information under the control of the company, was available but not openly presented by the firm. Overall, the firm does not "hype" its image in the same way as companies in other industries, but that is understandable considering the nature of its business. The predominant sources of information used were the business press and the Web sites of the regulatory bodies, in particular, the SEC, the USPTO, the FDA, Transium Business Intelligence, and CNNfn (see Figure 7.3). Of these, the most useful portals were the SEC, the FDA, and the Transium sites.

Information on Corporation B was obtained by first reviewing information presented on its own Web site, moving on to regulatory bodies, and then finally to the business press. This allowed us to easily compare the issues that Corporation B wished to disseminate with those of interest to external stakeholders. Corporation B disseminates information cautiously, but it does respond to concerns and provide information on its products and services as required or requested.

Chapter 8

Profiling Corporate Communications Styles

Have riots broken out as a result of your company's pipeline project, which just happens to be being built through the serene wilderness of the Andes? Is your firm logging a little bit too close to a centuries-old religious monastery? Has a mining operation owned and operated by your firm spilled toxic waste throughout a foreign nation's premiere fruit-growing region? Has your CEO publicly defended the actions of a management-consulting firm, actions that informed outside observers are labeling criminal in nature? If so, much of the task of slowing the descent of your firm's share price to the penny stock range probably falls on the shoulders of your CEO, acting in concert with his or her corporate communications team.

Aside from the management of obvious corporate crises, corporate communications professionals serve another important role—to effectively signal strategic intentions to competitors while guarding against the unintended disclosure of sensitive corporate information. Unfortunately, the use of the Internet for communications purposes has given rise to one more concern, the ability of one competitor to read the behavior of another.

As with products and services, many organizations continue to use communication strategies and styles that they have found successful in the past. This tendency creates an opportunity for the online analyst. The digital records left by a series of press releases disseminated through the Internet may leave an imprint. Thus, a firm's communications style can be profiled. Finally, in an age of limited employee loyalty, an overly zealous PR department can give away the store by indicating the real human resource talent in the organization. When might a profile be of use? Consider this example.

Your firm is ready to announce a new product launch in a market that has recently added a number of entrants to its list of competitors. These powerful newcomers have changed a previously stable operating environment into one fraught with uncertainty. No longer can the reactions of all adversaries be safely predicted. A failed launch will lead to layoffs and make the corporation an inexpensive acquisition target. Awareness of how the new entrants might react can stop you from making a bad decision.

A corporate communications profile can be invaluable to a competitor. As with the identity of its most valuable human assets, most senior managers would prefer that assessments of this nature could not be easily conducted. Although not all firms leave a distinct trail of their behavior, many do. A starting point for building a realistic portrait of a company's normal communications posture is a portfolio or chronology of online company press releases and independently written articles. The objective of this type of portrait is to enable an analyst to accurately predict responses to questions such as, "Will my competitor strike preemptively?" or, "Will it be aggressive in defending its turf?"

How might you develop a profile? First, identify the competitor(s) of interest. Then, for each, build two multiperiod chronologies of firm-specific communications. One of these chronologies or portfolios should track what the firm is saying about itself. These are the firm's public relations announcements or press releases. As with individuals, some organizations "talk" about themselves more than others do. Thus, an analyst may discover thirty press releases originating from one firm in any forty-five-day period, but only eight in a six-month period from another firm. A second chronology should provide insight from independent observers. These are the stories written by the news media. Given a particular group of competitors, an optimum set of data would commence at one point in time and allow researchers to track each move, independent assessment, and countermove.

Once this information is captured, develop a profile by answering a number of questions.[1] How often does the firm issue press releases? Is it known to announce actions and then take those actions at a much later date, or do announcements normally occur on or around the date of the action? Are press releases limited to major events in the life of the organization, or are media outlets bombarded with more mundane and normal operational activity? Does the firm normally communicate to its competitors by what it does or by stating its intentions? In general, how precise are the company's pronouncements, and are they to be accepted at face value or taken with a grain of salt? Is "aggressive" or "passive" a more accurate description of typical written communication? Finally, are communications or press releases tailored to each situation, or can the competitor be read like a book? Although fairly precise, these questions all have one characteristic in common: they seek to document patterns of regular and recurring behavior.

Where can you find this information? Sources of independent analysis or news reporting play an important role in deciphering actual from intended behavior. These sources allow an analyst to assess how a company responds to major external events and whether they do so on an immediate or a delayed basis. Does it mention the good along with the bad? Does it respond to each major move of a competitor or is it selective in its communication efforts? Information sources such as the Transium Business Intelligence Web site and the NorthernLight search engine clearly differentiate original information sources for researchers. The latter Web site and the NewsEdge allow researchers to limit their search of specific organizations to corporate press releases or independently written assessments as well as other important categories of inquiry.

Other independent news sources are numerous. The archives of online versions of media such as *Forbes, Fortune, Business Week,* and the *Wall Street Journal* are sources effective in their coverage of large corporations. In cases of less well-known firms, analysts might want to make use of search tools such as CEO Express, the Newspaper Association of America or News Directory.com to identify media aligned with the interests of a more specialized readership. Information specific to a corporate subsidiary or division is most effectively accessed through the online archives of a community newspaper than the national press or a generic search engine such as GO.com or NorthernLight. Ensure that an article retrieved from an online media source is not simply a reprint of the firm's press release. Analysts interested in examining press releases of subsidiaries of large companies such as General Electric or Siemens may also find them fraught with press releases from the parent company.

The direct route to company press releases is the company home page. A number of tools offer a means to identify company Web sites. These include a Company Locator link on the home page of NetPartners Internet Solutions, Inc., the portal of the Companies On-line Web site, and the Web site of NewsEdge. The first two of these sites identify and link researchers not only to the main company home page but also to those of any subsidiaries. Should these prove ineffective, recent company PR announcements can often also be found using the searchable news release databases of Business Wire and PR Newswire.

In addition to offering an opportunity to develop a communications profile, press releases can enlighten observers in other ways. Consider the example of ongoing internal crisis. Few competent managers wish to make bad news public. Yet, signals of internal strife may take many forms, including any obvious departures from regular, previously patterned public relations behavior. Consider whether the firm is now reactive in its press releases whereas previously its resources were focused on promoting its uniqueness. Are current communications efforts now focused solely on the CEO when, historically, announcements served to share the glory? Has there been a change in the frequency of news releases? Are previously uncommon periods of silence now quite normal? Affirmative responses may be indicative of financial instability, performance shortfalls, internal organizational turmoil, or an internal power struggle.

Press releases may also identify important power holders or extremely capable employees. In many instances, however, firms do not publicize the members of their executive team. Fortunately, a combination of the information found on the company home page and its chronology of news releases will often clearly indicate who is competent within the organization. Hints regarding competency may also be found by identifying backgrounds of success and tenure; whom the company is talking about; who has recently been written up in the major press; and whose area of the company has been growing, receiving resources, or receiving extended publicity.

Awareness of a competitor's human resource talent and an ability to read the signals of an ongoing internal organizational crisis may offer some firms a significant competitive advantage. These are both discussed in detail in other chapters of this book. Here, it is appropriate to examine the dissemination behavior of a typical industry combatant.

THE ANALYSTS' CHALLENGE: THE EXPECTED DISSEMINATION STRATEGY

How might professional communication experts play the game of information dissemination? Well, the obvious response is, "It depends." Each corporation has the capability to alter its public image by using the tools and communication or message characteristics discussed throughout this chapter. Thus, in instances when an organization chooses to proactively disseminate information about itself to the public, diligent observers should be able to observe distinct patterns among these characteristics.

How truthful are corporate public relations offerings? It depends upon whose viewpoint you choose to accept. Clearly, many of the public characteristics of a corporation are deliberately manufactured. But some of these may be more important and sensitive than others. Three of these are particularly noteworthy. Many firms will actively announce events well in advance of their expected occurrence but then not report on the events until well after the fact. Second, what many executives do not want made public is unreliable information, such as incorrect statistics regarding the use of a particular product or quotations taken out of context that are nonetheless used extensively to promote a service. Finally, a third issue that most firms will seek to protect from the curious is the actual accuracy of the messages that are put on public display. If a corporation promises hassle-free refunds to all customers who are not satisfied with its products, does it actually honor this commitment? Do its one-size-fits-all swim goggles really fit all types of faces? Beyond these areas of concern, one would not expect most firms to consciously protect or justify their intentions along other dimensions. These ideas are presented in Figure 8.1.

A Hypothetical Example

How might the ideas of this chapter be implemented? Let's consider the following example. As you are a newly minted MBA from a prestigious West Coast business school, your new employers are confident in your ability to add value to their main business line, management consulting. So confident are they that you are tasked to profile the behavior of a major new entrant into the management/information technology education market. A group of disenchanted alumni from a less prestigious East Coast MBA program identified a severe shortcoming of many existing graduate business degrees: graduates are technologically inexperienced. Seizing this opportunity, these entrepreneurs have quickly established a premium-price IT finishing school in major population centers across North America and have successfully gone public, all in the space of two-and-a-half short years. Targeting successful recent undergraduates and non-IT-competent members of the workforce who are willing to take or can obtain a nine-month leave from employment, I.T. Corporation is quickly making a name for itself.

The school's phenomenal success has garnered widespread publicity as well as a high level of criticism from defenders of the academic status quo. Beneath a veneer of high-minded if critical indifference, so concerned is a consortium of business school deans that your organization has been contracted to develop a strategic response to this threat. One important part of this response is a communication profile of this new entrant.

Your knowledge of the online information sources proves invaluable in your efforts to profile I.T. Corporation. In your first hour of research, you discover the depth of its proactive attempts to build a positive public image. A quick comparison of the news releases found on its home page and those obtained through Business Wire and the NorthernLight search engines point to an identical match.

With this established, your analysis begins with the revelation that I.T.

Figure 8.1
**Expected Information Dissemination Strategy—Profiling Corporate
Communications Styles**

	Good News	Bad News
Want You to Know	• Dominant form of communication • Speed to implementation • Information accuracy • Cost • Reliability of information • Behavior • Style	
Don't Want You to Know		• Speed to implementation • Accuracy • Reliability of information

Corporation's natural tendency is to announce upcoming activities well
in advance, with launch dates often announced six months in advance.
The company's normal strategy appears to be delayed action for these
costly undertakings.

I.T. Corporation is also prolific in its use of press releases to disseminate what could best be described as two forms of infomercials/position
papers. One set of articles, written by various nonacademic authors, is

Figure 8.2
Communications Profile of I.T. Corporation

Characteristic	I.T. Corporation
Dominant Form of Communication	• By Announcement
Speed to Implementation	• Delayed
Accuracy	• Precise
Cost	• Expensive
Reliability of Information	• Suspect
Behavior	• Docile, consistent
Style	• Unresponsive

openly critical of traditional business school programs but, interestingly, does not mention by name any of the poor performers. A second group of articles is somewhat more optimistic in nature, having in common a description of a digital future whose inhabitants all possess the skills offered by the I.T. Corporation program. The proactive dissemination of these two types of messages leads our analyst to suspect the accuracy of information used by I.T. Corporation in its efforts to shape its image. Best described as interesting reading, none of these articles offers insight that has been empirically tested or peer reviewed. Indeed, a leap of faith describes the mindset needed by an informed reader to consciously accept all of these ideas.

This communication package suggests other points about I.T. Corporation, summarized in Figure 8.2. With the exception of an announcement regarding its most recent financial performance and an early brief profile of its founder, the content of its publicity offerings has remained remarkably consistent. Each new location and program announcement also always occurs between the months of September and March, which are also normally the months when undergraduate students make decisions to enter graduate school and when corporations actively recruit on campuses. The believability of each announcement is, unfortunately, somewhat suspect. While the curious can clearly understand what this new entrant is trying to accomplish, how it is trying to do it, where it is trying to implement its plans, and when it would like to move forward, the believability of its announcements is somewhat suspect. For instance, a scan of the online Yellow Pages for the telephone numbers of four of the newly announced training facility locations found no listing for I.T. Corporation even though the target date had been surpassed by at least two months in all locations. Furthermore, its most recent 10K annual report filing on the Securities and Exchange Commission home page mentions the establishment of seven, not fourteen new training locations.

In order to assess its style, our researcher used the advance search option of the NorthernLight portal, seeking articles with terms such as "I.T. Corporation," "business education," and "information technology" in the title and/or text. Over a three-year period, forty-two articles were found that mentioned our target organization directly; of these, almost half appeared in reputable mainstream newspapers and business magazines. Of this latter group, fourteen articles were distinctly hostile and critical of I.T. Corporation. Somewhat surprisingly, a closer examination of its press releases indicated no instances where it directly responded to negative publicity. From this, our researcher came to the conclusion that, although proactive in its marketing and image-making efforts, I.T. Corporation is actually quite docile in its signaling behavior and does not generally respond to competitor's attacks.

Although somewhat brief, these insights allow diligent analysts such as our MBA to paint a portrait of a new predator on the loose in the management education industry.

This concludes our discussion of how the Internet might be used to assess the public relations posture of an organization. We now present in the following appendix a real-life case involving two high-profile computer industry combatants.

APPENDIX: CORPORATE COMMUNICATIONS AT ITC

OVERVIEW

In November of 1998, the president and CEO of Internet Tool Corporation (ITC), Dan Steeves, made a bold announcement. Facing declining market shares of its computer products, ITC switched its distribution channels away from retail sellers to a direct-to-consumer sales model. It was Steeves' goal for ITC to attract small business owners by customizing computer and Internet systems to meet individual needs and by providing ongoing hotline technical support. This bold move was necessitated by ITC decline of market share at the hands of rivals IEI and CPC, both of which employed a direct-to-consumer distribution model.[a]

It appeared that Steeves was banking on ITC's vast product line and industry image to bolster the success of this venture. As a Fortune Global 100 company,[b] ITC ranked in third place in Fortune's Computer Equipment sector,[c] with a product line that included such diverse offerings as enterprise computing solutions, fault-tolerant business-critical solutions, and enterprise storage products.[d] ITC's focus on the direct-to-consumer PC market signified its attempt to expand its share of that sector of the industry.

The change in its marketing trajectory had an immediate effect on the firm's financial heath. Profits fell through the floor, and the stock price declined. In the spring of 1999, the ITC board of directors announced that Steeves had resigned from his position as CEO.[e] The *Wall Street Journal* reported things a bit differently. Failing to have streamlined the firm's distribution system, Steeves was removed from his post the board of directors. Different versions of the same event are nothing new. However, can the communication style employed by a firm help analysts to understand its behavior?

An Issues Statement

How does Internet Tool Corporation employ press releases and announcements to communicate its objectives, and can the style it employs be categorized? As noted, ITC's version of events regarding its CEO differs remarkably from that of industry observers. Does this call into question the validity of the ITC's announcements? Does ITC rival Internet Entrepreneur Inc. (IEI) announce its plans and actions in a similar manner?

THE RESEARCH QUESTION

By reviewing the available online communication activities, can an observer interpret ITC's corporation communication efforts?

An Assessment and Identification of the Important Variables

Several variables are specific to this case. Both ITC and IEI employ press releases as a dominant form of communication. It is necessary to evaluate the speed of implementation of those announcements as well as their accuracy, cost and the reliability as indicated by past behavior. It is also useful to look at the style each firm employs to make announcements.

Prediction According to the Model of Chapter Two

The firm's reaction to favorable and not so favorable news is important to understand the communication process of the firm. When faced with "good news," ITC should want observers to know it and thus will promote that information with press releases and make senior officers available to the media for comment. When faced with "good news" that they may not wish to share, ITC should be less than forthcoming, but will not necessarily attempt to bury or protect that information. As seen in the case of the replacement of the CEO, ITC's reaction was to attempt to justify the information by placing a positive *spin* on it.

For an investigation of this type, the most useful portals should be those falling under the categories of news and journalism specialty business, corporate, and public relations. Most of these sites offer ITC's corporate announcements. Web sites found under the portal banners of news and journalism and specialty business news allow analysts an opportunity to compare announcements with outside opinion.

ANALYSIS

Through the use of the noted portal types, analysis of the available information points to a somewhat less than open communication style on the part of ITC. However, ITC certainly does not appear to go to great lengths to mislead observers. A more accurate assessment is that it chooses to amplify only certain forms of information and opinion that place it in a positive light. In most instances, it quickly follows announcements with action. Figure 8.3 summarizes its communication profile.

PREDICTIVE ACCURACY OF THE THEORY

The employment of this model of investigation proved to be effective. ITC's information dissemination tactics centered on the use of press releases and the availability of its CEO to respond to media concerns. Media portals, especially CNNfn and Transium Business Intelligence, proved useful when seeking to verify information emanating from the ITC corporate information dissemination effort. Very little delay existed between information posted on the corporate information site and the insight available from media sites. Information provided by the firm was at best limited in regard to the events surrounding the dismissal of the CEO. On other accounts, however, ITC does appear to be straightforward, leaving an honest impression in the mind of this writer.

The communication strategy the firm employs is uncomplicated in most instances. ITC is somewhat guarded in particular areas, but it does not misrepresent events to mislead stakeholders. Although it has faced difficulties in changing its marketing and distribution channels, ITC conveys a sense of honesty about the events and provides a positive spin.

Figure 8.3
Case Illustration: Communications Profile of ITC

Characteristic	ITC	IEI
Dominant Form of Communication	Press releases and action	Press releases
Speed of Implementation	High	High
Accuracy	High	High
Cost	Low	Low
Reliability of Information	Medium	High
Behavior	High	High
Style	Cautiously open	Open

Chapter 9 ───────────────────────

Spotting Indicators of Organizational Alteration

A recent article[1] in the *Academy of Management Review* contained an interesting observation. Over the last few decades, at least one million articles, books, and monographs have been written on the topic of change. Whether planned or not, change is the most important fact of corporate life. Unfortunately, despite a wealth of insight and research, the effective management of change remains a challenge for many managers.

As with many fields of study, more than one explanation is available to analysts seeking to grasp the complexities of an organizational transformation. This chapter adopts one existing framework[2] to demonstrate how online analysts might use the World Wide Web to spot and interpret signs of impending corporate change before they occur.

This perspective conceives of an organization as an entity in motion over time. Organizations and their designs are held in place or destabilized by a number of dynamics, including the operating context, the deep-seated values that hold sway among employees, the interests of the various groups within the organization, the degree to which any one group has power to implement its ideas, and the existence of a capacity to transform ideas into concrete actions.

By definition, major alterations affect the structures, systems, and meanings that form an organization's design. Analysts seeking to build a portrait of any organization need to take into account whether the existing design matches its competitive and internal operating environments.[3] In this framework, successful change involves the replacement of one design by another. Unsuccessful change occurs when an organization's design is no longer in sync with its environment. Signals of change in the offing normally point to a lack of fit in this regard.

In far too many instances, success is extremely difficult to discern, and many years may pass before the evidence is in. One plausible explanation for the failure of some change efforts is their unplanned nature. Caught by surprise, many firms are unable to meet the demands posed on them by an unforgiving competitive environment. This chapter discusses how the Internet might help an outside observer spot an organization in distress, before this knowledge becomes publicly available. It does so by matching important online indicators with the organizational dynamics of values, interests, power, capacity, and context.

CONTEXT

How important is the operating environment of a corporation to its long-term success? Some might suggest that little else truly matters. Indeed, one need simply think of Microsoft's recent struggles with the U.S. government to grasp the relevance of the expression, "No organization is an island unto itself." Major industry alterations rarely leave players unaffected.[4] Worrisome, for any manager, should be ongoing competitor activity in the area of mergers and acquisitions, initial public offerings, or government lobbying that comes as a surprise. In terms of the internal operating environment, outside analysts should be particularly interested in firms in the midst of extended financial decline. This can indicate an ongoing organizational crisis.

Corporations may have no choice but to respond to major alterations in the competitive environment. Such changes may be subtle, as in a program of creeping share acquisition of a marginal competitor by a much larger operating entity. They may also be quite overt, as when a giant such as Microsoft or General Electric publicly announces its intention to enter a new market through a new spin-off subsidiary. The changes may also occur at a societal level. For instance, consumer acceptance of furs disappeared literally overnight, resulting in a near decimation of the North American fur industry. Mergers and acquisitions, ownership alterations, the entrance of new players, and regulatory change are all important examples of industry alteration.

These examples can be identified by a number of means. The Security and Exchange Commission Web site offers access to the most recent filings. Firms that choose to combine are obliged to report such activity to the SEC using Form SC13D and Form 8K, a statement of material changes. Hoover's IPO Central offers researchers a searchable database that identifies firms whose shares have only recently started trading as well as those who have filed an S1 Prospectus Form but not yet begun to trade on U.S. stock exchanges. IPOs may be queried by geographic location, by company name, by industry, and by underwriter. IPO Central is of course a shortcut to the real source, the SEC EDGAR database. Another interesting site is operated by *Red Herring* magazine. Considered by many as the bible of the venture capital profession, it is extremely effective at monitoring merger and acquisition activity as well as documenting the development of IPOs. One need simply search by company name in the most recent issue or back issues to stay fairly current in this regard. Although biased towards technology stocks, it is nonetheless fairly broad in its coverage.

As noted, regulatory change is also an important form of competitive alteration. Tracking these changes or proposed changes can be a nontrivial task, but one good approach is to read what the lawyers read. Law Journal Extra Online provides access to a section of its home page titled Practice Areas. Each area of interest offers selected articles, columns, and legal memos that cover the major issues that no industry specialist would want to ignore. Communications, computer, environmental, and tax law are but a few of the areas covered. A second approach is to examine the portal of the regulatory agency or department of interest. Proposed changes and lobbying activity are normally well documented. Although the content of each Web site differs, many allow users to view letters submitted by interested parties or opinions rendered by the authority. In each site look for section headings such as "press releases," "dockets," or "statements." Researchers should also be on the lookout for links titled "reading room" or "freedom of information act."

One last possibility for identifying important upcoming changes to a competitive environment is to examine the Web sites of the relevant industry associations. The American Society of Association Executives offers access through its Gateway to Associations link to a large number of national associations. Many of these home pages provide a searchable database of press releases, formal statements, and executive speeches. Formal statements are often nothing more than responses to regulatory change proposals or consensus suggestions for altering the industry operating environment. They can also be very informative when they take the form of "state of the industry" addresses.

While top management teams ignore industry alterations at their own peril, few competent boards of directors ignore a more ominous internal sign, that of repeated poor financial performance. Financial statements can easily be found on the Internet if the stocks of the company under inspection are publicly traded on an American stock exchange. A good place to start is the Securities and Exchange Commission's (SEC) home page. Forms such as a 10K company annual report, a 10Q quarterly financial report, and an 8K statement of material changes will document any extended decline. Other tracking tools are numerous. Portals such as Market Guide, JustQuotes.com, and Zack's Investment Research provide tools, charts, financial statements, and share price indicators that will leave no doubt in the minds of analysts as to recent financial performance.

A most obvious sign of change in the offing is extended financial distress.[5] Other signals are often less obvious but just as important. These include organizational inertia or executive complacency,[6] uncharacteristic periods of silence on the firm-sponsored public relations front, extended product or service quality concerns, uncharacteristically heavy and negative discussion of the company's prospects in the online discussion forums, and ongoing loss of key personnel. These first two signs are discussed in the subsequent paragraphs. The latter three ideas are discussed further on in this chapter.

Explanations for executive complacency are numerous. The culture of a corporation may be overly rigid. Too many levels of hierarchy may shield the true decision makers from the realities occurring in the trenches. An entity may be controlled by a CEO with a strong personality, whose vision of the future is accepted by the entire top management team, whether it is correct or not. A weak board of directors may be under the control of an executive team and neglect their duties to protect shareholders. An executive suite might be paralyzed by political infighting or be staffed by managers whose level of competence is no longer appropriate for the contemporary marketplace. These same managers may simply ignore or not recognize poor financial performance. These are all signs that a firm is in trouble and may well reflect an inability to change for the better.

Despite these well-understood origins, only the pressures of bankruptcy appear strong enough to push some executive teams to act. Luckily, indicators of corporate inertia are not normally difficult to identify. Look for obvious news stories such as those that document periods of extended decline, openly question managerial inaction, discuss unfavorable changes in market share, or praise the rise to dominance of a competitor.

Analysts should also be on the lookout for what is not mentioned. Corporations normally announce new executive hiring initiatives, important promotions, or major improvement initiatives. Despite the negative connotations associated with layoffs, plant closings, and product line alterations, all are popular tools of turnaround specialists[7] and newsworthy subject matter for the business press. Analysts should be concerned if initiatives such as these are not evident when performance is below industry average. If performance is so poor, why are no changes occurring in the executive suite? Why are marketing campaigns not being mentioned? Where are the new product offerings? Silence or inactivity on the communications front can point to inactivity, internal paralysis, or turmoil.

Where might one look? Start a search on the company home page and look for the press release section. Company home pages can be accessed through portals such as Company Link or Companies Online. Most firms do not limit their public relations efforts to their own Web sites. External delivery sources such as PR Newswire or Business Wire are excellent public relations material providers and offer users the opportunity to search by company name or industry.

Take a peak at the Hoover's Online portals. A search by company name should provide a company capsule. Examine the selected stories at the bottom of the page. Another option is to peruse the sorted article abstracts available through the Transium Business Intelligence portal. Again, search by the company name and then sort the abstracts using the function option. This breaks the stories into categories such as financial forecasts, strategy, market development, and so on. A third option is to use the NorthernLight search engine. This portal clearly identifies information sources, allowing analysts to distinguish press releases from independent assessments and monitor corporate reactions to important competitive challenges. It also provides a lengthy historical record of company press releases where they exist and categorizes stories by folders according to the characteristics of the company under investigation.

VALUES

Along with contextual features, analysts seeking to spot a transformation in the making should pay attention to the values of the organization's human stakeholders, especially those that clearly deviate from those espoused by its top management team.[8] How important are values? One need simply think of a successful firm such as Andersen Consulting to realize their role in differentiating an industry leader from its followers. Signals of value shifts may take the form of illicit corporate behavior or may be apparent in online discussion forums.

In particular, overly negative, ongoing commentary should not be ignored. Corporations are rife with disgruntled insiders or former employees, who often seek a forum for sharing their viewpoints. These views may be worth gold to a competitor. Yahoo! offers a message board that may help distinguish corporate from employee views of the company. At this site, type in a ticker symbol and look for the online message board. Portals such as the Raging Bull and the Motley Fool specialize in discussion of particular stocks and industries and are well worth investigating. Other discussion forums can be found using services such as Deja.com, Internet Databases, Hotbot, and Reference.com.

Another sign of values inconsistent with those of a corporation is evidence of widespread corruption or illegal activity. Few members of any board of directors want to be associated with unethical or criminal behavior. Deviant behavior is often newsworthy and headline grabbing and may be difficult to hide. Illegal behavior also forces most boards to take direct action to preserve corporate integrity or even to restore a tarnished reputation. One need simply ponder the recent responses of the International Olympic Committee to accusations of misconduct on the part of a number its members.

Where should a search begin for signs of illicit behavior? Try the online popular business press. An article search using a general information portal such as NorthernLight or a news source such as CNNfn or Reuters may be the quickest route to uncovering any dirt. A different angle is to check out the media that lawyers read, such as the Law Journal Extra. This offers a long list of corporate lawsuits in the news. Another interesting site is that of Lawyer's Weekly online magazine. In this magazine, one can search by keywords such as the company name. The advantage or disadvantage here, of course, is that one may get a spin on events from legal commentators.

In other cases, an option may be to make use of the search capabilities of LawCrawler. Transcripts of court cases falling within federal court system may be queried by company name. Cases falling under the jurisdiction of state and local systems may be accessed using links from this research portal. This latter ability is most useful when investigating companies with offices or plants in more than one location.

INTERESTS

Along with context and corporate values, researchers may also want to be aware of any changes to the nature of internal stakeholder interests. Hiring and insider trading activity may offer insight into this important concern. Personnel turnover and new hiring is a fact of corporate life. Unfortunately, hiring activity can send ambiguous signals regarding the future of any corporation. In some cases, it may be the first signal of internal turmoil. Why is that new vice president being brought on board? What happened to the old one? In other cases, the signal can be a positive one, although managers may wish that the details of the signal remain publicly ambiguous. Why are two-hundred new mechanical engineers being hired in the Dallas facility? What could the competitor be up to? Answers to such questions can point out a new strategic initiative of interest to an outside analyst.

In instances of corporate growth, researchers may want to make note of whose department or division has been on the receiving end of any new positions or resources. The employment opportunities area of a company home page, a specialized job placement portal such as Mon-ster.com, or online local newspapers accessed through Web sites such as that of the Newspaper Association of America are good places to begin a search. Look for hiring activity that is out of the ordinary. This can mean hiring for newly created positions involving nontraditional skill sets or heavier-than-normal hiring for positions involving more tradi-tional skill sets. If this activity is abnormal, then it might be worthwhile to note whether this alters the relative position of a particular individual or department within the company. Decisions to hire or offer extra re-sources to a particular division or department are rarely made without debate.[9] Does this decision set a precedent within the company, or is it consistent with recent history? Insight into historical precedents may be obtained by reading an annual report obtainable through the Report Gal-lery portal, viewing the company home page using a search tool such as Companies Online or perusing the firm's most recent DEF 14A proxy statement.

As noted, hiring activity may not always be a good sign. A sure sign of a problem within a firm is evidence of an ongoing inability to retain valued employees. Look for a seemingly never-ending stream of job ad-vertisements or new executive hiring announcements without any cor-responding changes in strategic behavior or logical justification. Most important, pay particular attention to departures from the executive suite. These are not always announced, and in most instances ads are not openly posted seeking replacements. However, once a search effort has been completed, the identities of successful candidates are normally publicized. Again, the key is no significant hiring activity or number of departures. Company Web sites, professional and industry association home pages, and online public relations offerings are usually good sources for such information.

Heavy insider trading activity may also signify a large transformation in the making. For individuals with a lengthy tenure but no record of insider trading, any analyst should ask why they are trading now. Is an officer increasing his or her level of ownership? Is an executive preparing for a departure by selling off shares? Of course, insider trading may mean nothing more than an executive seeking to increase his/her per-sonal wealth. When considering insider trading, look at the big picture. Has the level of activity increased significantly? If yes, has the trading been primarily of a buy or a sell nature? What trend do you see from this new level of inside trading? All these questions may be answered by analyzing insider-trading activity.

A good place to start an analysis of such transactions is with the com-pany SEC filings. In particular, forms 3 and 5 offer an indication of who is considered to be an inside trader. Form 4 indicates who is undertaking legal inside trading. As noted, selling activity often sends an ambiguous signal. On the other hand, buying activity often indicates good fortune ahead.[10] A lack of buying activity on the part of recognized inside traders should be questioned, especially around times when a firm's business communications unit is actively promoting the extended benefits of a new product or service.

For very recent reports, try the *Wall Street Journal's* daily insider report or Yahoo! Business's company overviews. This latter portal identifies the company, the trader, the number of shares involved in the transaction, and the date of the transaction. Other sites that offer information on insider trading include Insider Trader and Stock Smart. While these sites charge a price for complete detailed information, most relevant information can be gathered from their free services.

POWER

Among the most important signals of an organizational transformation is a shift in the internal corporate power structure. In many cases, as power holders change, so too does strategic direction. Processes for identifying influential individuals are addressed in another chapter. As highlighted, powerful individuals are those who acquire important resources, absorb organizational uncertainty, do visible things, occupy offices with considerable formal authority, and make the firm dependent upon themselves for the successful completion of certain key activities.[11] Awareness and monitoring of the activity of individuals who meet these criteria can provide insight into important alterations to come.

CAPACITY

What is a firm capable of? What true skill sets does it possess? Answers to these questions are currently quite fashionable in academic circles. They are also extremely important but not always obvious, even to corporate insiders. Unfortunately, few actions are as effective at clarifying the definition of an internal capability as its loss. The departure of a key scientist may mean the loss of experience not so much in a specific area of inquiry as in the management of the challenges posed by the U.S. Patent and Trademark Office. At first glance, the loss of a forestry-sector chief financial officer may appear, to some observers, a minor setback, given the large number of well-qualified accountants in the contemporary marketplace. However, upon further examination, one may note the extensive experience of the previous incumbent in the area of forestry-related mergers and acquisitions. In a volatile marketplace, a lack of such expertise can lead to paralysis when swift and thoughtful decision making is most in need.

Indicators of a change in the capabilities of an organization are often subtle, but some are more obvious than others. Researchers might want to consider the ongoing level of effort toward innovation, the potential impact of new alliance agreements or long-term contracts, and the existence of any extended product or service quality concerns.

How might innovation be assessed? One means is to monitor a company's patent application and filing activity. Explanation of the contents of the U.S. Patent and Trademark Office home page and how it might be used are covered in another chapter. Be wary of any recent reduction in the frequency of patent or copyright filings or an increase in the number of filings by competitors. Such changes may indicate an organization with few strong ideas for the future or a competitor on the march. Simply type in the company name in the search box. If there are any current patents, they will be listed chronologically.

Innovative behavior can be indicated by other means. The Transium Business Intelligence Web site sorts articles by terms such as new product development, test marketing, and patents. Recent innovative activity may be documented or summarized in these abstracts. Along with the selected articles offered by Hoover's Online, this search tool will point an analyst to electronic journals dedicated to the industry of the interest. A query of articles in these journals may offer an assessment of the company and its products or services.

New contractual relationships or alliance agreements can signal a change in organizational capacity, especially when small firms link up with much larger firms. In this case, an alliance agreement may point to an ability gap of a larger firm that a smaller company is able to close or an area of new product development for the larger firm. It often also signals a new strategic direction for the smaller firm. For instance, in the case of a small software company with expertise in satellite mapping that links up with a major auto producer, it may not be unreasonable to assume that the smaller firm will now focus on the auto industry. Further, it may not be surprising if the automaker incorporates a satellite mapping program into its cars.

A number of portals are useful for identifying new collaborative relationships. For technology oriented firms, *Red Herring* magazine's online version lists alliance partners in its company profiles. If a firm of interest is actively involved in alliance relationships, then the online press services will probably have a story on file. Searching by company name or industry, doing so chronologically using sites such as PR Newswire, News Alert, or Transium Business Intelligence, should highlight any existing collaborative relationships.

Few companies make perfect products or develop perfect services. Yet, it is probably not too far-fetched to assume that a majority of American consumers equate technological progress with continuously improving product offerings. We expect that each new product will be superior to its previous generation. Acceptance of imperfection is, however, different from acceptance of defective products or ineffective services. Of worry for most managers would be a track record of quality concerns. Poor track records attract the attention of the market and, more often than not, force down share prices.

Quality problems are not an issue that most managers like to admit. Negative publicity of this nature is not normally corporate sponsored or disseminated. Thus, analysts must make use of proxy measures. At least five approaches are extremely effective in this regard. A first is to use a generic search engine such as Yahoo! or GO.com and conduct a keyword search by product, service, or company name. A story might simply pop up.

A second means is to explore online consumer reports regarding specific products or services. A lack of stellar reviews of a firm's product or service lines may point to an underlying problem such as inappropriate design, substandard parts, or poor assembly. As many products or services form part of a larger platform of offerings, problems with one may indicate weaknesses in many others. Unfortunately, the strongest signal of poor quality may be a lack of mention, as opposed to a strong critique. If the product or service lines of a player are consistently absent from consumer report forums or are mentioned but not in the same positive light as others, then this may be a vote of no confidence by the rating organization. A number of portals offer online consumer reports. These include Product Review Net, Consumer World, and Product Reviews Online. Free product comparisons using the services of Compare.net may be located on the consumer economy page of the Yahoo! portal.

A third means to assess extended product or service concerns is to build a multiyear chronology, or portfolio, of company news and public relations announcements. Given the wide swath of information found on many news and public relations Web sites, such a chronology offers an analyst a fairly complete portrait of a company's activities over time. A scan through these stories should allow important clues to surface if they do indeed exist. Of course, a given in any such discussion is to understand at which level to conduct an analysis. Searching on the term "G.E." may be much less effective than targeting a specific operating company of General Electric. As always, the company home page or online dissemination services such as Business Wire and PR Newswire are good sources for news releases.

A fourth idea is to use an online investigative tool such as Transium Business Intelligence. Search the available article abstracts by company name. Then use the Function category to sort the articles. In many instances, abstracts will be categorized under headings such as "product reviews," "product launch," and "product quality," which can speed up an analysis.

Finally, one further means to assess the ongoing strength of a firm's product and services offerings is to check the warning notices carried by organizations such as the Better Business Bureau, the Consumer Safety Protection Commission, the Food and Drug Administration, and the Federal Aviation Administration. Look carefully for a history of repeated product recalls. Is a change about to occur? Along with an understanding of other competitive dynamics, a researcher may also be interested in knowing whether its ability to meaningfully undertake important activities has changed. A record of innovative behavior, poor or superior quality, and an awareness of any new alliance relationships may provide the necessary evidence to make such a call.

Predicting the future is a messy challenge for most analysts. Despite the best of intentions, few of us are truly able to accurately read crystal balls. Understanding the behavior of large organizations without the benefit of hindsight is also a highly complex challenge. Indeed, the basis of this challenge has always been to apply the lessons of hindsight so that errors of previous actions would not be repeated. Analysts seeking to read important signals might pay particular attention to issues of context, values, power, interests, and capacity.[12]

THE ANALYSTS' CHALLENGE: THE EXPECTED DISSEMINATION STRATEGY

In a land called Utopia, managers and executives choose when to make decisions, when to implement decisions, and when to revisit decisions. Unfortunately, these same individuals are rarely afforded such luxury in the marketplace of the new millennium. The uncaring nature of the competitive landscape suggests that in many instances managers are caught by surprise, having to follow rather than lead, react rather than act in a proactive manner, forge ahead without the luxury of detailed planning or insight, and base decisions on matters related to survival rather than growth. The management of change may also be described in this manner. Unfortunately, even the most astute individuals are occasionally caught off guard and forced to hide their actions for reasons other than simply protecting sensitive strategies or tactics.

How might a competitor choose to handle information that can best be thought of as good news? Well, we will assume that most organizations will seek to *promote* corporate behavior or performance that is positively supported by a changing operating context, evidence that supports espoused corporate values, or indicators with the organization that sufficient managerial capacity or experience and talent exist to manage complex change initiatives or unforeseen alterations in the marketplace. In such cases, the corporate home page, public relations portals, industry association portals, and specialty business information Web sites should all prove useful to curious researchers.

In individual terms, rising to the level where one is able to determine corporate outcomes may be seen by many in career terms as a sign of success. Unfortunately, not all organizations want the identities of these power holders made public, as they often represent very attractive potential hires. Where money is spent is often indicative of the existing and future interests of the executive team. These as well are usually not the topic of open discussion beyond the confines of corporate boundaries. Indeed, we expect that Food Company will not proactively disseminate such information and instead will seek to *bury* it away from the business press and general public. In their quest for details of this nature, analysts will most likely spend much of their time reading independent business press coverage of Food Company as well as interpreting its SEC and or other regulatory filings. In line with this, one would suspect that specialty business and regulatory portals will be popular tools.

The dissemination of bad news is, of course, another issue. As noted in other chapters, poor financial performance involving publicly traded companies is hard to hide. In such instances, one would expect efforts to be made to *justify* such information, especially when it is within the domain of a changing operating context. In this instance, although efforts will be made to disseminate information, one would suspect that such information would be directed at the business communication and not the general public. Thus, attention should be given to public relations portals and specialty business portals.

In terms of other forms of bad news, one would expect a different dissemination strategy to be followed. Specifically, it should not be surprising if evidence that contradicts espoused corporate values, corporate behavior that is harmed by a changing operating context, signals of an insufficient executive capacity to manage significant change, evidence that serves to identify internal interests, and evidence that serves to identify internal power holders is *protected* or not openly publicized. For such cases, special interest portals, personal interactive Web sites and speciality business portals will probably prove useful.

Figure 9.1 summarizes the expected strategies in cases of organizational change.

A Hypothetical Example

Few topics command the interest of scholars, analysts, and CI professionals as does that of comprehending the implications of large-scale change. Unfortunately, despite the best of training and insight, seasoned observers are still often caught off guard. However, by matching the online resources of the World Wide Web with existing theoretical models, such instances may prove fewer and farther apart. The following example demonstrates one potential use of this perspective.

Food Company is a publicly traded entity operating primarily in the

Figure 9.1
Expected Information Dissemination Strategy—Identifying Signs of Organizational Change

	Good News	Bad News
Want You to Know	Promote • Corporate behavior or performance supported by a changing operating context • Evidence that supports espoused corporate values • Sufficient capacity to manage significant change	Justify • Corporate performance harmed by a changing operating context
Don't Want You to Know	Bury • Evidence that serves to identify internal interests • Evidence that serves to identify internal power holders	Protect • Evidence that contradicts espoused corporate values • Corporate behavior harmed by a changing operating context • Insufficient capacity to manage significant change • Evidence that serves to identify internal interests • Evidence that serves to identify internal power holders

Northeast. It owns approximately one hundred and fifty grocery stores located in lower-density population centers. Competing in a low profit margin industry, firms such as Food Company have been hard pressed to find ways to make the most effective use of retail space while taking advantage of expensive but potentially cost-effective new store technology. Food Company is also an acquisition candidate of your organization. Unfortunately, you are new to your position and have had little exposure to this organization. However, as an analyst, you understand the importance of internal organizational stability for predicting the success of corporate decision making. You are thus quite sensitive and extremely interested in any signals of unexpected changes to Food Company or its operating environment.

Your initial research leads you to understand that attaining economies of scale in all aspects of operation are increasingly crucial to the long-term survivability of market players in this industry. Indeed, this assertion is supported in a food industry profile found on the Hoovers.com home page that suggests that an industry-wide concentration is underway. Further, analysis of docket submissions found on the Department of Transportation Web site suggest that improved cold-storage technology may soon loosen stringent regulations regarding the cross-border transportation of perishables and frozen products and thus leave traditional food retailers open to new forms of competition in their own backyards. Not surprisingly, you conclude that the impact of a changing regulatory environment, new transportation technologies, and large competitors will be an increasing downward pressure on the profits of players unable to keep up with the frenetic pace of needed investment.

Food Company's Web site proves extremely useful for new job seekers. Using Yahoo!, interested database marketers discover an opportunity to manage its new Internet-based home delivery program. Information found on its home page, accessed through Companies Online, also provides insight into Food Company's longer-term human resource strategy. One statement offers, "We seek to build our future with young, non-traditional university graduates who seek employment in a workplace with few bureaucratic barriers to success."

By coincidence, a scan of the Food Industry Association Web site discovered using the ASAE home page offers details of the recent election of a Food Company vice president as its president. In her first speech to the association, she outlines the advantage to recent technology-literate college graduates of employment in this industry and outlines a new prototype career place being developed by Food Company.

Unfortunately, this carefully managed portrayal of a stable, confident organization is undermined by a brief examination of a number of other important information sources. Using News Directory.com as an entry portal, an examination of the online archives of the newspapers serving the population surrounding the Food Company headquarters suggests that its employment opportunities may be somewhat too abundant and may indeed point to a revolving-door workforce. To reinforce this suspicion, a search is made of the Monster.com Web site by the term "Food Company." Indeed, an examination of entries over the past year suggests that in many instances candidates were requested for a particular full-time, noncontractual position. Further, Food Company's hiring activity appears to be three times as intense as that of its major competitors, with no apparent justification for such a large gap. The three most recent 10K form filings of Food Company attest to this, suggesting no notable increase in the overall number of corporate-wide employees and no special hiring initiatives. Clearly, others are thinking the same thoughts. A recent story found in the CNNfn archives suggests difficulty in its efforts to retain highly skilled employees. As a pattern starts to unfold, a detailed peek at the archived press releases found on Food Company's Web site indicates that at least nine separate individuals have been welcomed into the five vice-presidential offices over the last thirty months.

Besides placing doubt on the accuracy of the values portrayed by the company on its home page, this body of evidence also suggests a change in the structure of interests of the internal power holders. Of the five offices of vice president, two had been held by younger executives who departed after having held the positions for seven years. Backgrounds of these individuals obtained from the corporate SEC DEF 14A form suggest that they were originally hired by the current CEO. Both had track records of success, one growing her divisional revenues over four-hundredfold, while the other had positioned Food Company among the most efficient in the industry. These departures, along with the growing visibility in the business press of a third, long-serving, revenue-enhancing, but previously poorly known executive, suggests a new home is being found for scarce corporate resources.

Indeed, a detailed examination of Food Company's 10K annual reports for the last four years points to a philosophical shift in its capital budgeting priorities. With the exception of the most recent year, the allocation of resources has focused on supporting a strategy of growth through the acquisition of small independent competitors or the construction of new retail outlets. However, in the past year, a close examination of the notes attached to the financial statements suggests a shift into fund initiatives to counter the Y2K threat and development of an Internet strategy.

The divisiveness of this internal power struggle and its impact on the actual values of employees becomes very apparent when one observes the content of a chat group discussion about the organization found on the Raging Bull Web site. Over the span of two weeks, four self-described employees describe the Food Company workplace as chaotic and paralyzed, with workers demoralized and leaderless.

From these points, it becomes evident that the espoused values of Food Company may be inconsistent with those held by its employees, the interests of the executive team may be unclear, and the identities of key power holders may not yet be known.

The exit of the two formerly influential vice presidents highlights a further important concern for shareholders of Food Company—the competence of the existing top management team in managing the turbulence of the existing marketplace. While its average revenue and profit performance for the last seven years is impressive, evidence from its three most recent SEC 10Q quarterly reports leaves much to be desired. Indeed, a comparison of its most recent revenue performance with that of its major competitors, using the research tools of Market Guide, suggests that its good fortune is at an end. A recent article in Business Week Online documenting in-store sales per square foot reveals a retail strategy out of sync with the current demands of consumers. Most important, however, the exit of these two executives leaves Food Company without any experienced creative minds. Further, a review of recent merger and acquisition activity in the food industry points to a need for Food Company to continue using this form of collaboration as an engine for future growth. Unfortunately, a peek once again at its most recent DEF 14A form filing and executive profiles on its home page suggests that few members of the execuive team have significant expertise operating in turbulent competitive environments. These points are illustrated in Figure 9.2.

This concludes our discussion of how the Internet might be used to identify signals of change in an organization. A related case study follows in the appendix.

Figure 9.2
Signs of Organizational Change at Food Corporation

Concept	Assessment	Evidence	Sources
Context	Turbulent	Stagnating profits, large competitors, increasing use of technology.	www.hoovers.com www.dot.com www.sec.gov www.marketguide.com www.businessweek.com www.asaenet.org
Capacity	Uncertain	Questionable ability to managing in turbulent environments. Little remaining strength in acquisition integration.	www.sec.gov Corporate home page
Power	Unclear	Exit of previous power holders leaves a vacuum with little clarity regarding who is really calling the shots.	Corporate home page
Values	Confused	Chat group dialogue suggests workplace values at odds with espoused corporate values.	www.ragingbull.com www.yahoo.com www.monster.com Corporate home page
Interests	Shifting	Traditional support for growth through acquisitions displaced by technology upgrade program and Internet initiative.	www.yahoo.com www.monster.com www.sec.gov www.cnnfn.com www.newsdirect.com

APPENDIX: INDICATORS OF ORGANIZATIONAL ALTERATION AT BUYFROMUS

AN OVERVIEW

Within the first five years of its operation, the online business BuyFromUs has developed a virtual brand-name identity synonymous with traditional brick-and-mortar stores. Its principal corporate offices are located in the Pacific Northwest, with regional distribution centers across the country.[a] BuyFromUs (BFU) went public three years after incorporation and experienced continued stock growth.[b] Its current home page suggests that customers can purchase everything they need online from its Web site.[c]

The BuyFromUs customer base and product offerings have grown significantly since incorporation. It now serves customers in more than 160 countries and has proven that online shopping is far more than a niche market.[d]

In a manner similar to the way upscale brick-and-mortar stores use elaborate window displays or architectural details to attract clients, BFU offers online services in an effort to win over consumers. Special incentives include a personalized shopping guide, a twenty-four-hour customer service department, and a number of supporting Web sites to enhance customer satisfaction.[e] BuyFromUs has also partnered with a number of other online firms to provide a vast product line to entice customers. Pharmaceuticals, sporting goods, groceries, household products, and pet supplies are among the products offered, as are books, CDs, DVDs, videos, electronics, video games, toys, and software. More than 10 million customers have been convinced to purchase at least one product from its Web site. It projects a customer base of more than 125 million by 2002, to be serviced by dozens of product categories.[f]

Of the "dot.com" firms that have battled to gain dominance in the e-commerce sector, BuyFromUs is among the best known. Originally viewed as an alternate source of books not available locally, BuyFromUs has departed from the domain of the Internet enthusiast willing to trust his or her credit card information to the Net to a household name exceeding all expectations. Established brick-and-mortar stores, seeing the growing sales levels of BuyFromUs and seeking to imitate its success, are now responding through the use of hybrid strategies that combine traditional storefronts with e-commerce divisions. Not only has Buy-FromUs gained the lion's share of e-commerce sales, it has also has challenged traditional retailers for part of their market share.[g]

An Issues Statement

The expeditious growth of BuyFromUs has surprised even the most optimistic of observers. Despite rising revenues, stock price, and public awareness, Buy-FromUs has yet to make a profit.[h] Increasingly, a concern of investors is how safe, in the long run, is their money.

THE RESEARCH QUESTION

Of interest to analysts is the availability of online signals that might indicate whether changes truly are being undertaken by BFU to become profitable. Are there online information sources that might help outside analysts determine the specific measures being taken by BFU to transform itself into a profitable concern?

An Assessment and Identification of the Important Variables

Efforts to assess the signals of ongoing or future change at BuyFromUs should take into account a number of variables.[i] One such variable is the context within which a company operates. Important internal and external factors impact the chances of transformational success and are normally very accessible using the online resources of the World Wide Web. The values of BFU's human stakeholders are a second important variable and are critical for understanding the direction of change efforts. Is there evidence of internal dissent or ideas emanating from stakeholders of BFU that are inconsistent with those communicated by its top management team or official communications? The makeup of internal interests is a third variable. Changes in values can be signaled by trends in new hiring activity, employee turnover, insider trading, and aspects of a firm's online communications style. Who are BFU's power holders? Are they the same familiar faces? Should they be the same familiar faces, given the financial picture of BFU? A final variable of importance is an assessment of what BFU is capable of accomplishing, specifically, what BFU can do today that is different from what it could do yesterday.

Prediction According to the Model of Chapter Two

BuyFromUs is a media darling that is featured extensively in the online specialty business press and through public relations and media outlets.[j] It promotes good news that advances its public image. Its state can best be described as an organization experiencing dramatic growth. Unfortunately, some observers question its ability to control its destiny. As a result, one might speculate that it is in the best interest of BuyFromUs to *promote* certain types of "good news" to the public. "Good news" is reassuring, leaving many to think of its originator as a ship well on course to its final destination. Data and insight regarding growing revenues, sales, and product offerings are thus plentiful. However BuyFromUs does not promote other forms of good news that might tip off competitors and inadvertently offer a more detailed portrait of its intended trajectory.

"Bad news" is also used in a positive sense. During peak seasons such as Christmas, BuyFromUs occasionally runs low on inventory. When this type of bad news arises, BFU is up front with consumers, notifies affected customers through its Web site, places the affected items on back order, and then ships them as they become available.[k] BFU *justifies* this public disclosure as evidence of its efforts to provide exceptional customer service. It is somewhat more *pro-*

tective of other forms of bad news. For instance, its nonprofitability is not mentioned in great detail in its press releases.

Of the online information sources used in this analysis, most prominent are those that originate with regulatory, news and journalism, specialty business, and corporate portals. Because of the nature of the these sources, the expected level of information correctness is moderate.

ANALYSIS

Context is the first variable to be considered when seeking signs of impending change. Imitation is among the most powerful forms of flattery. It is also a signal of industry respect. BuyFromUs employs an e-commerce business model that is extensively copied and envied by competitors around the world.[l] Indeed, a look at its Web site suggests that its use and adoption of Internet-enabled technology is a prime determinant of its future prosperity.[m]

In performance terms, BFU dominance is such that it seems to be rivaled only by the growth of the Internet. On the surface, its capacity to manage increased sales levels appears limited only by demand, given its strategy of building its product and service base through partnership agreements with other e-commerce firms.[n] Of course, operationally, this may be an oversimplification of the true state of affairs. Realistically, one might suggest major limits to the growth of this portal, such as shareholder intolerance for poor profit performance (at the moment, this is for the most part absent); the existence of a life cycle for e-commerce companies that includes a mature phase (this may not even be an appropriate model); litigation from existing and new competitors seeking to slow its ascent (this is occurring with some frequency);[o] and the ability of BuyFromUs to meet online consumer demand (recent activity to open new geographically distinct distribution facilities as highlighted by job postings on the Monster.com Web site suggests that it is acting on this concern).[p]

If imitation is the greatest form of flattery, litigation is the worst form of jealousy. BuyFromUs has been no stranger to the courts but has for the most part ended up on the winning side of its legal altercations. Indeed, its recent 10K forms list a series of competitor-initiated legal proceedings, most of which have been voluntarily dismissed by the filers. One important example is a complaint by a competitor that BuyFromUs violated trade-secret legislation by soliciting and successfully recruiting a key employee. Although originally dismissed, the case remains before the courts in the form of an appeal. Context matters to BFU, as it does to all corporations. In this instance, however, it appears that contextual alterations are being managed by BFU in an effective manner.

A stable core of competent power holders can be an important force for long-term success. Judging from the relationship of the starting dates of members of its top management team hired since BFU's incorporation (as suggested by brief personal histories listed in its SEC 10K and DEF14A form filings)[q] and important development milestones, its CEO has grown his inner circle in a nonfrivolous manner. New executive-level hires are brought on based on merit and their previous personal histories of success in managing new product lines, relationships, or challenges in e-commerce operating environments. Not only has the core of original power holders remained stable, it has strengthened itself judiciously to manage online growth. Press releases obtained from its home page suggest a CEO who runs the shop and is its chief spokesperson.[r] Signals from this perspective suggest that any near-term future changes will take the form of new talent being added as opposed to anyone's being dropped from the executive roster.

The status of its cadre of power holders also offers insight into the shifting nature of internal interests. Where do interests lie? Well one suggestion is "in line with its product lines and acquisition and alliance behavior." As new product lines and online service offerings are established, BFU simply adds more to its popular mix. As it branches out into new areas of opportunity and uncertainty, it adds to its portfolio the necessary human, financial, and infrastructure resources necessary to make the venture succeed. Interests certainly shift in BFU, but they do not do so in the context of a zero-sum game, whereby by one area gains at the expense of another. Rather, interests shift as support for new areas of activity is offered while the resources for existing areas of revenue generation are maintained.

The organizational values of BuyFromUs are observable to researchers. A search of news abstracts from Transium Business Intelligence, OSHA administrative actions, and stories retrieved following a search of the World Wide Web using the NorthernLight search engine failed to turn up evidence of a disgruntled workforce, cases of employee litigation, or special interest groups critical of BuyFromUs.[s] A name search using the identities of senior management did not result in evidence of unethical or illegal activity.[t] Abstracts obtained from the Transium Business Intelligence information portal suggests that BuyFromUs has a low level of employee turnover and with no listed employee litigation issues.[u]

Stories originating in the popular business press suggest a corporate culture that is flexible, with young, hard-working, focused, and committed individuals who are compensated with competitive salaries and stock options.[v] Signals emanating from this important perspective suggest a contented and growing workforce whose main concern is being able to hire new staff fast enough to meet the needs associated with the increasing demand for its products.

Capacity is a final issue that may offer signals of change in the offing. Is BFU's senior management team capable of managing growth and making it a profitable entity? Does it have the in-house experience to manage exponential growth in a controlled fashion? Is there evidence to suggest otherwise? It appears that the team does have an internal capacity to manage large-scale change. BuyFromUs has developed expertise in two areas critical to its future success: alliance and acquisition implementation and relationship management. As noted, it has also recognized its shortcomings and weaknesses and developed a solid track record of acquiring the necessary talent in a timely fashion to fill important gaps as they arise.[w] Although it is still not profitable, its losses have been decreasing at a steady pace. It appears that, if anything, BFU is on the road to financial stability through its capacity to master the learning curve of a business model that it alone is creating.

PREDICTIVE ACCURACY OF THE THEORY

How credible is the information used to make this assessment? The answer in this case is, "moderately credible." The relative youth and dramatic growth of BuyFromUs has focused most observers' attention on its performance. Much of the information regarding its internal workings is generated by the company itself through its Web site and press releases or through specialty business portals. However, this was balanced by a significant amount of detail available through regulatory portals such as the Securities and Exchange Commission Web site.

How well did our model work to identify signals of ongoing or future corporate alteration? The answer is, "pretty well." An examination of relevant online information accessed through various portals suggests that change at Buy-FromUs is ongoing, predictable, and controlled (see Figure 9.3). That BFU is experiencing growing pains should be of little surprise to an informed observer. However, that it will experience dramatic transformation in a manner other than normal expansion is not evident from the findings. Nor is strong evidence yet available, aside from key personnel additions, that it will soon become a profitable concern.

Figure 9.3
Case Illustration: Signs of Organizational Change at BuyFromUs

Concept	Assessment	Evidence	Sources
Context	Uncertain	Yet to show profits, leader in sector, competitors follow, effectively utilizes technology.	www.hoovers.com www.sec.gov www.about.com www.cnnfn.com
Capacity	Uncertain	Growth rate needs to slow at some point. Strong partnering history.	www.herring.com Corporate home page databex.transium.com
Power	Certain	Founder/CEO is a visionary of E-commerce. Strong management team.	Corporate home page databex.transium.com www.cnnfn.com
Values	Certain	Corporate values appear established and focused. Ethical actions.	www.northernlight.com Corporate home page www.yahoo.com www.monster.com
Interests	Directed	Unique organization in the marketplace. Leader in E-commerce. Sales & stock prices are strong. Utilizes available technology to maximise consumer exposure.	www.monster.com www.sec.gov www.cnnfn.com Corporate home page databex.transium.com

Chapter 10 ——————————————————

Identifying Competitors

> It's a time of such tumult and confusion that no one can agree on what's happening now, much less what is coming next.[1]

The preceding quotation or similar ones are probably quite familiar to anyone seeking to understand the impact of the World Wide Web and the Internet on a particular industry, sector, or market. Indeed, to clearly grasp its applicability, ask eight friends to dinner, take a peek at the recent merger and acquisition activity in the telecommunications industry, and then ask, "Where is this industry headed?" It is probably an understatement to suggest that a consensual response would be difficult to achieve.

The speed of change brought about by the Internet has also left others, besides one's friends, scrambling to explain and understand the new dynamics of Web-enabled commercial activity. This chapter responds to this concern by exploring how the free online information resources of the World Wide Web can help analysts make informed choices regarding the identities of existing and future competitors. As we shall see, competitor identification is not always a straightforward task; it is an example of how personal knowledge of the Web can often prove to be a double-edged sword, serving both to simplify and to complicate tasks.

For instance, consider the task of identifying important adversaries. On the surface, this may appear a trivial undertaking. Yet when placed in the context of the following questions, it may no longer appear so simple. Who are the key players in the Internet industry? Where do the boundaries of the telecommunication sector begin and end? In what industry does Microsoft compete? Such queries are now quite common. However, satisfactory responses are not.

There is no shortage of examples of firms that appropriately fit within the response domain of each question. Nor is the time necessary to track down such examples overwhelming. What is troublesome is a lack of clarity regarding the accuracy of conceptual responses. Indeed, what are the boundaries of the Internet industry? Can we meaningfully define telecommunications in the new millennium? If we can pin down Microsoft's competitive domain, is it meaningful? One reason for this uncertainty is an inability of many corporate decision makers to clearly identify future competitors that may not yet exist.[2] A second reason is the exponential growth of players seeking entry into competitive landscapes impacted by the Internet. How many midsized to large companies are not formulating a response to challenges and opportunities presented by the online world? As never before, identification of relevant competitors matters. Indeed, awareness is building of the frustrations faced by managers and analysts alike in defining current and future adversaries.[3]

In one sense, these frustrations are perplexing. Online analysts have at their fingertips instant access to the contents of the world's largest library. Given the increasing sophistication of commercial search engines, one might argue for the use of a portal such as Excite, Lycos, Yahoo!, or NorthernLight. However, evidence also suggests existing search engines are losing the battle to index the growing body of digital information being placed on the Web daily. Indeed, one study argues that even the best of search engines are capable of capturing only a small fraction of online information.[4]

Academia has also struggled to keep up with the overwhelming changes to the competitive landscape. Traditionally, scholars from various disciplines have led the development of tools and processes useful for understanding competitors and their behavior. Among theorists, one might suggest agreement that in the eyes of the customer one firm competes with another when its products or services can do a number of things. They may satisfy the same need, provide benefits by resolving important problems or concerns, perform a similar function, serve a similar market, or appeal to the same customer group.[5] Unfortunately, putting theory into practice has not always been easy. For instance, in the eyes of a twenty-six-year-old with $3,000 to spend, a cruise line operator may compete head on with a home entertainment system retailer. This is, of course, quite different from the perspective of a family of four in the need of a new dishwasher. In that case, competitors may go by the name of Maytag or Sears.

This evidence points to the need for alternative digital research strategies. One such strategy is an awareness that knowledge of original information sources might also lead to accurate responses at the press of a button. In this vein, increasingly, responding to questions such as "How do I determine who my competitor is" often takes a back seat to "where should I look to identify my competitor."

Understanding this distinction has implications for managers operating in resource-scarce corporate environments. The most important implication is a reduction in the need to expend valuable time and energy chasing answers to such questions. Indeed, the ability of an analyst to identify online sources with readily available answers should be a given. However, not all current and future competitors are so easily identified, and few business concerns are so trivial as to be resolved at the push of a button. In the next few paragraphs, we explore the task of identifying competitors and different strategies for doing so.

In earlier chapters, we suggested the use of the *arena* metaphor to put into perspective the ongoing struggle between outside analysts seeking to understand how particular corporations practice commerce and corporate executives seeking to build a friendly public portrait of their company's activities. In exploring the topic of online competitor identification, we continue the use of a metaphorical approach, using the ideas of Gareth Morgan.[6] Morgan, an organizational theorist, suggests that effective analysis is often the result of an individual's ability to develop skills that allow him or her to read complex situations. From this perspective, most situations can be conceived of as metaphors or implicit images that we can see and understand.[7] For instance, in his work on organizations, Morgan effectively argues for the use of metaphors as diverse as prisons, machines, and brains to describe contemporary corporate work environments. This same style of thinking may also apply to this discussion.

The use of implicit images as a means to understand adversaries, either real or emerging, offers CI professionals a degree of analytical flexibility that goes beyond most rigid conceptual models. This approach also implies that competitors may be analyzed from different levels, angles, or viewpoints, with the underlying metaphor serving both to distinguish reasonable analysis from daydreaming and to suggest reasonable digital alternatives.

A MODEL

A metaphor useful in understanding the organization of online information sources is the weather. Analysts, as noted earlier, seek to understand the behavior of their target, organizations. The idea of a sporting arena can be furthered by thinking of these analysts as members of a crowd at an outdoor stadium. The conditions of the day impact the abil-

Figure 10.1
Organizing Information Sources—Identifying Competitors

	Temporal	
Cognitive	Emerging and Apparent Rainy Conditions	Mature and Apparent Crystal Clear Conditions
	Emerging and Non – Apparent Foggy Conditions	Mature and Non – Apparent Snowy Conditions

ity of analysts to see the field or to understand how organizations compete on the playing field. These conditions can range from sun to rain to snow to fog and serve as useful descriptions of groupings of online information sources.

To illustrate these points, let's consider a simple framework (see Figure 10.1) that incorporates two dimensions—the cognitive and the temporal. On the cognitive side of things (e.g., in the mind of an analyst), the identities of adversaries may be apparent or nonapparent. That Lucent Technologies competes with Cisco Systems is probably not a surprise to most habitual readers of the business press. However, that Walmart's major long-term competitor in its new foray into the European grocery market may become not the existing European food chains, but rather the global construction behemoth Bechtel Group is probably not as obvious.[8] If one considers the temporal dimension, adversaries may also be thought of as emerging or mature.

Today, as a year ago, Prudential Bache Securities competes with Merrill Lynch and others in the retail brokerage industry. Yet, both face the threat of an onslaught of new Web-based competitors, such as E*trade, and others that may currently be operational but are not really on the radar screen. Together, these cognitive and temporal dimensions form the basis of four categories useful for identifying important or potentially soon-to-be-important adversaries. They are as follows:

- Mature competitors that are apparent to an informed observer
- Mature competitors that are not or may not be apparent to an informed observer
- Competitors that are emerging or may not already be in existence but are apparent to any informed observer

- Competitors that are emerging or may not already be in existence that are not or may not be apparent to any informed observer

Along with an important yet simple framework for classifying online means of competitor identification, this approach also suggests that the way one conceives of a question or metaphor impacts the result. To begin, let's consider examples of competitor identification sources that fit within the first quadrant of our framework. In metaphorical terms, this is a playing field on a *sunny* day that is *crystal clear* for spectators sitting in the crowd. These sources that allow identification of *mature competitors that are apparent to an informed observer* are also trivial undertakings. These include Web sites or portals that allow an analyst to search for corporate names by SIC code or product review. They may also refer to competitors commonly mentioned in business press articles as such, those that are mentioned in the regulatory filings or the communications of the company under study, or those that are commonly grouped together by frequently used specialty business portals such as Justquotes.com, Quicken.com, Hoovers.com or Yahoo! Business.

Who does the company think are its competitors? Surprisingly, this angle is often forgotten. Where might one first look to answer this question? How about the filings that the company submits to the organization that regulates much of its activity? Publicly traded firms are obligated to identify and report on the activity of their competitors to the Securities Exchange Commission through a 10K annual report filing and an S1 initial filing. Other Web sites useful for accessing the SEC filings are FreeEdgar, Hoover's Online, and Edgar Online.

If information found in the SEC filings is vague, a second good source for a company's own views is its Web site. Most firms maintain their news releases online and do so in chronological order. In many instances, where appropriate, firms will mention competitors by name. A number of tools offer a means to identify company specific Web sites. These include, but are not limited to, Companies Online, NetPartners Internet Solutions, Inc., InfoSpace and NewsEdge Corporation Company Lookup.

Who does the mainstream business media think are its competitors? Online portals including CNNfn, Fortune.com, or NorthernLight will allow an analyst to develop a list of news articles about specific companies or industries. NorthernLight's power search option will, of course, allow researchers to track articles with terms such as the company name in the title and words such as "competitor" in the text of the article. These can be quickly skimmed for mention of any specific competitors. In cases of technology industries, company profiles found on the Red Herring Web site will list major competitors. Further, most of the specialty business portals will link interested readers to recent articles.

Along with the financial markets, the U.S. government also provides a tool for identifying important competitors. SIC Codes (Standard Industrial Codes) are numerical assignments designated to specify and categorize different types of businesses. If you are unsure which firms compete in a particular industry or under a particular code, then you might want to try the World Pages Web site. If, on the other hand, you are interested in knowing under which codes a particular firm is classified, then you should make use of the WhoWhere? Web site. In this case, a search by company name will often identify more than one code, each representing a different industry.

An alternative approach is to make use of the SIC code search key on the FreeEdgar Web site. FreeEdgar identifies the predominant code under which each publicly traded corporation is categorized and in turn, upon identification of a specific code, identifies other publicly traded firms operating in the same arena. Unfortunately, this tool has its limitations. One need simply think of a firm such as IBM in order to understand the shortcoming of using only one SIC code per firm. Currently, the SIC codes are being updated and replaced by the North American Industrial Code System. However, for this task, the SIC codes are still extremely effective in many cases.

In some instances, identifying a specific product or service may be too detailed. A more appropriate angle of attack might be to use a larger net. For instance, what companies does the market identify as competing in the same industry or sector? A widely used online database is offered by Market Guide Inc. This company acquires, integrates, condenses, and publishes financial and other information on over ten thousand publicly traded companies and markets this information to the financial, investment, and credit communities. At this Web site, hit the "research" link. At the next site, press on the "sector" or "industry" link. This will offer you a selection of different industries or sectors to choose from and will list the publicly traded organizations competing in each. A second useful source for such information is the corporate profile section of the Hoover's Web site. Each profile suggests to readers the three or four major competitors of the firm in question. Although identifying adversaries of great importance, it omits competitors in non-core-product lines. Quicken.com is another online portal that offers comparative opportunities that suggest the most obvious adversaries.

Online product reviews are another interesting source for spotting the obvious. Who sells dishwashers? Looking for desks for the office? Who makes them, and how are they priced? How about hardware or software? No shortage exists of Web sites dedicated to this function. An interesting approach is to make use of the free, downloadable, search engine software available on the Copernic Web site. From a pool of approximately sixty search engines, when faced with a specific query such as a product comparison, Copernic chooses the most relevant and uses these focused tools to respond to the query.

In the second quadrant of our framework we find information sources that allow online researchers to identify a different type of competitor. These are sources useful for identifying *competitors that are emerging or may not exist but are apparent to any informed observer*. Typically, this is the domain of the press release, announcement, or news story. Such a playing field is *rainy*. The audience may have to look a bit harder to see the field, but it is still there. More often than not, the effort necessary to identify these adversaries is insignificant. These new entrants are the topics of many a daily online business briefing, a trait of a media whose passion for merger rumors, alliance announcements, and IPO registrations never seems to abate. New entrants are also a continual worry for many firms in many industries. Thus, any public hints, rumors, speculation, or confirmations of such are normally followed quite closely.

The Internet is particularly effective at disseminating knowledge in this regard. One need simply to ponder the trade name "Netscape Navigator" to understand the potential of some IPOs to transform entire industries. IPO candidates seeking to raise equity by offering shares of ownership to the public must file an S-1 form or prospectus with the Securities and Exchange Commission. IPOs in registration can be quickly identified using Hoover's IPO Central.

Merger and acquisition activity by publicly traded companies must also be disclosed to the SEC through a number of form filings, including SC13 D and 10C, in the case of firms with shares traded on NASDAQ. Such activity is captured by free commercial online databases such as those found on the Web site of Wall Street Net. When announced, future intentions to merge or acquire can be identified through business-related search tools such as CNNfn, Transium Business Intelligence, Reuters, Yahoo! Business, Quicken.com, and others or a search engine such as NorthernLight.

Competitor identification sources that fit within the third quadrant of our framework are somewhat different. Although conceptually simple, identification of competitors using these tools can be tricky. These sources refer to those that allow the identification of *mature competitors that are not or may not be apparent to an informed observer*. The word "tricky" is used cautiously. An assumption underlying their use is knowledge by the researcher of obvious, existing competitors—the knowledge obtained by sources highlighted in Quadrant A. Field conditions in this quadrant are *snowy*. Players know the field in good weather, but snow makes the boundaries difficult to judge. In a simple sense, understanding the obvious allows for identification of the exceptional or unexpected. As noted earlier, one industry of interest is food retailing. Seeing companies such as Walmart or Safeway Inc. listed as competitors should be of little surprise to most people. Finding Bechtel Corporation among proposed competitors is, however, noteworthy. Analysts interested in this type of competitor may want to pay close attention to listings of online manufacturer's guides, new patent registrations in particular areas of endeavor, recently announced merger and acquisition behavior, and new product development efforts.

In this quadrant, examples of competitors worthy of attention are those with deep pockets that have traditionally operated at the fringe of an industry other than the one that outside observers consider their home. In their home industries, these companies are usually powerful and prominent. Examples of such competitors would include firms such as Microsoft, Monsanto, Intel, Enron, or Walmart. In which companies have powerful firms such as these undertaken a minority equity investment? With which firms have such large corporations formed alliance agreements?

In order to uncover such information, one may examine the home page–located press releases of existing industry players for announcements of alliances, leases, or distribution agreements. Look at the names of companies touted as members of "resource networks," "partners for leveraging expertise," "family members," and the like. What skills or contributions do these firms bring to the mix? One may also consider using the Transium Business Intelligence online database. Type the name of the competitor of interest. Then, sort the list of abstracts by "company." A series of company names should pop up. If not apparent from the article or its abstract, a next laborious step would be to visit the home pages of these organizations or their most recent 10K form filings and then search for the name of the competitor firm. Given that the competitor firm, if it is an investor, is almost always larger than the firm it funds, its equity investment will also most likely be large relative to the overall capitalization of the funded firm.

Finally we come to examples of online competitor identification sources that fit within the fourth quadrant of our framework. These are useful for discovering *competitors that are emerging or may not exist that are not or may not be apparent to an informed observer*. Relevant sources include the minority equity investments of large powerful corporations not currently considered major competitors in the industry and a number of state and federal regulatory Web sites or portals that disclose the identifies of new companies registering for the right to deliver particular regulated services. They also include venture capital firm Web sites that identify young companies that they have awarded seed capital, the U.S. Patent and Trademark Office patent database, and online chat forums. Were one to suggest a ranking of quadrants by importance to a CI professional, this last quadrant would find itself at the top of most lists. As André Trudel suggests in the concluding chapter of this book, CI is about predicting the future and the unknown, not the past. Quadrant four is the domain of CI professionals, and the metaphor that best describes such a playing field is *foggy*.

Where might one look for the unknown? Try the realm of inventors—the patent office! From the point of view of the U.S. Patent and Trademark Office, competitors are "those firms that are listed as patenting or holding patents on structures, processes, features or products which fall under the same SIC code or make use of similar prior art to that of the organization." Aside from simply searching by subject, knowing the assignee and inventors of existing patents may also prove useful. Has the inventor of a key patent or series of patents found new employment? Has the corporate assignee itself been acquired by another organization? Changes of this nature may signal the onset of a new adversary.

A second angle is to monitor or participate in chat group discussions. Chat groups are online forums in which Internet users can discuss topics that vary from stock market trends to concert events. An individual may pose a question or make a comment that other newsgroup subscribers around the world respond to. Simply posing the question, "Who are the emerging competitors of Company X?" may offer a surprising hint of the future. These discussion forums can be found using services such as Deja.com or Internet Database. Of particular importance may be discussions of upcoming product launches or research efforts underway in other firms that are a little too close for comfort.

A third angle is associated with discovering the minority equity investments of established corporations that at best would currently be considered fringe players in the industry. It is the recipients of such aid that should be tracked and monitored carefully, as they often represent future acquisition targets of powerful outside corporations, should they wish to be become important forces in the industry. Unfortunately, this task is in most instances a nontrivial undertaking. Indeed, it is the exceptional firm that makes available to the public information of this nature.

Using the sorting capability of the Transium Business Intelligence home page offers one means to focus on this type of information. First, a search by industry will offer links to one to two paragraphs of article highlights. These article highlights can then be further sorted by industry topic and then by company name. Often the information provided can be extremely revealing. For instance, when searching for information regarding routers, Cisco Systems may appear. A further sorting exercise will turn up articles on the topic of Lucent Technologies as well as Nortel. But what would be the reaction of an analyst if a company such as energy giant Williams Co. or global construction behemoth Bechtel popped up under the function heading of "new product development"? Clearly, these associations would raise the curiosity of any informed observer and make worthwhile a quick search of their regulatory filings to identify the existence of a minority equity investment in the industry. A brief perusal of article highlights sorted by "companies" will invariably identify other competitors along with suppliers and customers.

Angle four would focus analyst attention on the Web site of government regulators. If the industry in question is regulated, a search of the Dockets section will list companies, public and private, that recently have been granted the opportunity to conduct business in the industry.

Finally there appears the case of young, private companies that have successfully built a business case powerful enough to attract venture capital funding to themselves. These are the organizations and people that probably should be watched. One Web site, Vfinance.com, allows researchers to sort its lengthy list of venture capital firms by the industries that they fund. It then offers a series of links to the Web sites of these venture capital firms. From this point on, many of these companies will list the portfolios of start-up companies that they currently fund and, in turn, provide links to each Web site. Although not a short process, this exercise provides an opportunity to discover the next generation of adversaries, products, or services.

Clearly, being able to identify an emerging competitor before it becomes obvious to most stakeholders is a useful skill for any CI professional. One need simply ponder the example of Netscape Navigator and its impact on the wired world to appreciate why relative obscurity should not be ignored. Luckily, for every "Netscape" success story, there are hundreds of less successful efforts. This poses a quandary for analysts. Knowing that success is the exception rather than the rule, which start-ups, once spotted, should be tracked over time? Or, which truly have the potential to be important competitors?

THE CONTRIBUTION OF ORGANIZATION THEORY

One means to narrow the band of possibilities is to examine the potential of the competitive environment of any young firm to nurture new ideas, products, services, and organizations. "Potential" refers to resources sufficient to sustain and grow a number of companies as well as an aura of legitimacy in the eyes of important stakeholders. *Population ecology theory* is the theoretical basis for pondering the adequacy of resources for signalling future success. *Institutional theory* is one school of thought from which the ideas of legitimacy originate. These terms are explained further in the following paragraphs.

Population ecology theory seeks to explain why some forms of organization survive over time while others do not. From this perspective a population refers to all entities that compete for the same set of resources in a specific environment. For example,[9] IBM, Compaq, Dell, Gateway, and the other personal computer companies constitute a population. They all seek to attract the same environmental resources, in this case, the money consumers spend on personal computing. Some organizations within a population often choose to focus on different environmental *niches*, or sets of resources. For example, Dell Computer chose to focus on the mail-order niche of the personal computer environment. IBM and Compaq originally focused on the business niche, while Apple focused on the higher-education niche.

According to Population Ecology theory,[10] the availability of resources determines the number of organizations in a population by limiting the population density or the number of similarly focused organizations that can coexist. Generally, this perspective assumes that the growth in the number of new start-ups in a new environment will always be rapid in the beginning, as new organizations are founded to take advantage of the prospect of new resources. Two factors account for this rapid birth-rate. First, as new organizations are founded, there is an increase in the knowledge and skills available to generate other similar new organizations. Second, as successful new companies break a path, they make it easier for others to attract investment and needed resources.

Institutional theory is a second perspective useful for understanding the relative level of danger posed by emerging competitors. It suggests that organizations that deal with similar environments tend to gravitate towards similar organizational structures. As with many social perspectives, it also means different things to different people.[11] One useful perspective views organizations in the context of their operating environments. Institutional environments are characterized by the elaboration of rules and requirements to which individual organizations must conform if they are to receive support and legitimacy. Organizations conform to a set of institutionalized beliefs because they are rewarded for doing so through increased legitimacy, resources, and survival capabilities.[12]

A good analogy to these ideas may be found in the world of fast-food restaurant chains. Most newer ones mirror the two most popular chains, Macdonald's and Burger King. Yet, even these two industry leaders seem less the product of unique ideas and more the product of careful comparison and imitation. Popularity improvements to the operations or product of one chain are usually quickly adopted in some faintly altered form by the other. Generally, the layouts are similar, as are the menus, labor forces, and promotional gimmicks. Interestingly, competitors that are too different from these industry front-runners rarely survive, for a number of reasons.[13] One reason for such similarity may be economic. If a firm is making slight adjustments that appear to increase efficiency, other adversaries are also likely to incorporate these changes to keep up. Exemplary financial performance by one firm may prove too tempting for others. Success alone may serve as a strong reason for imitation. Conformity may also be the result of industry regulations. Often, laws are enacted that affect all industry players and force all managers to comply. Equally influential are the bylaws and policies of the various professional associations and bodies whose policies regulate the conduct of employees in so many industries.[14] Finally, few firms wish to be perceived as illegitimate. Those that break industry norms often become less socially acceptable to the general public, stakeholders and shareholders.[15] Thus, if industry norms are consistent corporate goals, it is in the best interest of the business to conform. One need simply ponder the fate of the former Canadian Airborne Regiment to understand the importance of legitimacy. Following evidence of torture by some of its members in the Somalia campaign of the early 1990s, this proud unit was disbanded.

Combined, insights from these two theories provide guidance regarding the survival prospects of emerging competitors. Population ecology[16] suggests that in most new industries, resources do exist to promote long-term survival. Unfortunately, these resources are limited. Not all start-ups will be able to take advantage of them. Institutional theory complements this perspective, suggesting that those firms that conform to institutional beliefs, follow industry rules, and meet generally accepted competitive requirements will be perceived as legitimate and increase their chances for survival.

SIGNALS

The challenge for CI professionals is to identify those young firms capable of surviving. Evidence of external funding or acceptance for funding suggests a significant level of legitimacy in the eyes of the market. Yet survival is rarely assured. Indeed, chances for survival may range from high in the case of a highly successful venture that is in registration as an upcoming IPO, to that of one that has caught the attention of a larger corporate entity in the form of a minority equity investment, to that of membership in the portfolio of companies being funded by a particular venture capital firm. Firms that fit within this last category of funding are the most difficult to assess for survivability. Yet, signals regarding the hospitality or resources of a particular competitive environment for nurturing younger firms to maturity may also be fairly obvious. In particular, if a young firm is well funded and an affirmative response meets most of the following queries, its behavior and growth should be monitored very carefully.

• Do journals or magazines exist, online or otherwise, that target their content toward readers employed by firms such as the one under study? As noted earlier, users of the Transium Business Intelligence online database can sort news-story abstracts by journal to respond to this query.

- Do professional or industry associations exist that meet the needs of firms such as the one under study? The Web site of the American Society of Association Executives is one that responds to this challenge by offering a search tool to find online association Web sites.

- Among firms such as the one under study, is there a healthy industry growth rate, as measured by any number of financial measures? Various online specialty business portals such as Quicken.com and Market Guide suggest performance measures that meet this demand.

- If regulators play a role in this industry, is a significant amount of their attention now being focused on firms such as the one under study? This can be addressed directly or indirectly. Directly, each government regulator will normally offer information regarding issues of importance to it. Indirectly, industry association Web sites, accessible through ASAENET.org, will normally document the issues that they seek to discuss with regulators.

- Do professional service firms or practice areas within them and supporting industries exist that meet the resource requirements of firms such as the one under study? Again, this question may be responded to directly or indirectly. Indirectly, one approach is to read the popular online literature read by lawyers, engineers, accountants, and so on. Legal News Network is an example of one online magazine that targets lawyers. Is it discussing issues of interest to the type of firm under study? Does it reference or sort articles according to related specialties that impact the firm of interest? Directly, scan the home page of a number of professional service firms. Are they chasing business in this area? Do they list partners, managers, or employees with expertise in this area of expertise?

If knowledgeable and competent, the attention of CI professionals should be predominantly directed towards building a realistic portrait of future adversaries and their actions. These are the adversaries of quadrant four. For many industries, online discussion forums, regulatory authority registration and patent databases, and business news story sorting tools such as Transium Business Intelligence offer examples of information sources that can be used fairly efficiently to spot emerging adversaries as they arise. Within this grouping, among the most difficult to identify are those funded as minority equity investments of a cash-rich corporation that at best is considered a fringe player in the current competitive environment and those funded as part of a venture capital firm's portfolio of investments. These are the adversaries that may dramatically change the future competitive landscape. They should be tracked and monitored carefully over time.

Chapter 11

Concerns for the Future of the Internet: Literacy Development, Technology, and the Workplace

Sonya Symons

A large portion of the workforce is ill prepared for the literacy demands placed on them today. The rate at which information is made available and the haphazard way in which technology is changing demand more from workers today than ever before. In order to meet the literacy demands of the twenty-first century, educators will have to emphasize more practical literacy skills than traditionally, and information technology specialists will have to take human factors into consideration as they develop resources such as the Internet.

Until recently, most people have equated literacy with basic reading skills. Now literacy experts consider literacy to be multifaceted and to include mathematical and practical skills such as the ability to understand graphs and charts. In 1995 the Organization for Economic Co-operation and Development (OECD) published "Literacy, Economy and Society,"[1] an international adult literacy survey that included Canada, Germany, Netherlands, Poland, Sweden, Switzerland, and the United States. The participating countries defined literacy as "using printed and written information to function in society, to achieve one's goals, and to develop one's knowledge and potential."[2] This definition of literacy is much broader than the ability to "read words" and incorporates problem-solving and higher-level thinking skills.

Recognising the complex nature of literacy, most literacy surveys, including the OECD survey, measure three domains of skills: (1) Prose literacy is the knowledge and skills necessary to understand and use information from text. Prose literacy is what most people think of when they hear the word "literacy." It involves reading and understanding written text. Prose literacy is the aspect of literacy emphasized in school settings. (2) Document literacy, the knowledge and skills involved in locating information contained in text and various graphic formats, is "reading for a purpose," the type of reading most often performed at work. (3) Quantitative literacy is the knowledge and skills involved in arithmetic operations.

In the next decade, literacy surveys will likely include a fourth component, computer literacy, since most jobs require some degree of technical skill.[3] In this chapter, I will focus on prose and document literacy and, because of the dynamic nature of computer literacy, speculate on how this "new" literacy will affect the ability of the workforce to keep pace with the demands placed on it.

THE NATURE OF WORKPLACE LITERACY

Analyses of jobs ranging from executive vice president to forklift operator reveal that virtually all jobs (i.e., 98%) require literacy skills.[4] People spend an average of two hours per day reading at work. Material read at work is written at a relatively complex level, usually at the grade 9 to grade 12 level. Considering that the average newspaper article is written at a grade 6 level, workplace reading requires well-developed literacy skills.

Depending on the job classification, 50 percent to 80 percent of workplace reading can be described as task-oriented.[5] Workplace reading often involves locating and reading information that is used to perform a task, make a decision, or solve a problem. Adults report, for example, that the purpose of 29 percent of their reading time is to find information.[6] They may be using charts, graphs, diagrams, pay stubs, or schedules to locate specific information, or they may be using a database or the Internet to find information needed to answer a question or solve a problem.

Workplace reading differs greatly from leisure reading. First, people spend twice as much time reading at work than anywhere else. Second, people read mostly brief documents and reference materials at work, whereas leisure reading includes newspapers, magazines, and novels. Of course, workplace reading practices differ considerably depending on the occupation. Clerical workers, for example, spend an average of nearly three hours per day reading brief documents. Managers and professionals are the only job classification that engages in reading any news and business or society and science journal articles at work. Due to the nature of their work, technicians and skilled workers spend an average of 50 minutes per day reading reference materials. With increased use of technology, technical, semiskilled, and clerical workers are reading more complex materials requiring new skills, such as computer programs.

This high volume of task-oriented, complex reading demands well-developed literacy skills. Workplace reading requires both prose and document literacy skills. Most jobs also require some degree of computational and computer literacy. Do workers have these literacy competencies? The investment that many businesses are making in on-site literacy programs suggests that the answer to this question may be "no."

THE LITERACY PROBLEM

The OECD's international Adult Literacy Survey[7] classifies literacy according to five levels on each of the three measured dimensions: prose, document, and quantitative literacy. Different literacy levels are required of workers in different occupations. For example, most clerical workers have level 3 document literacy skills. Approximately 75 percent of managers and professionals function at the highest literacy levels. Results of the survey reveal, however, that many adults do not have the literacy skills required of clerical or management professional workers. In the United States, 46 percent of adults are at the two lowest literacy levels. Higher literacy levels are associated with income and job classifications. Not surprisingly, approximately 50 percent of adults with no income have the lowest literacy levels.

Document literacy (the ability to locate and use information) is an important aspect of workplace literacy, as it is the literacy task performed most frequently in a wide variety of occupations. The international adult literacy survey indicated that 24 percent of American adults were unable to make a literal match on the basis of a single piece of information. An example is identifying from a sales chart the dollar figures associated with any one sales location or finding the dosage of medicine for a person of a specific age on a medication label. With the growth of the Internet and the World Wide Web, the ability to locate information efficiently is becoming even more important. Unfortunately, this area of literacy seems to be particularly difficult for many people. Most people report problems when they attempt to use the Internet for the purpose of seeking information. In a large online survey of Internet users, 46 percent reported that finding new information was problematic and 25 percent cited the organization of Web sites as posing a problem when trying to locate information.[8] At least two factors may be causing the difficulties experienced when trying to locate information on the Web. The first is the ability of the user to locate information in any written document. The second is the nature of the Web itself, where information is often poorly organized or indexed in a way that may make logical sense to a computer programmer but not to a person accustomed to using indexes and tables of contents to locate information.

Beyond the fact that illiteracy is associated with unemployment and poverty, employers associate many problems with illiteracy. There are safety concerns when employees cannot read or understand warnings or written directions. In many cases, this leads to staff turnover and its associated costs. Companies report that growth is slowed by poorly educated workers and that career development and advancement of workers is often limited by basic skill deficiencies. In the early 1980s American companies were surveyed about the skill levels of their workers. Thirty percent noted that secretaries had difficulty reading at the level required by the job, 50 percent reported that managers and supervisors were unable to write paragraphs free of mechanical errors, and 50 percent noted that skilled and semiskilled employees, including bookkeepers, were unable to use decimals and fractions in math problems.[9] Added to these concerns are problems of global competition and an increasing reliance on technology.

How Can the Problem Be Rectified?

A large portion of the population appears unable to meet the literacy demands of today's workplace. Why is this so, and what can be done to improve the situation? The explanation heard most frequently is that the type of reading found in the workplace is new to most workers. The types of skills needed to perform well in school are not the skills needed to perform well in the workplace. Comparisons of high school and workplace settings indicate that there is a mismatch between literacy acts in the workplace and in the schools. First, textbooks constitute 95 percent of the reading materials of high school students, whereas middle-level workers (clerical, retail, service) read much more varied materials including textbooks, manuals, computer screens, flyers, brochures, and forms.[10] Many workplace tasks involve using more than one of these formats in order to complete a task. Middle-level workers are more competent than high school students at applying what they are reading, by identifying important aspects, summarizing, and suggesting applications. The average worker spends more time reading at work than does the average high school student, including time spent on homework. High school students classify 66 percent of their reading time as "reading-to-learn," whereas workplace reading involves "reading to do" or accomplishing a task, with learning occurring as a consequence of completing the task.[11] When high school students are asked about the strategies they use to help them learn, the vast majority report rereading, or rote rehearsal, whereas middle-level workers report a variety of more effective strategies such as problem solving, using notes and underlining, and relating new material to what they already know. In sum, it would appear that high school students read less than do middle-level workers, that the materials they read are less varied in format, and that high school students read for the purpose of learning the material rather than accomplishing a task.

One recommendation is that educators encourage children at all ages to read more varied materials and that there be purposes associated with the reading that go beyond reading to memorize the material. I am encouraged in the trends that we see in schools these days, with students taking more self-direction in their learning; yet there needs to be increased emphasis, certainly in the elementary grades, on reading materials that are not narrative. The majority of material that children are reading in school would be classified as fiction; children enjoy but read very little informational text.

A related concern regarding the preparation of today's graduates for the workforce is the nature of literacy instruction. A concern is that students are not taught explicitly workplace literacy skills. Students are often expected to gather information for projects, but are rarely given instruction in how to locate information in text or in electronic media. High school and post-secondary students display poor information-seeking strategies. If educators taught students procedures for locating information in the way that they teach procedures for studying and comprehending text, we might see an improvement in document literacy skills. Figure 11.1 displays a general problem-solving model of the search process that could inform educators about how to teach the skills needed for seeking information on the Internet.

First, the reader forms a goal by deciding what he or she is looking for in specific terms. Keeping the goal in mind as the search proceeds helps in maintaining the searcher's focus and in generating terms to use in search engines. Goals are often refined as the searcher generates either too much or not enough information while searching the Internet. After forming a goal, the searcher selects categories to help decide which Web sites to search in more detail. This stage involves planning ("How do I find the information I need?") and time management ("What is the fastest, most efficient route to satisfying the search goal?"). Choosing a category may involve using the organizational aids such as a search engine or subject directory to locate specific World Wide Web sites that may contain the desired information. After Web sites are located, the searcher extracts information by slowing their reading rate until they come upon the desired information. When searching for information in text, a very common error is that the reader misses the information, even after examining the appropriate section of text. This is even more likely to happen when reading text on a computer screen than when reading text on paper. The searcher next monitors whether or not the identified infor-

Figure 11.1
Applying a Problem-Solving Model of Information-Seeking to Internet Search Tasks

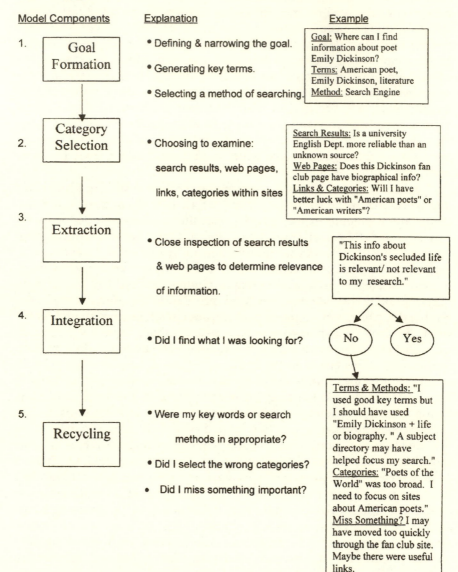

mation makes sense in terms of the search goal ("Did I find what I was looking for?"). Finally, the searcher recycles through the previous stages until the sought-after information is located. The searcher may reevaluate the original goal and planning process or retrace the steps taken to arrive at the point where information was extracted. An educator following this model of information seeking would be encourage students to be playful and to monitor how well they are achieving their search goal.

In addition to a general problem-solving approach to Internet searching, many specific strategies can be taught. These can vary from one search engine to the next and tend to change frequently. Many search engines and subject directories have built-in features that are user-friendly, provided that searchers know that they exist and how to use them. The fastest way to search for an organization's home page, for example, is to guess its Web address, or URL. A URL has a "grammatical" structure, like a sentence or mathematical equation. All URLs begin with "http://" (hypertext transfer protocol). In fact, the server (e.g., Netscape or Internet Explorer) usually automatically generates this, which is typically followed by "www" (World Wide Web). The next component is the organization's name, abbreviated name, or acronym. The top-level domain caps off a URL sentence and is usually one of the following: ". com" for commercial sites, ".org" for organizations, and ".edu" for educational institutions in the United States. This particular strategy is most effective when the searcher is looking for a specific, known Web site and is willing to make more than one attempt to guess the correct URL. For example, when I introduced university students to this strategy, to locate the home page of the Columbia Sportswear Company, most guessed *"http://www.columbiasportswear.com"* when the correct address was "http://www.columbia.com." Most students did not persevere with this strategy. If they did not locate the desired Web site on the first attempt, they gave up.

Many search engines offer help options for searchers who may be having difficulties. Three effective search tips include phrase searching, joining key terms, and searching within a search. Some search engines automatically recognize when searchers are trying to locate a phrase. Other search engines will look for the phrase only if quotation marks are placed around the information request (e.g., "War of 1812"). If the searcher typed in War of 1812 (without quotation marks), then the search engine might locate sources that discuss the War of 1812 and others that discuss "war" or include the number 1812 in some capacity, producing many irrelevant search results. Similarly, when trying to find two or more keywords that must appear together in a search summary, searchers should include "+" signs between the terms (e.g., "ltaly + flag" if the searcher is looking for an image of the Italian flag). If the searcher fails to include the "+" sign when joining two or more words, the search engine will locate an unmanageable number of search results. Some Web sites would produce information about the flag of Italy, but others would contain irrelevant information pertaining to flags in general or Web sites about the country of Italy.

Some search engines give searchers the option of entering their search questions verbatim. The user simply types in a complete question on the appropriate area of the screen. The results obtained by this request are fairly specific and useful. The success of this feature depends on the quality of the searcher's question. Good questions contain information relevant to the search goal and help the search engine narrow the search field. In addition, the information should be arranged in a logical order. Suppose someone were interested in finding out about law programs at American universities. If the searcher asked, "Where can I find information about American universities and law programs?" then the database might locate sites about American universities and law programs separately, yielding a lot of irrelevant information about international law programs. However, if this question were modified to read, "Where can I find information about law programs at American universities?" then the server would locate more specific information.

Searching within a search is an option provided by most search engines. If the user makes a search request, such as "rap music," the database will locate all of its sites about rap music. If the searcher then types in "female groups" and chooses to "search within a search" instead of opting to "begin a new search," then it will locate only sites pertaining to female rap music groups. This strategy, along with phrase searching and joining key terms, can help the searcher to specify the field of inquiry and to reduce the number of irrelevant responses.

Many people get distracted from their goal when they are searching because they have to remember the goal as they inspect numerous Web sites and keep track of the search terms that they have used. Generating a map may be a useful approach, in that it may serve as a physical reminder of the goal and the plan for achieving it. A map may also assist the searcher in generating terms to use with the search engines. "Semantic" maps have been recommended by educators as a way of improving reading comprehension for many years, but they may also serve a useful function when searching the Internet. A tree diagram connecting concepts might assist students in generating key terms and keeping track of routes already used. A semantic map is a visual representation of major ideas and their interrelationships. Maps have two elements—*nodes* that represent ideas and *links* that represent relationships between ideas. Figure 11.2 presents an example of a semantic map that a student might use to search for an appropriate college.

Consider the following example:

Figure 11.2
Semantic Map for Locating Information on the Internet to Choose a College

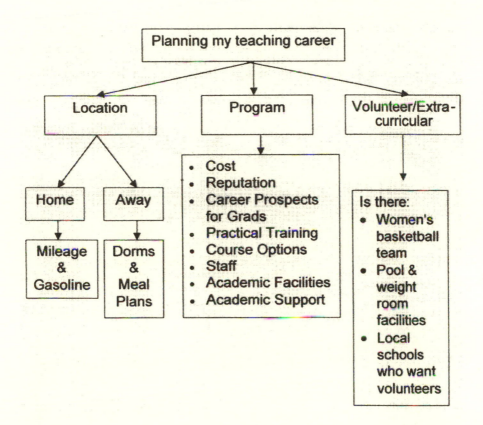

The school year is drawing to a close once more at Kalamazoo High. Mr. Rupert, the guidance counselor, is busy trying to get the seniors on the right future path. Molly, a graduating student, has decided on a career as a teacher. Now she must choose schools to apply to. Mr. Rupert suggests that Molly use the Internet to locate information about different programs. He also tells her that she should create a semantic map to facilitate her search process.

This activity allows Molly to think about what she is looking for in furthering her education. After prioritizing her goals, she decides on the following: She wants to attend school away from her hometown but would like to stay in *New England*. Therefore, she is looking for programs in Maine, Vermont, and New Hampshire. She decides to live in *an all-female residence* her first year to make new friends. Since she is a *vegetarian*, her school of choice should have a good salad bar and a menu of meat-free options. Athletic facilities and opportunities to play basketball and volunteer at a local public school are essential. Molly is also looking for a reputable school that offers scholarships, since cost is an issue. *Alumni* information is also important, because Molly wants to ensure that other students have succeeded after graduation. She also believes that *practica* are an asset to a teacher-training program, and she wants to take courses that focus on helping special-needs children. Since this is the first time she will venture away from home, Molly would prefer a small school with a *population* of 5–10 thousand students and a friendly, supportive campus. Now Molly is ready to surf the Net. She restricts her search to the New England states and uses her keywords (in italics here) to facilitate her scan of various educational institutions.

Semantic maps can help people organize their search options, formulate search goals, generate key search terms, and keep track of what has already been searched.

I have recently tried teaching grade 9 students in a high-tech high school a two-pronged approach to locating information on the Internet. All of these students were familiar with the Internet; many had computers at home and had daily Internet access at school. I taught the students specific strategies such as described, and I have taught them to draw maps of what they are searching as they use the Internet. Students who were taught to search using this approach found information faster than did students who were not taught the approach. Based on this preliminary evidence and evidence that I have from younger children whom I have taught very successfully to locate information in text using a playful, problem-solving approach, I am optimistic that educators can teach students better document literacy skills that better them for the workforce.

CONCLUSION

Workplace literacy is a complex concept that includes much more than being able to read words. Too many people are ill-prepared for the complex and multifaceted nature of the literacy skills that today's workplaces require. The movement in education to having students complete real tasks for real purposes is a step in the right direction for addressing this serious problem. Changing the types of materials that students read throughout their school years would also help to reduce the gap between school and workplace literacy. Locating information is an important literacy skill that is challenging for most people.

While the Internet increases the accessibility of information, inherent problems such as lack of structure and massive volume may make it even more challenging to use than traditional media. In this chapter I have attempted to demonstrate that taking a problem-solving, strategic approach to the task can increase the likelihood of success in finding information on the Internet. As society becomes increasingly reliant on computers and global communication, information-seeking skills will become even more indispensable in working and learning environments.

Chapter 12

The Future: Proactive, Agent-based CI

André Trudel

This book has one major aim—to offer to practitioners examples of how knowledge of original online information sources can be matched with analytical or theoretical frameworks to help analysts solve important business concerns. An assumption underlying this initiative is that computer software is currently incapable of replacing the knowledge and know-how that form the basis of decision making for most competitive intelligence professionals. Despite significant advances, software has yet to capture the human or nonrational side of decision making, the essence of which is described by terms such as intuition, experience, knowledge of history, and emotion. To conclude, André Trudel, an Intelligent Software Agent researcher at Acadia University, offers some thoughts on the future of CI and how technology is pushing closer to capturing many of the human qualities of decision making.

Who are my competitors? If a company is using competitive intelligence (CI) resources to answer this and similar questions, it has probably missed the boat. Accurate responses to such queries are increasingly becoming available to researchers through the push of a button. If existing Web-enabled laptop technology does suggest one point, it is that CI resources should not be used to identify today's problems or concerns. Instead, these same resources should be directed toward identifying opportunities that can be proactively managed, ahead of time.

CI is really about understanding tomorrow. In the short and long terms, who will be my emerging competitors? This is the type of query on which CI efforts will concentrate in the future. CI is about identifying problems and opportunities with enough lead time to allow decision makers to respond with maximum effectiveness.

Currently, CI is practiced by many means. Unfortunately, an all-too-common and ineffective approach involves one or more humans surfing the Internet. Even with improvements in search engine capabilities and the advent of powerful but easy to use online commercial databases, Web sites still need to be continually monitored, on a regular basis. Unfortunately, the tools currently available to access the Internet are primitive. If a search engine does manage to find the correct answer, it is usually buried within a mountain of related but unimportant information and more often needs to be analyzed by a team of CI experts to be given true meaning.

Where lies the future of CI? Consider the following scenario.

In the not-too-distant future, an executive will receive e-mail whenever a new competitor emerges on the horizon. The e-mail will not originate from his or her team of CI experts. Instead, the e-mail will be sent by an information agent. This agent will be part of a CI team of intelligent software agents freely roaming the Internet. The agents will have the built-in knowledge and capabilities to seek, gather, assimilate, and summarize pertinent information from Internet Web sites. This information will be forwarded to another collection of agents residing at the parent company. These resident agents will collect reports from the mobile agents on the Internet. They will further analyze the information and decide on an appropriate course of action, such as sending a notification e-mail to an executive.

Does this sound far-fetched? If it does, then read on. If it does not, the following discussion may strike a chord. Few things are certain in life, but one area of research that you may want to pay attention to is that of Artificial Intelligence (AI). In the near future, AI will probably come to play a dominant role in any analyst's efforts to monitor competitor behavior. Indeed, the ultimate goal driving research in the AI field is to make computers easier to use by delegating part of the decision-making process to the computer. The subfield of AI that will directly benefit CI is intelligent software agents.

INTELLIGENT SOFTWARE AGENTS

An agent is a software system that engages and helps users. The scope of agent applications ranges from the mundane to the smart. The following are examples of existing agent systems.

Microsoft paperclip. The paperclip in Microsoft Word is an example of a simple and sometimes annoying agent that monitors the user's input and offers assistance when a common task is recognized.

Visitor hosting system. This example[1] of an agent-based system is built to deal with the time-consuming task of making up schedules for scholars visiting Carnegie Mellon University (CMU). Task- and information-specific agents cooperate to create and manage a visitor's schedule to CMU. Via the Internet, they determine the visitor's status and areas of interest. They then use this information to identify faculty members who may be interested in meeting with the visitor. Finally, the agents use e-mail to book meetings and distribute the visitor's schedule.

License management application. Not surprisingly, the Central Intelligence Agency (CIA) has been active in this area. It has been using the Tally Systems CentaMeter since 1993. CentaMeter includes intelligent agents that automatically detect the personal computer's operating environment and then launch the appropriate agents. The agents keep track of licensed software and its usage on the machine.

WebCrawler. An indispensable tool when surfing the Internet is software for searching. Currently, popular search programs include Alta-Vista, Excite, Lycos, and Northern Light. Another popular search engine is called WebCrawler. WebCrawler has a database, which contains a list of references (URL links) to both visited and unvisited pages on the Internet. Visited pages are indexed. WebCrawler indexes unvisited pages by sending out agents to retrieve specific pages and to index and store them. New links are added to the database by doing a breadth-first search of the Internet. (A breadth-first search occurs when all of the URL links on a specific page are retrieved at once.)

CISCO Systems. CISCO Systems, the communications equipment vendor, has developed electronic commerce agents that interact directly with the customer. A *status agent* helps customers to determine the status of their orders in real time. This popular agent is used 12,000 times per week. A *pricing agent* provides price information and assists the customer in applying discounts to which he or she is entitled. "The CISCO configuration agent helps not only the company's own personnel but also the customer in confirming the availability and suitability of the products he or she wants."[2] CISCO is also using agents to solve technical support problems online. This very popular service had 450,000 log-ins in 1996.

Air Traffic Control. The Australian Artificial Intelligence Institute has built an agent-based air traffic control system named OASIS for the Sydney airport in Australia. When an aircraft enters the Sydney air space, it is assigned to an agent. Air traffic control agents are then responsible for managing the aircraft agents. How does it work?

OASIS accurately estimates landing times, determines the sequence of aircraft to land giving the least total delay, and advises air traffic controllers of appropriate control actions to achieve this sequence. It also monitors and compares actual progress of aircraft against the established sequence, and notifies the air traffic controller of significant differences and appropriate action to correct the situation. OASIS is designed to be responsive to sudden changes in environmental conditions (such as meteorological conditions or runway configuration) and changes in user objectives (such as aircraft operational emergencies or requirements).[3]

Extremely promising in its potential, the system has started field trials at the airport.

Definition

The dynamic and complex nature of both information and applications require that software not merely respond to user's requests but also intelligently anticipate, adapt, and help the user. Such systems are called *intelligent software agents*.

The study of agents is as old as the field of Artificial Intelligence (AI). John McCarthy, one of AI's founders, conceived the idea of an intelligent software agent in the mid 1950s. The term "agent" was coined by Oliver Selfridge a few years later:

They had in view a system that, when given a goal, could carry out the details of the appropriate computer operations and could ask for and receive advice, offered in human terms, when it was stuck. An agent would be a "soft robot" living and doing its business within the computer's world.[4]

From its humble beginnings in the 1950s, the study of intelligent agents has grown into an active research area. There are now many academic workshops, conferences, journals, and books dedicated to this important topic.

What is an intelligent agent? There is no single agreed-upon definition. One researcher[5] believes there is a convergence of opinion and suggests that an agent is a computer software system whose main characteristics are as follows:

- *Situatedness*. The agent receives input from and can perform actions to modify its environment. Examples of environments include the real world and the Internet.
- *Autonomy*. The agent acts without human guidance and has control over its actions.
- *Adaptivity*. The agent is capable of

  Reacting and adapting to changes in its environment.

  Taking proactive goal-directed initiative when appropriate.

  Learning from its past performance, environment, and interactions with others, with a goal of improving performance over time.

- *Cooperation.* The agent is a social creature that must interact with humans and other agents via a communication language that is usually quite sophisticated.

These four properties must all be present in a software system for that system to be considered an "agent." This definition excludes most traditional computer applications (e.g., databases, accounting packages, spreadsheets) from being called "agents" because

- They are not autonomous. The application must wait for a command from the user.
- They cannot take a proactive course of action.
- They are brittle. If the environment changes, the program usually crashes (e.g., using an editor with a type of file it has not been programmed to deal with).
- They do not learn.
- They do not collaborate with other programs to solve a problem.

Two other researchers[6] take a narrower view of agents. They consider agents to possess all of these properties except for situatedness and learning.

To demonstrate the frailty of consensus, evidence from a series of alternative studies suggests the existence of other agent attributes.[7]

- *Mobility.* Agents are situated in a static location or given the ability to migrate in a self-directed way over networks.
- *Deliberative versus reactive.* Deliberative agents possess an internal symbolic model of the problem domain used to plan to achieve goals. Reactive agents do not have an internal model. Instead, they automatically react to the present state of the environment.[8]
- *Temporal continuity.* Agents must have a persistence of identity and state over time.

It does not take much imagination to picture an extraordinary range of agent types waiting to be created by talented scientists and programmers. Eight popular types are as follows:[9]

- *Collaborative agents.* These are autonomous and co-operative.[10]
- *Interface agents.* These are autonomous and capable of self-learning.[11]
- *Mobile agents.* These are mobile.[12]
- *Information agents.* These are mobile World Wide Web agents.[13]
- *Reactive agents.* These are reactive.[14]
- *Hybrid agents.* These agents are made up of two or more of the above types.[15]
- *Heterogeneous agent systems.* These systems contains agents from two or more of the above types.[16]

• *Smart agents.* These are autonomous, cooperative, and capable of self-learning (unfortunately they are yet to be fully implemented).

APPLICATION AREAS

Where might intelligent agents be put to good use? IBM[17] has identified eight major application areas for agent technologies, as follow.

Systems and network management. Management is one of the earliest application areas to benefit from intelligent agent technology. Primarily because of the increasing popularity of LANs and network-centric computing, systems and networks have become increasingly more difficult to manage. Administrators require intelligent system management software. Agents can be used to aid in management, detect and correct errors, and deal with dynamic changes to the networks.

Mobile access and management. As computing becomes more pervasive and network centric computing shifts the focus from the desktop to the network, users want to be more mobile. Not only do they want to access network resources from any location, they want to access those resources despite bandwidth limitations of mobile technology such as wireless communication, and despite network volatility. Intelligent agents which reside in the network rather than on the users' personal computers can address these needs by persistently carrying out user requests despite network disturbances or intermittent connection. In addition, agents can process data at its source and ship only compressed answers to the user, rather than overwhelming the network with large amounts of unprocessed data.[18]

Mail and messaging. Agents currently exist that can organize and prioritize e-mail. Either the user can specify rules to personalize the behavior of the agents, or the agents can modify their operations based on observing the user.

Information access and management. Information access and management is an area of great activity, given the rise in popularity of the Internet and the explosion of data available to users. Users need to find the *right* information, and they need it organised in a way that makes it *easy to understand.* Intelligent agents are helping users not only with search and filtering, but also with categorization, attentional prioritization, selective dissemination, annotation, and collaborative sharing. Intelligent agents can traverse the Internet, corporate databases, and local workstation data looking for data which is of interest. They can do this while running on the user's workstation or on a server in the network, without actually having to "go" anywhere. They can apply sophisticated filters to data to locate just the right information. They can even *learn* what the user really wants to see.[19]

Collaboration. Computer networks allow physically separated users to collaborate. An infrastructure is required to dynamically manage the sharing of data and computing resources. Tools are also needed to help create and manage collaborative teams of people. A natural model for this problem is a group of agents (each team member being represented by at least one agent) that collaborate together on the team's behalf. For example, the agents could schedule the team's activities.

Workflow and administrative management. Administrative management includes both workflow management and areas such as computer/telephony integration, where processes are defined and then automated. In these areas, users need not only to make processes more efficient, but also to reduce the cost of human agents. Much as in the messaging area, intelligent agents can be used to ascertain, then automate user wishes or business processes.[20]

Electronic commerce. Electronic commerce users, which include both buyers and sellers, must automate their "electronic financial affairs." On the Internet, agents can shop for a user by taking their specifications and finding the best places to purchase a product. They can also act as salespeople for sellers. Agents can assist a company involved in Electronic Data Interchange (EDI). Agents could electronically advertise a tender, collect bids, prioritize them, and ultimately select one.

Adaptive user interfaces. Traditionally, users have had to learn and adapt to an application's method of operation. As applications become more complex and sophisticated, this is the wrong way to build Graphical User Interfaces (GUI). Instead, the onus should be on the application to adapt to the user. Interface agents can be used to learn user habits and preferences and to help out when the user is in trouble. Through interface agents, the application becomes customized for each individual user.

For each application of the eight areas just described, many companies offer agent-based products. For instance, IBM either currently has or plans to have in the near future many commercial products in all of these areas. Their most popular product using agents is Lotus Notes, which is considered to be a part of the "collaboration" application area. Indeed, it is acknowledged that "IBM has done considerable work in products, advanced development, and research that exploit intelligent agents."[21]

THE FUTURE

In the not-too-distant future, how and why analysts, researchers, and CI professionals, among others, use the World Wide Web will change. Consider the possibilities beyond merely identifying emerging competitors. Consider how useful software agents will be that are capable of answering questions such as the following. Worried about a marketplace moving too quickly to comprehend? Where is it headed? Are there opportunities for alliances with other industries? Where will the next technology-industry breakpoints come from? Universities? Competitors? New start-ups? Who are good candidates to run the new operating division and why? In the next eight weeks, which firms should be targeted for acquisition and in what order should the deals be prosecuted? Now imagine a workplace in which your computer resolves these concerns for you. Picture a world in which more of your time is spent thinking, rather than reacting. Also, consider a world in which deadlines are met consistently within the confines of a forty-hour workweek and a balanced lifestyle. The future of CI will lie with artificial intelligence. The future is almost here!

Appendix: List of Information Portals

Title	How to Access the URL	Why This Web Site Is Important
Alliance for Justice, Washington, DC	http://www.afj.org/	This is a multifaceted umbrella association for advocacy organizations.
Alta-Vista, Digital Equipment Corporation, Palo Alto, CA	http:// www.altavista.com/	This is a generic search engine.
Anonymizer Anonymizer Inc., San Diego, CA	www.anonymizer.com	This Web site offers some free software that protects the online privacy of users.
Antitrust homepage at St. Olaf University, St. Olaf College, Northfield, MN	http://www.stolaf.edu/ people/becker/ antitrust/antitrust.html	This homepage offers a searchable database of antitrust case summaries.

Antitrust Policy Homepage, Owen Graduate School of Management, Nashville, TN	http:// www.antitrust.org/	This Web site offers information on antitrust issues.
ASAE Gateway to Associations, American Society of Association Executives, Washington, DC	http:// www.asaenet.org	This Web sites directs researchers to professional and industry association Web sites.
Ask Jeeves, Ask Jeeves Inc., Berkeley, CA	http:// www.askjeeves.com	Ask Jeeves is a search engine or provider of natural-language question-answering services on the Internet for consumers and companies.
Baobab's Corporate Power Information Center, Baobab Computing, Durham, NC	http://www.baobab computing. com/corporatepower/	This Web site offers a collection of essays on the ethical actions of selected companies.
Yahoo Finance, Yahoo! Inc., Santa Clara, CA	http:// finance.yahoo.com	This Web site offers researchers a wide selection of business information including company profiles, SEC filings, analyst estimates, fundamentals, corporate and industry performance charts, and recent press headlines.

Business Week, online McGraw-Hill Companies, New York, NY	http://www.businessweek.com	This is the online version of the print periodical.
Business Wire.com Business Wire, San Francisco, CA	http://www.businesswire.com/	This Web site provides corporate press releases and public relations information for the U.S. business market.
Center for Science in the Public Interest, Washington, DC	http://www.cspinet.org/	This is a consumer watchdog group that addresses health and safety concerns.
CEO Express, AlphaSight Online Strategists, Inc., Boston, MA	http://www.ceoexpress.com	This Web site offers a well-organized series of business information sources for researchers seeking quick access to business and news publications.
CNNfn Cable News Network America, Inc., Atlanta, GA	http://www.cnnfn.com	This Web site provides readers with current business news.
Companies Online, Dun & Bradstreet, Lycos Inc., Murray Hill, N.J.	http://www.companiesonline.com/	This Web site, among other functions, links researchers to company home pages.
Company Link Individual, Inc., Burlington, MA	http://www.companylink.com	This Web site, among other functions, links researchers to company home pages.

Compare.net, Microsoft Corporation, San Francisco, CA	http:// www.compare.net/	This Web site offers researchers product information, product comparisons and reviews, side-by-side charts, discussion groups, and shopping Web site links.
Consumer.net, The Consumer Information organization, Washington, DC	http:// www.consumer.net/	This Web site offers consumer protection information and tracks the direct mail and telemarketing industries.
consumer reports On-line, Consumers Union of U.S. Inc., Yonkers, NY	http://www.consumer reports.org	This Web site offers consumer information on a wide range of products and services.
Consumer World, Charlestown, MA	http://www.consumer world.org/	This Web site provides links to consumer protection information.
Copernic 2000, Copernic Technologies Inc., Ste. Foy, Quebec	http:// www.copernic.com	A meta search engine that simultaneously consults a group of Internet search engines that are grouped into six categories labeled as: The Web, Newsgroups, E-mail Addresses, Buy Books, Buy Hardware, and Buy Software.

Corporate Watch, Transnational Resource & Action Center San Francisco, CA	http:// www.corpwatch.org/	This Web site tracks corporate activity with special attention toward issues of globalization, human rights, worker health and safety, and the environment.
CorpTech Corporate Technology Information Services Inc. Woburn MA	www.corptech.com	This searchable database offers a information on high-tech manufacturers and developers.
deja.com deja.com Inc., NY, NY	http:// www.dejanews.com	This is a search engine for online discussion groups.
DLJ Direct, DLJdirect Holdings Inc., Jersey City, NJ	http:// www.dljdirect.com	This Web site offers researchers a wide selection of business information including company profiles, SEC filings, analyst estimates, fundamentals, corporate and industry performance charts, and recent press headlines.
DOGPILE Go2Net, Inc Seattle, WA	www.dogpile.com	This is a meta-search engine.
ECONET, Institute for Global Communi-cations, Menlo Park, CA	http://www.igc.org/igc/ gateway/enindex.html	The Institute for Global Communications website provides environmental information.

Edgar Online EDGAR Online Inc., Norwalk, CT	http://www. edgaronline.com/	A free online search tool that focuses its efforts on effectively retrieving information from corporate regulatory documents filed with the Securities and Exchange Commission.
enews.com enews.com Inc., Washington, DC	http:// www.enews.com/	This Web site offers links to online newspapers around the world.
Environmental Protection Agency Research Triangle Park, NC	http://www.epa.gov/	This is the Web site of the chief U.S. regulatory body responsible for the protection of environment.
Essential Information, Washington, DC	http:// www.essential.org/	This Web site offers a searchable directory of articles as well as information on activist organizations around the world.
Excite, Excite@Home Redwood City, CA	http:// www.excite.com/	This generic search engine offers search, chat, and investment information.
FedWorld.gov U.S. Department of Justice Springfield, VA	http:// www.fedworld.gov/	This Web site offers a searchable directory of all U.S. government sites.

Federal Judiciary Homepage, Administrative Office of the U.S. Courts, Washington, DC	http://www.uscourts.gov/	This Web site allows researchers to query the contents of all federal judiciary publicly available documents by selecting the search option.
Federal Trade Commission Washington DC	http://www.ftc.gov	This is the Web site of an important U.S. regulator.
The Business Law Site, Ferguson Methven and Associates, Berkeley, CA.	http://members.aol.com/bmethven	This law firm home page provides informational articles on patents.
FT.com Financial Times, London, UK	http://www.ft.com	This is the online version of the print magazine. It offers a searchable archive of articles.
Find.com idealab! Pasadena, CA.	www.find.com	Find.com is a search engine.
FindLaw, Internet Legal Resources, Palo Alto, CA	http://www.findlaw.com/	A search engine that returns information on legal issues.
Forbes.com, Forbes Magazine, New York, NY	http://www.forbes.com	This is the online version of the print magazine. It offers a searchable archive of articles.
Fortune.com Fortune Magazine, New York, NY	http://www.fortune.com	This is the online version of the print magazine. It offers a searchable archive of articles.

Free Edgar, EDGAR Online Inc., Norwalk, CT	http:// www.freeedgar.com,	A free online search tool that focuses its efforts on effectively retrieving information from corporate regulatory documents filed with the Securities and Exchange Commission.
Greenpeace.org Greenpeace International, Amsterdam, Holland	http:// www.greenpeace.org/	A worldwide environmental and consumer watchdog group.
Hoover's Online Hoover's Inc., Austin, TX	http:// www.hoovers.com	This Web site offers researchers a wide selection of business information including company profiles, SEC filings, analyst estimates, fundamentals, corporate and industry performance charts and recent press headlines.
Hoover's IPO Central, Hoover's Inc. Austin, TX	http:// www.ipocentral.com	IPO Central provides a database of information regarding successful IPOs and those in registration since May 1996.
Hotbot, Lycos, Inc., Waltham, MA.	http:// www.hotbot.com	This general search engine also offers a search engine for news groups.

Hotbot Wired Digital Inc., San Francisco, CA	www.newsbot.com	Newsbot is a search engine specializing in news information.
IBM Intellectual Property Network, IBM Corporation, Armonk, NY	http://www.patients.ibm.com/ibm.html	This is a powerful search engine for patent information.
Inc.com Inc. com Inc., Charlestown, MA	http://www.inc.com	This is the online version of the print magazine. It offers a search ability of its archives.
InfoSpace.com InfoSpace.com Inc., Redmond, WA	http://www.infospace.com	This Web site links researchers to company home pages.
GO.com, Santa Clara, CA	http://www.go.com/	This Web site offers researchers a wide selection of business information including company profiles, SEC filings, analyst estimates, fundamentals, corporate and industry performance charts, and recent press headlines.
Infospace.com Infospace Inc., Redmond, WA	http://www.infospace.com	Infospace is an online tool that allows researchers an extensive capacity to conduct online business research.
Insider Trader, New York, NY	http://www.insidertrader.com/	Insider Trader provides information on just that, inside trading.

igc internet Institute for Global Communication, Menlo Park, CA	http://www.igc.org/ igc/	This Web site offers researchers an alternative viewpoint of industry and corporate behavior through banners such as: Peacenet, Econet, Labornet, Conflictnet, and IGC Projects
Internet Databases, Martin Bohnet Markt Consulting KG, Hessen, DE	http://www.Internet database.com/ usenet.htm	This Web site connects users to Internet news groups.
InterNIC Network Solutions, Inc., Herndon, VA	http://interNIC.net/	This Web site provides domain name registration information, including server and technical specifications.
Invest Quest, Invest Quest Inc., Hilliard, OH	http:// www.investquest.com/	This Web site claims to provide information on over 10,000 public companies in more than 145 countries.
justquotes.com Just Ventures Company, Wenonah, NJ	http:// www.justquotes.com/	This Web site offers researchers a wide selection of business information including company profiles, SEC filings, analyst estimates, fundamentals, corporate and industry performance charts, and recent press headlines.

Labor Net Headlines Archive, Menlo Park, CA	http://www.igc.org/igc/labornet/	This Web site of daily international labor news offers links to labor-related sites.
LawCrawler Legal Web Search, Palo Alto, CA	http://www.Lawcrawler.com	This search engine returns information on litigation in the U.S.
Lawyers Weekly, USA Lawyers Weekly Inc., Boston, MA	http://www.lweekly.com/	This is an online journal of legal news and information.
Macrocosm USA, Inc., Macrocosm USA Inc., Cambria, CA	http://www.macronet.org/	This Web site offers researchers alternative viewpoints regarding industry or corporate behavior.
Market Guide, Market Guide, Inc., Lake Success, NY	http://www.marketguide.com	This Web site offers a large sortable company information database.
McSpotlight, McSpot, Amsterdam, NE	http://www.mcspotlight.org/	This Web site monitors consumer and environmental issues as well as human rights violations around the world.
Media Finder, Oxbridge Communications Inc., New York, NY	http://mediafinder.com	This Web site helps researchers find industry publications.
Metacrawler, Go2net, Inc., Seattle, WA	http://www.Metacrawler.com/	This a meta search engine.

Moody's Investors Service, New York, NY	http:// www.moodys.com	This Web site offers online corporate bond ratings.
Fool.com, The Motley Fool, Alexandria, VA	http://www.fool.com/	This site offers news and profiling information on companies and chat links.
Multex.com, Multex.com Inc., New York, NY	http:// www.multex.com	This Web site hosts a database of Wall Street analysts consensus estimates and recommendations.
National Technology Transfer Center, Wheeling, WV	http://www.nttc.edu/	This Web site provides access to federal R&D information and links to government sites.
NetPartners Internet Solutions, NetPartners Internet Solutions, Inc., San Diego, CA	http:// www.netpart.com/	This Web site locates company home pages through its "company locator" option.
New York Times, New York Times Company, New York, NY	http:// www.nytimes.com	The *New York Times*!
News ALERT, NewsAlert Inc., New York, NY	http:// www.newsalert.com	This Web site provides a source for business news.
News Directory.com Ecola Design, Beaverton, OR	http://www.news directory.com/	This Web site provides links to online English-language newspapers and magazines.

individual.com, Individual, Inc., Burlington, MA	http://www.individual.com/	This Web site provides news and information on selected industries.
NewsEdge Company Look-up, Individual, Inc., Burlington, MA	http://www.companylink.com	This Web site states that it provides, "news, research and contacts for over 100,000 companies."
NEWS Index New York, NY.	www.newsindex.com	NEWS Index is a search engine specializing in news information.
Newspaper Association of America, Newspaper Association of America, Reston, VA	http://www.naa.org/	This Web site links users to North American newspapers with online editions through its HOTLINKS option.
Northern Light.com, Northern Light Technology LLC, Cambridge, MA	http://www.northernlight.com/	This is a search engine.
Notess.com The Greg Notess Web site	notess.com	This Web site tracks and discusses activity in the search engine business.
Monster.com, Online Career Center, Indianapolis, IN	http://www.occ.com	This Web site hosts online job postings.
PPPP.Net, PPPP.net, New York, NY	http://www.pppp.net/	This Web site is a source for business news.
PR NEWSWIRE, PR Newswire, Jersey City, NJ	http://www.prnewswire.com/	This Web site hosts corporate press releases.

PRODUCT REVIEW NET, Rain Corp, Cambridge, MA	http://www.product reviewnet.com/	This Web site reviews consumer products and services and compares them for quality and reliability.
Quicken.Com, Intuit, Mountain View, CA	http:// www.quicken.com	This Web site offers researchers a wide selection of business information including company profiles, SEC filings, analyst estimates, fundamentals, corporate and industry performance charts, and recent press headlines.
Raging Bull, Raging Bull, Inc., Andover, MA	http:// www.ragingbull.com/	This Web site hosts a highly respected corporate discussion forum.
Red Herring, The Red Herring, San Francisco, CA	http:// www.redherring.com	This online magazine is the bible of the venture capital industry.
Reference.COM, Sift Inc., Sunnyvale, CA	http:// www.reference.com/	This Web site helps users locate newsgroups, e-mailing lists, and web forums.
Report Gallery, IntraGrafix, Santa Ana, CA	http://www.report gallery.com/	A service of Zack's Research Reports that hosts online annual reports.
Researching Companies Online, Debbie Flanagan, Houston, TX	http:// home.sprintmail.com/ ~debflanagan	This Web site offers readers an online business research tutorial.

Right to Know Network, DMB Watch, Washington, DC	http://www.rtk.net/	This Web site provides researchers with a capability to quickly search of OSHA and EPA warning letters and actions.
Road Way Express, Road Way Express Inc., Akron, OH	http:// www.roadway.com/ shippers/sbrc.html	This Web site categorizes and offers direct links to hundreds of online information sources useful to small businesses and their owners.
Savvysearch CNET Inc. San Francisco, CA	www.savvysearch.com	Savvysearch is a meta-search engine.
Search Engine Watch internet.com New York, NY	www.search enginewatch.com	This Web site tracks and discusses activity in the search engine business.
Securities and Exchange Commission, Washington, DC	http://www.sec.gov/	This federal regulator Web site hosts the EDGAR database, the online repository of securities filings provided by corporations whose shares trade publicly in the United States.
Silicon Investor, VB Web Partners, San Jose, CA	http:// www.techstocks.com	This Web site hosts a discussion forum for technology stocks.
Sixbey, Friedman, Leedom, McLean, VA	http:// www.sixbey.com/	This law firm's Web site provides informational articles on patents.

Society of Competitive Intelligence Professionals, Alexandria, VA	http://www.scip.org	This is the home page of the industry association for CI professionals.
Society of Environmental Journalists, Erdenheim, PA	http://www.sej.org/env_subj.htm	This Web site offers links and resources about the environment.
Standard and Poor's Ratings, Standards & Poors, Inc., New York, NY	http://www.ratings.com/	This Web site offers online corporate bond ratings.
Stanford Securities Class Action Clearinghouse Robert Crown Law Library Stanford University School of Law	securities.stanford.edu	An interactive database that monitors class action litigation and related issues.
The Third Voice, Third Voice Inc. Redwood City, CA	http://www/thirdvoice.com/	A free service that allows users to put public group or personal notes on any Web page.
Thomas Register, Thomas Publishing Company, New York, NY	http://www.thomasregister.com/	An online manufacturers' guide.
Transium Business Intelligence, Transium Corporation, Los Altos, CA	http://www.transium.com	An online database of business press and news stories. It allows users to sort abstracts by a number of means including function, journal, geography, industry and company

Trial Lawyers for Public Justice, The TLPJ Foundation, Washington, DC	http://www.tlpj.org/	This Web site offers a series of useful legal resources and Web links
U.S. Attorney General, Washington, DC	http://www.usdoj.gov/usao/ghindex.html	The Attorney General's archives are searchable using the "Glimpse HTTP Search" function.
U.S. Department of Justice (DOJ), Washington, DC	http://www.usdoj.gov	Researchers can query the Department of Justice online archive of cases and decisions or link to courts around the country.
U.S. Patent and Trademark Office, Washington, DC	http://www.uspto.gov	This Web site offers a searchable database of full text patents and patent abstracts as well as trademarks.
University of California at San Diego Science and Engineering Library	http://scilib.ucsd.edu/subjectdir/patents.html	This Web site offers a patent-searching tutorial.
University of Texas Engineering Library, Austin, TX	http://www.lib.utexas.edu/Libs/ENG/PTUT/ptut.html	This Web site offers a patent searching tutorial.

University of Virginia School of Law, Charlottesville, VA	http:// www.law.virginia.edu/ Library/govadm.htm	This Web site offers direct links to federal administrative decisions and other actions found on the various regulatory portals.
Vfinance.com, The Venture Capital Resource Library, Vfinance Holdings Inc. Delray Beach, FL	http:// www.vfinance.com	This is an online resource library for venture capitalists.
Virtual Pet.com, Polson Enterprises, Stillwater, OK	http:// www.virtualpet.com/	This Web site offers an example of how a researcher might conduct an industry analysis.
Wall Street Journal, Princeton, NJ	http://www.wsj.com	*The Wall Street Journal*!
Wall Street Journal's Daily Insider Report, CDA Investment Technologies, Rockville, MD	http://www.cda.com/ investnet/daily/ wsj.html.	This Web site provides a daily account of insider trading.
Wall Street Net, Internet Resource Pages, Milford, CT	http://netresource.com/ wsn	This Web site offers a listing of publicly traded firms involved in merger and acquisition activity.

Wall Street Research Network, Greenwich, CT	http://www.wsrn.com	This Web site offers researchers a wide selection of business information including company profiles, SEC filings, analyst estimates, fundamentals, corporate and industry performance charts, and recent press headlines.
Washburn University School of Law, Topeka, KA	http:// www.washlaw.edu/	This Web site offers great links to legal information.
WhoWhere? Who Where Inc., Mountain View, CA	http:// www.whowhere.com/	This Web site offers links to company home pages through its "companies" option. It also offers a means to search for companies by SIC code.
WomensNet, igc internet Inc., Menlo Park, CA	http://www.igc.org/igc/ womensnet/	This Web site offers information on the women's rights movement worldwide.
World Pages.com, Web YB, Inc., San Francisco, CA	http://www.world pages.com/	This Web site provides many online information tools including SIC codes
Yahoo!, Santa Clara, CA	http://www.yahoo.com	This is a multipurpose search engine.

Zacks.com Zack's Investment Research, Chicago, IL	http://www.zacks.com/	This Web site offers researchers a wide selection of business information including company profiles, SEC filings, analyst estimates, fundamentals, corporate and industry performance charts, and recent press headlines.
Zpub, Z Publishing, San Francisco, CA	http://www.zpub.com/	This Web site offers links to online annual reports.

Notes

CHAPTER 1: INTRODUCTION

1. Paul C. Judge, BusinessWeekOnline[Online]. Available: http://www.businessweek.com/reprints/99–11/b3620001.htm [1999, November 22].

2. Ibid.

3. Ibid.

4. Ibid.

5. Ibid.

6. Company A credo. [Online] Company A. Available: http://www.companya.com/who_is_companya/contributions/r_credo.html [1999, October 7].

7. Harrison Brown, Lawrence A. Cremin, et al., *The World Book Year Book*. (Chicago, IL: World Book, 1983).

8. Company A Company History. [Online] Company A. Available: http://www.companya.com/who_is_companya/hist_index.html [1999, October 7].

9. Company A Homepage. [Online] Company A. Available: http://www.companya.com/home.html [1999, October 7].

10. Brown, Cremin, et al., *World Book Year Book*.

11. Richard T. De George, *Business Ethics* (Englewood Cliffs, NJ: Prentice-Hall 1995).

12. Ibid.

13. Brown, Cremin, et al., *World Book Year Book*.

14. De George, *Business ethics*.

15. Hoover's Online [Online] Hoover's Inc. Available: http://www.hoovers.com/capsules/7/0,10xx,xx077,00.html [1999, August 27].

16. ABC Corporation 1998 Annual Report. [Online] ABC Corporation. Available: http:abccorporation.com/annualreport.html [1999, August 22].

17. Ibid.

18. Ibid.

19. ITC Fights Off Pack CNNfn.com[Online] CNN The financial network. Available: http://cnnfn.com/1998/11/11/technology/ITC [1999, September, 14].

20. ITC press release: [Online] Internet Tool Company. Available: http://www1.ITC.com/pressrelease/0,1494,wp~85_2!ob~9238_1_1. 000.html [1999, August 22].

21. Ibid.

22. [Online] Transium ITC Computer. Available: http://transium.com/backgrounder/pro . . . %22&stag+2&r=1.tbusr ef.I54430007 [1999, October 15].

23. BFU press release: [Online] BuyFromUs Inc. Available: http://www1.BFU.com/exec/obidos/subst/misc/jobs/culture.htm   1/102-8011706–5781646 [1999, August 22].

24. [Online] CNN The financial network. Available: wysiwyg://57/http://cnnfn.com/1998/11/11/technology/ITC [1999, October 15].

CHAPTER 2: THE CHALLENGE

1. News Releases [Online] Cisco Systems. Available: http://www.cisco.com/warp/public/146.html. [1999, November 27].

2. News Releases [Online] Nortel Networks. Available: http://www.nortelnetworks.com/corporate/news/newsreleases/press_8-99.html. [1999, November 27].

3. James Kinsella (1999, August 20). Excel deal just one of Lucent's many purchases. [Online] *Cape Cod Times*. Available: http://www.lucent-sas.com/news/excel_14.shtml [1999, November 27].

4. Joseph Alois Schumpeter, *The Theory of Economic Development: An Inquiry into Profits, Capital, Credit, Interest, and the Business Cycle*, translated from the German by Redvers Opie (Cambridge, UK: Harvard University Press, 1934).

5. Jay B. Barney, "Types of Competition and the Theory of Strategy: An Integrative Framework," *The Academy of Management Review* (Mississippi State) 11(4) (October 1986): 791.

6. Mark Evans. "Cisco Head Unfazed by Nortel Networks," *The Globe and Mail*, November 17, 1999, p. B4.

7. Bernard Wysocki, Jr., "Corporate America in Search of Its Core," *Wall Street Journal*, November 9, 1999.

8. Guy Kolb, (1999, November 27). An Introduction to CI [Online]. Society of Competitive Intelligence Professionals. Available: http://www.scip.org/education/online_edu.html [1999, November 27].

9. Scip.org. [Online]. Society of Competitive Intelligence Professionals. Available: http://www.scip.org/ci [1999, November 27].

10. Kolb, An Introduction to CI [Online].

11. Stephen Miller (1999, October). Actionable Intelligence [Online]. Society of Competitive Intelligence Professionals. Available: http://www.scip.org/news.html [1999, November 27].

12. Kolb, An Introduction to CI [Online].

13. John Ralston Saul. *The Doubter's Companion: A Dictionary of Aggressive Common Sense* (Toronto, ON: Viking Penguin, 1994), p. 251.

14. Mats Alvesson, "A Critical Framework for Organizational Analysis," *Organization Studies* 6(2) (1985): 117–138.

15. Saul, *Doubter's Companion* 5, p. 251.

CHAPTER 3: THE POWER OF SEARCH ENGINES

1. Deb Canale, "Searching the World Wide Web: A Tutorial," *Transportation and Distribution* (May): 37–40.

2. *Time Magazine*, Canadian Edition, "The Start-Ups: Life at Warp Speed," October 4, 1999, p. 23.

3. Shailagh Murray, "1998 Special Report: Convergence. The Spying Game. Intelligence Goes Corporate as Global Players Seek a Competitive Edge with Sharper Tech Tools," Dow Jones and Company Inc., File No. 066 06/29, pp. 2–7.

4. Jennifer L. Schenker, "Chasing the Data. The Latest Tech Tools Are Designed to Boost the Bottom Line," Dow Jones and Company Inc., File No. 066 06/29, 1998, pp. 7–11.

5. News Release [Online] Ask Jeeves. Available: http://www.askjeeves.com.html. [1999, November 27].

6. For an interesting discussion of field and phrase searching, please see Canale, "Searching the World Wide Web."

7. Search Engine Watch.com[Online] Available: http://www.searchenginewatch.com/reports/reviewchart.html [1999, November 5].

8. News Release [Online] Copernic 2000. Available: http://www.copernic.com.html. [1999, November 27].

9. News Release [Online] The Third Voice. Available: http://www.thirdvoice.com/demo/.html. [1999, November 27].

10. Michelle DeWitt, *Competitive Intelligence, Competitive Advantage*. (Grand Rapids, MI: Abacus, 1997).

11. Bill Mark, Ontologies as the Representation (and Re-Representation) of Agreement. [Online] Stanford KSL Network Services. Available: http://www.ksl.stanford.edu/KR96/BillMarkPosititonPaper.html [1999, November 27].

12. Tom R. Gruber, What Is an Ontology[Online] Stanford KSL Network Services. Available: http://www-ksl.stanford.edu/kst/what-is-an-ontology.html [1999, November 27].

CHAPTER 4: A THEORY

1. Joseph Alois Schumpeter, *The Theory of Economic Development: An Inquiry into Profits, Capital, Credit, Interest, and the Business Cycle*, translated from the German by Redvers Opie (Cambridge, MA: Harvard University Press, 1934).

2. Richard A. Bettis, and Michael A. Hitt, "The New Competitive Landscape," *Strategic Management Journal* 16 (1995): 7–19.

3. Ibid.

4. Ibid.

5. Janet Fulk, and Gerardine DeSanctis, "Electronic Communication and

Changing Organisational Forms," *Organisation Science* 6 (4) (July–August 1995): 337–349.

6. Henry Mintzberg, *Structure in Fives: Designing Effective Organizations* (Englewood Cliffs, NJ: Prentice Hall, 1983).

7. B. H. Burris, *Technocracy at Work* (Albany, NY: State University of New York Press, 1993).

8. William Ouchi, "Markets, Hierarchies and Bureaucracy," *Administrative Science Quarterly* 25 (1980): 129–142.

9. W. H. Davidow and M. S. Malone, *The Virtual Corporation* (New York: Harper Business, 1992).

10. J. L. Badarraco, Jr., *The Knowledge Link: How Firms Compete Through Strategic Alliances* (Boston, MA: Harvard Business School, 1991).

11. W. W. Powell, "Neither Market nor Hierarchy: Network Forms of Organization," in L. L. Cummings and B. M. Staw (eds.), *Research in Organizational Behavior* 12 (1990): 295–336.

12. W. Heydebrand, "New Organizational Forms," *Work and Occupations*, 16 (1989): 327.

13. Richard L. Daft and Karl E. Weick, "Toward a Model of Organisations as Interpretation Systems," *Academy of Management Review* 9 (2) (1984): 284–295.

14. John J. McGonagle and Carolyn M. Vella, *Protecting Your Company Against Competitive Intelligence* (Westport, CT: Quorum Books, 1998), p. 5.

15. Daft and Weick, "Toward a Model of Organizations."

16. Ram Charan and Geoffrey Colvin, "Why CEOs Fail," *Fortune* (June 1999), pp. 68–78.

17. Ron Ashkenas, Dave Ulrich, Todd Jick, and Steve Kerr, *The Boundaryless Organization: Breaking the Chains of Organizational Structure* (San Francisco, CA: Jossey Bass, 1995).

18. Bettis and Hitt, "New Competitive Landscape."

19. McGonagle and Vella, *Protecting Your Company*.

20. SEC.

21. Form 10K, [online], Partes Corporation, Available: http://www. freedgar. com.[1999, July 20].

22. Shaker A. Sahra and Sherry S. Chaples, "Blind Spots in Competitive Analysis," *Academy of Management Executive* (1993): May 7–28.

23. Jeffrey Pfeffer, "Four Laws of Organizational Research," Implications of Perspectives, 409–418.

24. Ibid.

25. Ibid.

26. Omar A. El Sawy and Thierry C. Pauchant, "Triggers, Templates and Twitches in the Tracking of Emerging Strategic Issues," *Strategic Management Journal*, 9 (1988): 455–473.

27. John Ralston Saul, *The Doubter's Companion: A Dictionary of Aggressive Common Sense* (Toronto, ON: Viking Penguin, 1994), p. 251.

28. Ibid.

29. J. P. Liebeskind, "Knowledge, Strategy, and the Theory of the Firm," *Strategic Management Journal* 17 (Winter 1996): 93–109.

30. McGonagle and Vella, *Protecting Your Company*.

CHAPTER 5: IDENTIFYING POWER HOLDERS

1. Jeffrey Pfeffer, *Managing with Power* (Boston: Harvard Business School Press, 1992).

2. Deborah C. Sawyer, *Tradecraft: A Sourcebook of Competitive Intelligence Tactics* (New York: Information Plus, 1995).

3. William H. Starbuck, "Keeping a Butterfly and an Elephant in a House of Cards: The Elements of Exceptional Success," *Journal of Management Studies*, 30(6) (1993): 885–921.

CHAPTER 6: PERFORMING A SOCIAL RESPONSIBILITY AUDIT

1. A. B. Carroll, "A three-dimensional model of corporate social performance," *Academy of Management Review*, 4(4): 497–505.

2. Researching Corporations: How to investigate a TNC. [Online], Corporate Watch. Available: http://www.corporwatch.org. [1999, July 23].

3. William Starbuck, Anders Greve, and Bo Hedberg, "Responding to Crisis," *Journal of Business Administration* (Spring 1978): 111–178.

4. Melissa S. Baucus and Janet B. Near, "Can illegal corporate behaviour be predicted? An event history analysis," *Academy of Management Journal*, 34(1): 9–36.

5. National Technology Transfer Center. [Online].Available: http://www.nttc.edu.gov. [1999, July 23].

CHAPTER 7: PERFORMING DUE DILIGENCE

1. Robert P. Lynch, *The Practical Guide to Joint Ventures and Corporate Alliances* (New York: John Wiley & Sons, 1990).

2. Stuart Bochner, How to read an annual report. [Online], ABC News and Starwave Corporation. Available: http://www.abcnews.go.com. [1999, June 12].

3. Researching Corporations: How to Investigate a TNC. [Online] Corporate Watch. Available: http://www.corpwatch.org. [1999, June 12].

4. Debra Meyerson and Joanne Martin, "Cultural Change: An Integration of Three Different Views," *Journal of Management Studies* 24(1998): 623–648.

5. Mats Alvesson and Peter O. Berg, *Corporate Culture and Organizational Symbolism* (Berlin /New York: de Gruyter, 1992).

6. Michael Tushman and Elaine Romanelli, "Organizational Evolution: A Metamorphisis Model of Convergence and Reorientation," *Research in Organizational Behavior* 7(1985):171–122.

7. Oliver Williamson, *Markets and Hierarchies: Analysis and Anti-trust Implications* (New York: Free Press, 1975).

CHAPTER 8: PROFILING CORPORATE COMMUNICATIONS STYLES

1. George Day, and David Reibstein, *Wharton on Dynamic Competitive Strategy* (New York: Wiley, 1997). Robert Grant, *Contemporary Strategy Analysis*, 3rd ed. (Malden, MA: Blackwell Business, 1998).

CHAPTER 9: SPOTTING INDICATORS OF ORGANIZATIONAL ALTERATION

1. Andrew H. Van de Ven and Marshall Scott Poole, "Explaining Development and Change in Organizations," *Academy of Management Review* 20(3) (1995): 510–540.

2. Christopher Hinings and Royston Greenwood, *The Dynamics of Strategic Change* (London: Basil Blackwell, 1988).

3. Danny Miller, *The Icarus Paradox* (New York: Harper Books, 1991).

4. Michael Tushman and Elaine Romanelli, "Organizational Evolution: A Metamorphisis Model of Convergence and Reorientation," *Research in Organizational Behavior* 7(1985): 171–122.

5. Ibid.

6. Bill Starbuck, Anders Greve, and Bo Hedberg, "Responding to Crisis," *Journal of Business Administration* (Spring 1978): 111–178.

7. Victor L. Barker and I. M. Duhaime, "Strategic Change in the Turnaround Process: Theory and Empirical Evidence," *Strategic Management Journal* 18(1997): 13–38.

8. Debra Meyerson and Joanne Martin, "Cultural Change: An Integration of Three Different Views," *Journal of Management Studies*, 24(1988): 623–648.

9. Jeffrey Pfeffer, *Managing with Power* (Boston: Harvard Business School Press, 1992).

10. Pfeffer, *Managing with Power.*

11. Alan Chai, The Insider. [Online], Hoover's IPO Central. Available: http://www.ipocentral.com. [1999, July 20].

12. Hinings and Greenwood, *The Dynamics of Strategic Change.*

CHAPTER 10: IDENTIFYING COMPETITORS

1. Robert D. Hof, The Internet Age: Bright Hopes and Terrible Fears. Business Week Online, October 4, 1999. http://www.businessweek.com/1999/99_40/b3649001.htm [1999. October 20].

2. Gary Hamel and C. K. Prahalad, "Competing for the Future," *Harvard Business Review*, 72(4) (July–August 1994): 122.

3. David Hussey and Per Genster, *Competitor Intelligence: Turning Analysis into Success* (New York: John Wiley & Sons, 1999), p. 2.

4. Steve Lawrence, "Accessibility of Information on the the Web," *Nature* 400(674) (July 8, 1999): 107.

5. George S. Day and David J. Reibstein, *Wharton on Dynamic Competitive Strategy* (New York: Wiley, 1997), p. 25. Robert M. Grant, *Contemporary Strategy Analysis*, 3rd ed. (Oxford: Blackwell Publishers, 1997).

6. Gareth Morgan, *Images of Organisation* (Thousand Oaks, CA: Sage Publications: 1986).

7. Gareth Morgan, *Images of Organisation* (Thousand Oaks, CA: Sage Publications, 1997) p. 4.

8. Hof, Internet Age.

9. V. K. Naraynan and R. Nath, *Organization Theory: A Strategic Approach*. (Homewood, IL: Richard D. Irwin, 1993), pp. 144–145.

10. M. T. Hannan and J. H. Freeman, *Organizational Ecology* (Cambridge, MA: Harvard University Press, 1989).

11. W. R. Scott, "The Adolescence of Institutional Theory," *Administrative Sciences Quarterly* 32(1987): 493–511.

12. Ibid.

13. P. J. DiMaggio and W. W. Powell, "The Iron Cage Revisited: Institutional Isomorphism and Collective Rationality in Organizational Fields," *American Sociological Review* 48(1983): 147–160.

14. Naraynan and Nath, *Organisation Theory*.

15. M. C. Suchman, "Managing Legitimacy: Strategic and Institutional Approaches," *Academy of Management Review* 20(3)(1995): 571–610.

16. Hannan and Freeman, *Organizational Ecology*.

CHAPTER 11: CONCERNS FOR THE FUTURE OF THE INTERNET

1. Statistics Canada, *Literacy, Economy and Society* (Ottawa, Canada: Organisation for Economic Co-operation and Development, 1995).

2. Ibid., p. 14.

3. Ibid.

4. L. Mikulecky and R. Drew, R. Barr et al., "Basic Literacy Skills in the Workplace," *Handbook of Reading Research* 2(24)(1991): 671.

5. L. Mikulecky, "Job Literacy: The Relationship Between School Preparation and Workplace Actuality," *Reading Research Quarterly* 17(1982): 400–419.

6. J. T. Guthrie, W. D. Schafer, and S. R. Hutchinson, "Relations of Document Literacy and Prose Literacy to Occupational and Societal Characteristics of Young Black and White Adults," *Reading Research Quarterly* 26(1991): 30–48.

7. Statistics Canada, *Literacy, Economy and Society*.

8. Georgia Tech College of Computing 1998. Graphics, Visualization, & Usability (GVU) Center's WWW User Surveys.

9. Mikulecky and Drew, "Basic Literacy Skills."

10. Mikulecky, "Job Literacy."

11. Ibid.

CHAPTER 12: THE FUTURE: PROACTIVE, AGENT-BASED CI

1. K. Sycara, "Intelligent agents and the information revolution" (London: UNICOM Seminar on Intelligent Agents and Their Business Applications, November 1995), pp. 143–159.

2. D. Chorafas, *Agent Technology Handbook* (New York: McGraw-Hill, 1998).

3. M. Georgeff, and A. Rao, "Rational Software Agents: From Theory to Practice," in *Agent Technology*, edited by Jennings and Wooldridge (New York: Springer-Verlag, 1998), pp. 140–160.

4. A. Kay, "Computer Software," *Scientific American*, 251(3) (1984): 53–59.

5. K. Sycara, "The Many Faces of Agents," *AI Magazine* 19(2) (Summer 1998): 11–12.

6. N. R. Jennings and M. J. Wooldridge, "Applications of Intelligent Agents," in *Agent Technology*, edited by Jennings and Wooldridge (New York: Springer-Verlag, 1998), pp. 3–28.

7. O. Etzioni and D. Weld, "Intelligent Agents on the Internet: Fact, Fiction, and Forecast," *IEEE Expert*, 10(4)(1995): 44–49. S. Franklin and A. Graesser, "Is it an agent or just a program? A taxonomy for autonomous agents," in *Proceedings of the Third International Workshop on Agent Theories, Architectures, and Languages* (New York: Springer-Verlag, 1996). H. S. Nwana, "Software Agents: An Overview," *Knowledge Engineering Review* 11(3): 1–40.

8. R. Brooks, "Intelligence Without Representation," *Artificial Intelligence* 47(1991): 139–159.

9. Nwana, "Software agents: An overview."

10. M. Georgeff, "Agents with Motivation: Essential Technology for Real World Applications," First International Conference on the Practical Applications of Intelligent Agents and Multi-Agent Technology, London, UK, April 24, 1996.

11. A. Chavez and P. Maes, "Kasbah: An Agent Marketplace for Buying and Selling Goods." in Proceedings of the First International Conference on the Practical Application of Intelligent Agents and Multi-Agent Technology (PAAM '96), London, March 22–24, 75–90.

12. P. Wayner, *Agents Unleashed: A Public Domain Look at Agent Technology* (Boston, MA: AP Professional, 1995).

13. O. Etzioni and D. Weld, "A Softbot-based Interface to the Internet," *Communications of the ACM* 37(7)(1994): 72–76.

14. Brooks, "Intelligence Without Representation."

15. B. Hayes-Roth, "An Architecture for Adaptive Intelligent Systems," *Artificial Intelligence* 72(1–2)(1995): 329–365.

16. Brooks, "Intelligence Without Representation."

17. Hayes-Roth, "An Architecture for Adaptive Intelligent Systems."

18. M. R. Genesereth and S. P. Ketchpel, "Software Agents," *Communications of the ACM* 37(7)(1994): 48–53.

19. D. Gilbert, M. Aparicio, B. Atkinson, S. Brady, J. Ciccarino, B. Grosof, P. O'Connor, D. Osisek, S. Pritko, R. Spagna, and L. Wilson, "The Role of Intelligent Agents in the Information Infrastructure" (white paper, Research Triangle Park, NC: IBM, 1995).

20. Ibid.

21. Ibid.

Appendix Notes

CHAPTER 5

a. ABC Corporation Homepage, Annual Report 1998. [Online]. Available: http://www.ABC Corporation.com. [1999, October 01].

b. ABC Corporation Homepage. (1999) [Online]. Available: http://www.ABC Corporation.com [1999, October 01].

c. CNET, Inc. [Online]. Available: http://www.news.com/News/Item/0,4,36929,00.html. [1999, October 01].

d. Infoseek and Hoovers Online Company Profile for ABC corporation. [Online]. Available: http://infoseek.go.com, [1999, October 01].

e. USPTO Search on ABC corporation Corp. (1999). [Online]. Available: http://www.uspto.gov. [1999, June 21].

CHAPTER 6

a. Fortune Online Company Snapshot No. 51 Company A. [Online] Fortune Inc. Available: http://cgi.pathfinder.com/cgi-bin/fortune500/csnap.cgi?r96=51/ [1999, May 27].

b. Standard and Poors Ratings. (1999).[Online] Available: http://208.243.115.130/search97cgi/vtopic?action=view&VdkVgwKey=http%3A%2F%2Fwww%2Estandardandpoors%2Ecom%2Fratings%2Fcredit week%2Fstuv%2Ehtm&DocOffset=2&DocsFound=16&QueryZip=%3CAnd%3E%28%3CMany%3E%27companya%27%2C+%3CMany%3E%27companya%27%29&Collection=Coll1&SearchUrl=http%3A%2F%2F208%2E243%2E115%2E130%2Fsearch97cgi%2Fvtopic%3FQueryZip%3D%253CAnd%253E%2528%253CMany%253E%2527companya%2527%252C%2B%253CMany%253E;

pc2527companya%2527%2529%26Filter%3Dsrchflt%252Ehts%26ResultTem
plate%3Dresults%252Ehts%26QueryText%3Dcompanya%2Band%2Bcompanya
%26action%3DSearch%26Collection%3DColl1%26ResultStart%3D1%26R   esult-
Count%3D10&ViewTemplate=docview%2Ehts&ServerKey=Primary&AdminI
magePath=&Theme=&Company= [1999, May 27].

c. Climate wise, about climate wise [Online]. US EPA Washington DC. (1999). Available: http://www.epa.gov/oppeinet/oppe/climwise/cwweb/about.htm [1999, July12].

d. Climate wise, climate wise company partners by name [Online]. US EPA Washington DC.(1999). Available: http://www.epa.gov/oppeinet/oppe/ climwise/cwweb/about.htm [1999, July 12].

e. Right to Know Network (1999). [Online] Available: http://www.rtk.net [1999 July 12].

f. Company A Homepage Awards & Recognition, Fortune magazine's second annual ranking of global corporate reputations, which are based on reputation, quality of management and products/services. [1999 July 12]. http://www.companya.com/who_is_companya/factbook/backup/ 98fb_awards.htm [1999 October 01].

g. U.S. Food and Drug Administration, Washington DC. [Online]. Available: http://www.fda.gov/ [1999, August 03].

h. U.S. Consumer Product Safety Commission, Washington DC. [Online] Available: http://www.cpsc.gov [1999, August 03].

i. Awards and Recognition, Company A Home page. (1999). [Online]. Available: http://www.companya.com/who_is_companya/awards.html [1999, August 01].

j. US Occupational Safety and health Administration. (1999). [Online]. Available: http://www.osha.gov [1999, August 01].

k. Company A, Balancing Work & Family Program, Company A home page. [Online]. Available: http://www.companya.com/job_postings/prog/famwork_index.html

l. Company A Homepage Social Responsibility. [Online]. Available: http://www.companya.com/who_is_companya/sr_index.html [1999, June 01].

m. Council on Economic Priorities. (1999). [Online]. Available: http://www.cepaa.org/ [1999, July 21].

n. Company A Homepage, Our Environmental Commitment. (1999). [Online]. Available: http://www.companya .com/who_is_companya/env_index.html [1999, June 01].

CHAPTER 7

a. Corporation B 10K Report to the US securities and exchange commission, (1999). [Online]. Available: http://www.sec.gov [1999, August 03].

b. Corporation B 10K Report to the US securities and exchange commission, (1999). [Online]. Available: http://www.sec.gov [1999, August 03].

c. Search on the USPTO web Site, [Online]. Available: http://www.uspto.gov [1999, July 15].

d. Corporation B 10K Report to the US Securities and Exchange Commission.

(1999). [Online]. US Securities and Exchange Commission Available: http://www.sec.gov [1999 August 03].

e. Ace Consensus Estimates for Corporation B. (1999). [Online] Multex.com, Inc Available: http://www.multex.com/ [1999, July 10].

f. Corporation B 10K Report to the US Securities and Exchange Commission. (1999). [Online]. US Securities and Exchange Commission. Available: http://www.sec.gov [1999, August 03].

g. Corporation B Corporate Profile, Zacks.com. (1999). [Online]. Available: http://zacks.com [1999, August 07].

h. US FDA Docket. (1999). [Online]. Food and Drug Administration. Available: http://www.fda.gov [1999, June 13].

i. Corporation B Homepage, A Woman's Voice. (1999). [Online]. Corporation B Available: http://www.Corporation Bcorp.com/voicebody1.html [1999, June 23].

j. US FDA, Consent Decree with Corporation B and Corporation B Texas, Inc. regarding the manufacture of silicone gel and saline breast implants, May 05, 1999. [Online]. Food and Drug Administration. Available: http://www.fda. gov/ bbs/topics/ ANSWERS/ ANS00867. html [1999, July 02].

k. Oldham, Jennifer, Companies Debut 1st Ads for Saline Breast Implants, Jennifer Oldham 99–05–20. [Online]. Los Angeles Times. Available: http://www.polyzine.com/siliconeact.html [1999, July 02].

CHAPTER 8

a. ITC fights off pack, [Online] CNN The Financial Network. (1999). Available: wysiwyg://57/http://cnnfn.com/1998/11/11/technology/ITC [1999, July 24]

b. Fortune Online Fortune Company Snapshot No. 28 ITC . [Online]. Fortune Inc. (1999). Available: http://cgi.pathfinder.com/cgi-bin/fortune/fortune500/csnap .cgi?r96=28 [1999, August 01].

c. Fortune Industry Snapshot: Computers, Office Equipment. (1999). [Online]. Fortune Inc. Available: http://www.pathfinder.com/fortune/fortune500/ind8.html [1999, August 01].

d. ITC press release: ITC board of directors forms office of the chief executive under leadership of chairman Jan Boz. Dan Steeves, and Margaret D'Angelo resign as CEO and CFO. (1999). [Online]. BOSTON, April 18, 1999–Internet Tool Corporation. Available: http://www1.ITC.com/pressrelease/0,1494,wp~ 85_2!ob~ 375_1_1,00.html [1999, August 01].

e. ITC could have averted missteps; insiders say board ignored major warning signs; actions came too late. [Online]. Wall Street Journal 99–04–20. Transium Business Intelligence. Available: http://www.transium.com/backgrounder/pro . . . %22&stag=a&pa ge=2&r=1.tbusref.I54430007 [1999, July 30].

CHAPTER 9

a. BuyFromUs Home page [Online] BuyFromUs Inc. Available: http://www.amazon.com / exec / obidos / subst / misc / jobs / index.html/103–2985737–1137421 [1999, Dec 9].

b. SEC 10K <SEC-DOCUMENT>0000891020–99–000375.txt : 19990308 [On-line] Securities and Exchange Commission. Available http://www.sec.gov [1999, Dec 9].

c. BuyFromUs Home page [Online] BuyFromUs Inc. Available: http://www.amazon.com/exec/obidos/subst/home/home.html/ [1999, Dec 9].

d. BuyFromUs Home page [Online] BuyFromUs Inc. Available: http://www.amazon.com/exec/obidos/subst/misc/jobs/culture.html/103–2985737–1137421 [1999, Dec 9].

e. BuyFromUs Home page [Online] BuyFromUs Inc. Available: http://www.amazon.com/ [1999, Dec 9].

f. BuyFromUs home page [Online] BuyFromUs Inc. Available: http://www.amazon.com/exec/obidos/subst/misc/jobs/culture.html/103-2985737–1137421 [1999, Dec 9].

g. "BuyFromUs Gains from November Online Buying; Online Pharmaceuticals Solidify positions" PRNewswire/ Dec. 09/1999 [Online] Available: http://info-seek.go.com/Content?arn=PR876 . . . v=IS&lk=nofra mes&col=NX&kt=A&ak=news1486 [1999, Dec 9].

h. Disclosure-Investor.com "BUYFROMUS INC (BFU) [Online] Available: http://www.disclosure-inves . . . KEY=BFU&ITEM_FORMAT=HTML&ORDE R_ID=&.pdf [1999, Dec 9].

i. CNNfn.com search results- [Online] Available: http://search.cnnfn.com/ query.html?rq=0& . . . &qm=1&st=1&nh =10&lk=1&rf=1&qt=BFU [1999, Dec 9].

j. BuyFromUs Home Page [Online] BuyFromUs Inc. Available: http://www.BFU.com [1999, Dec 9].

k. BuyFromUs Home page [Online] BuyFromUs Inc. Available: http://www.BFU.com/exec/obidos/subst/misc/jobs/culture.html/103-2985737–1137421 [1999, Dec 9].

l. Buckalew, Toby, About.com,- "Buy From Us Grows Again"- [Online] Available: http://computers.about.com/ . . . htm?rnk=r8&terms=buyfromus &PM=112_300_[1999, Dec 9].

m. Hoovers Online "BuyFromUs Inc." [Online] Hoovers Inc. Available: http://www.hoovers.com/co/capsule/3/0,2163,51493,00.html [1999, Dec 9].

n. CNNfn.com search results- [Online] CNN Financial Network Available: http://search.cnnfn.com/query.html?rq=0& . . . &qm=1&st=1&nh =10&lk=1&rf=1&qt=BuyFromUs [1999, Dec 9].

o. Buy From Us SEC 10K <SEC-DOCUMENT>0000891020–99–000375.txt : 19990308 [Online] Securities and Exchange Commission. Available: http://www.sec.gov [1999, Dec 9].

p. FindLaw.LawCrawler [Online] Available: http://lawcrawler.findlaw . . . ry=buyfromus &sites=wlegal&focus=checked [1999, Dec 9].

q. "How BuyFromUs kept a top idea guy" Herring.Com [Online] Red Herring Inc. Available: http://www.redherring.com/insider/1999/0908/vc-vcps.html/ [1999, Dec 9].

r. Monster.com "BuyFromUs" [Online] Available: http://jobsearch.monster.com/jobsearch.asp?cy=US&q=BuyFromUs [1999, Dec 9].

s. BuyFromUs Home page [Online] BuyFromUs Inc. Available: http://www.

buyfromus/exec/obidos/subst/misc/jobs/culture.html/103-2985737–1137421
[1999, Dec 9].

t. 'BuyFromUs Gains from November Online Buying; Online Pharmaceuticals
Solidify positions" PRNewswire/ Dec. 09/1999 [Online] Available: http://info-
seek.go.com/Content?arn=PR876 . . . v=IS&lk=nofra
mes&col=NX&kt=A&ak=news1486 [1999, Dec 9].

u. "BuyFromUs Navigating" Herring.com [Online] Red Herring Inc. Available: http://www.redherring.com/mag/issue43/angler.html [1999, Dec 9].

v. CNNfn.com search results- [Online] Available: http://search.cnnfn.com/
query.html?rq=0& . . . &qm=1&st=1&nh=q10&lk=1&rf=1&qt=BFU [1999, Dec
9].

w. CNNfn.com search results- [Online] Available: http://search.cnnfn.com/
query.html?rq=0& . . . &qm=1est=1&nh=10&lk=1&rf=1&qt=BFU [1999, Dec.
9].

Recommended Readings

Alvesson, M., and P. O. Berg. 1992. *Corporate Culture and Organizational Symbolism*. Berlin/New York: de Gruyter.

Ashkenas, Ron, Dave Ulrich, Todd Jick, and Steve Kerr. 1995. *The Boundaryless Organization: Breaking the Chains of Organizational Structure*. San Francisco, CA: Jossey-Bass.

Calof, Jonathon. "For King and Country and Company." *Business Quarterly* (Spring 1997): 32–37.

Campbell, Andrew, Michael Goold, and Marcus Alexander. 1995. "The Value of the Parent Company." *California Management Review* 38(1) (Fall): 79–97.

Clegg, S. 1975. *Power, Rule and Domination*. London: Routledge & Kegan Paul.

Collis, David J., and Cynthia Montgomery. 1995. "Competing on Resources: Strategy in the 1990's." *Harvard Business Review* (July–August): 118–128.

Cvitkovic, Emilio. 1989. "Profiling Your Competitors." *Planning Review* (May–June): 28–30.

Dance, S. X. 1967. *Human Communications*. New York: Holt Rinehart & Winston.

Day, George, and David Reibstein. 1997. *Wharton on Dynamic Competitive Strategy*. New York: John Wiley & Sons.

Dewitt, Michelle, 1997. *Competitive Intelligence, Competitive Advantage*. Grand Rapids, MI: Abacus.

Dunphy, Dexter, and Doug Stace. 1994. *Beyond the Boundaries*. Sydney: John Wiley & Sons.

Euske, E. J., and R. Stephen Player. 1996. "Leveraging Management Improvement Techniques." *Sloan Management Review* (Fall): 69–79.

Fahey, L. 1999. *Competitors*. New York: John Wiley and Sons.

Fisher, B. A. 1978. *Perspective on Human Communication*. New York: Macmillan Publishing.

Foucault, M. 1980. *Power/Knowledge*. New York: Pantheon.

Ghemawat, Pankaj. 1999. *Strategy and the Business Landscape*. Cambridge, MA: Harvard Business School Publishing.

Ghoshal, Sumantra, and Christopher Bartlett. 1996. "Rebuilding Behavioural Context." *Sloan Management Review* (Winter): 23–36.

Goffee, Rob, and Gareth Jones. 1996. "What Holds the Modern Company Together." *Harvard Business Review* (Nov.–Dec.): 133–148.

Grant, Robert M. 1991. "The Resource Based Theory of Competitive Advantage." *California Management Review* (Spring): 114–135.

Grant, Robert M. 1998. *Contemporary Strategy Analysis*, 3rd ed. Malden, MA: Blackwell Business.

Hardy, C. 1990. *Retrenchment and Turnaround*. Berlin: de Gruyter.

Hinings, C. R., and R. Greenwood. 1988. *The Dynamics of Strategic Change*. London: Basil Blackwell.

Keidel, Robert. 1994. "Rethinking Organizational Design." *Academy of Management Executive* 8(4): 12–27.

Lynch, Robert P. 1990. *The Practical Guide to Joint Ventures and Corporate Alliances*. New York: John Wiley & Sons.

McGonagle, John J., and Carolyn M. Vella. 1998. *Protecting Your Company Against Competitive Intelligence*. Westport, CT: Quorum Books.

Miles, Raymond, Henry Coleman, Jr., and Douglas Creed. 1995. "Keys to Success in Corporate Redesign." *California Management Review* (Spring): 128–145.

Miller, D. 1990. *The Icarus Paradox: How Exceptional Companies Bring About Their Own Downfall*. New York: HarperCollins.

Mintzberg, Henry. 1998. *Strategy Safari: A Guided Tour Through the Wilds of Strategic Management*. New York: The Free Press.

Morgan, G. 1986. *Images of Organizations*. Los Angeles: Sage.

Nystrom, P. C., and W. H. Starbuck. 1984. "To Avoid Crises, Unlearn." *Organizational Dynamics* 12(4): 53–65.

Pearson, Christine, and Jan Mitroff. 1993. "From Crisis Prone to Crisis Prepared: A Framework for Crisis Management." *Academy of Management Executive* 7(1): 48–59.

Pfeffer, J., and G. Salancik. 1978. *The External Control of Organizations: A Resource-Dependence Framework*. New York: Harper & Row.

Porter, Michael. 1987. "From Competitive Advantage to Corporate Strategy." *Harvard Business Review* (May–June): 43–59.

Porter, Michael. 1993. "How Competitive Forces Shape Strategy." *Harvard Business Review* (March–April): 137–145.

Prahalad, C. K., and G. Hamel. 1990. "The Core Competence of the Corporation." *Harvard Business Review* (May–June): 80–91.

Saul, John Ralston. 1994. *The Doubter's Companion: A Dictionary of Aggressive Common Sense*. Toronto, ON: Viking Penguin.

Shoemaker, Paul. 1995. "Scenario Planning: A Tool for Strategic Thinking." *Sloan Management Review* (Winter): 25–40.

Strebel, Paul. 1997. "Breakpoint: How to Stay in the Game." *In the Financial Times: Mastering Management*. London: Pitman Publishing, pp. 543–547.

Ulrich, D., and D. Lake. 1990. *Organizational Capability: Competing from the Inside Out*. Toronto: John Wiley & Sons.

Watson, Gregory H. 1997. "Understanding the Essentials of Strategic Benchmarking." In *Strategic Benchmarking: How to Rate Your Company's Performance Against the World's Best*. New York: John Wiley & Sons, pp. 39–79.

Zahra, Shaker, and Sherry Chaples. 1993. "Blind Spots in Competitive Analysis." *Harvard Business Review* 7(2): 7–28.

Index

About the Author and Contributors

CONOR VIBERT is an Assistant Professor of Business Policy at the Fred C. Manning School of Business of Acadia University in Wolfville, Nova Scotia. He has presented his work at conferences of the Academy of Management, the American Psychological Association, the Administrative Sciences Association of Canada, and the Atlantic Schools of Business and has published in the *Competitive Intelligence Review*. At Acadia University, Conor teaches Business Policy, Change Management, and Organisation Theory, while his current research interests focus on the management of higher risk alliance partners and the application of the Internet to contemporary business issues. He is a member of the Society of Competitive Intelligence Professionals and may be reached at conor.vibert@acadiau.ca. or http.CI.ACADIAU.CA.

CHRISTINA McRAE is a free-lance writer and editor based in Wolfville, Nova Scotia, Canada. She specializes in scientific and literary communications and can be reached at editworks@ns.sympatico.ca.

SONYA SYMONS has expertise in the areas of educational psychology and applied cognition. Her research examines the psychology of reading to locate information and comprehension and recall strategies. Currently, she is conducting research on factors that affect information-seeking on the Internet and how Internet technology affects adult literacy development. She is the Head of the Department of Psychology at Acadia University and has published in *Contemporary Educational Psychology* and *Reading Research Quarterly*. Sonya can be contacted at sonya.symons@acadiau.ca.

ANDRÉ TRUDEL is a researcher specializing in the areas of Intelligent Software Agents and Artificial Intelligence. He is the Director of the Jodrey School of Computer Science at Acadia University as well as the Intelligent Information Technology Research Centre. He has published in *Computational Intelligence*, the *International Journal of Intelligence*, and the *International Journal of Expert Systems*. He can be contacted at andre.trudel@acadiau.ca.